The
Beta Sigma Phi
International

FONDUE
& BUFFET

COOKBOOK

Congratulations and thank you . . .

to each Beta Sigma Phi whose recipe was selected to be part of this *Fondue and Buffet* cookbook, surely one of the most unusual cookbooks in the entire Beta Sigma Phi series.

I am pleased to be able to introduce to homemakers everywhere this collection of fondue, chafing dish, and buffet recipes. From last-minute suppers to formal buffets — you will find great recipes and unusual suggestions for entertaining both family and friends. And homemakers can prepare each recipe with confidence, knowing that it has been tested in the kitchen of a Beta Sigma Phi and approved by her for flavor, ease of preparation, and visual appeal.

Beta Sigma Phi is an international sorority offering opportunities for friendship, development of cultural appreciation, and community service. Founded in 1931 by Walter W. Ross, the organization has grown rapidly. Beta Sigma Phi is the largest, most outstanding women's organization of its kind in the world.

Today there are 225,000 Beta Sigma Phis dedicated to the belief that the only right they have is the right to be useful. Organized into approximately 10,000 chapters, the membership represents every state in the United States, every province in Canada, and fourteen other countries. Kansas City, Missouri is the location of the international headquarters.

The Beta Sigma Phi International Cookbooks are very meaningful to the communities of participating members. The profit on each cookbook goes directly to the individual chapters who use these funds for their current local service projects.

Bill Ross

WALTER W. ROSS III
President
International Executive Council
of Beta Sigma Phi
Kansas City, Missouri

Favorite Recipes Press © MCMLXXII
Post Office Box 3396, Montgomery, Alabama 36109
Library of Congress Card Catalog Number 72-81736

PREFACE

Your friends drop by in the evening for a quick before-the-theater meal. You suddenly discover tomorrow is the day you've invited ten guests for dinner. Your husband comes home announcing an unexpected promotion. Your children bring home especially good report cards. What do you do to highlight the occasion with a memorable meal? Do as thousands of America's most innovative cooks do, and celebrate with fondue, chafing dish, or buffet foods. These foods are gaining in popularity across the country as more and more people discover how very easy they are to prepare, how festive they look, and how they bring a new flavor spectrum to the dinner table.

A wonderful new collection of recipes for fondue, chafing dish, and buffet foods is yours in this *Fondue and Buffet* cookbook. Here you'll find recipes for meat fondues, including sauces to accompany them; seafood; cheese; vegetable; and even dessert fondues. In short, in the first section of this book, you'll find everything you need for the complete fondue party! If the elegance of chafing dish cooking and serving appeals to you, you'll be delighted to find an entire section devoted to meat, chicken, seafood, cereal, egg, cheese, pasta, vegetable, and dessert recipes for chafing dishes. Or do you prefer the prepare-in-advance ease of buffet service? In this book, we've included a collection of recipes that are almost tailored for buffets.

Prefacing each of this book's three major sections are pages of informative, illustrated material suggesting how to choose your equipment, how to plan a party days in advance so that it runs smooth as clockwork, how to match menus and color schemes, and much more. For every bit of entertaining you do in your busy world, depend on this one cookbook. It's a reliable guide to every aspect of fondue, chafing dish, and buffet cooking.

CONTENTS

FONDUE

There is a long-standing quarrel between the Welsh rabbit or rarebit and the Swiss fondue over which is the oldest cheese dish invented. The fondue dates from the thirteenth century and, while we may not be able to determine for certain that it is older than the rabbit, we do know that it has been enjoyed in Europe for several hundred years. The word "fondue" comes from the French word *fondre,* meaning "to melt". Originally applied only to bread and melted cheese dishes, today fondue encompasses a complete range of foods. There are meat fondues, seafood fondues, vegetable fondues, even dessert fondues. And in this section, you'll find page after page featuring home-tested recipes for all types of fondue.

No one knows where the idea of using pieces of meat and seafood in fondues (called fondue Bourguignonne) originated, but almost everyone agrees that these fondues make unusual and enjoyable main courses. The dessert fondue was invented by a clever New York public relations woman — and is now as popular in Switzerland as it is here!

You'll begin learning more about fondues in the section that follows. Turn the page, and you'll find diagrams of fondue pots, information on how to buy pots and heating units for your specific needs and how to care for your equipment as well as suggestions for memorable fondue-centered parties. This illustrated information precedes page after page of fondue recipes that have won the stamp of approval from American families. Some of these recipes are so quick and easy, you can serve them for hurry-up supper. Others are more elaborate recipes you'll want to reserve for those very special evening parties.

But begin to explore the entertainment possibilities of fondue now, and picture yourself as the most talked-about hostess in town when you feature fondue at your next dinner or supper party.

fondue
FUNDAMENTALS____

There is a legend in Switzerland that says that the fondue was invented by accident. The Swiss bake bread and make cheese during the fall and summer months and whatever they produce during that time has to last them through the long, cold winter. Needless to say, before summer comes around again, the bread and cheese can become very hard! The legend has it that a Swiss woman left a piece of cheese too near the stove, and it melted. Rather than see the liquid cheese go to waste, she cut a chunk of hard bread and dipped it into the cheese. The result: the first fondue.

Like all folk legends, this one has to be taken with some reservations. But however fondue developed, it has become one of the world's great dishes. And today, there is a wonderful variety of equipment awaiting you in gourmet shops, housewares sections of department stores, cheese stores, and even in discount stores.

EQUIPMENT

Of all the fondue equipment available, the pots are absolutely essential. There are three types of *fondue pots;* two are earthenware and the other is metal. When planning the equipment you'll need for a fondue, allow one pot for four people. Look for sturdy pots with wide trays to catch spills and prevent burns.

Cheese fondues are traditionally prepared in round, heavy pottery dishes called *caquelons,* with wide mouths and heavy handles. If you don't have one, try substituting a heavy chafing dish. A smaller version of this pot is used to prepare dessert fondues.

The third type of fondue pot is a metal one wider at the bottom than at the top and deeper overall than the earthenware pots. This metal pot is used to prepare meat, seafood, and vegetable fondues that require hot oil. The metal can tolerate the 360 degrees of heat needed to keep oil hot without cracking, as would an earthenware pot. The pot's shape – narrower at top than at bottom – helps keep the oil from spattering as foods are cooking. The better metal pots are enameled steel with an extra-heavy bottom and come in a wide range of colors that will complement virtually every room decor. Other metal fondue pots may be made of stainless steel, copper, or sterling silver. If you choose a fondue pot of either copper or sterling silver, be certain it is clad with a heavier metal inside and on the bottom or you'll spend a good deal of time and money having it reclad.

The *heat source* you choose will depend upon the kind of fondue you are preparing. Cheese, meat, seafood, and vegetable fondues need more intense heat than do dessert fondues. For the latter, choose a *candle warmer.* A dessert fondue is usually prepared on the kitchen stove over very low heat and is poured into a fondue pot. The pot is carried to the table, and the only heat needed from that point on is enough to keep the dessert warm.

For all other fondues, choose from alcohol lamps, canned heat, or electricity. There are two types of *alcohol lamps,* both illustrated here. One has a wick that is raised and lowered by turning a screw and also has a bottom compartment that holds alcohol. The

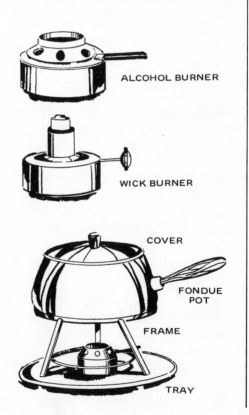

ALCOHOL BURNER

WICK BURNER

COVER

FONDUE POT

FRAME

TRAY

other type has cotton wool in its base. Alcohol is poured over the cotton, ignited, and the degree of heat is controlled by a cover that opens and closes vents on the side of the lamp.

When using either type of alcohol lamp, never fill the base more than half full. One tablespoon of alcohol gives about twelve minutes' cooking time. Denatured alcohol is the best kind to use in alcohol lamps: it is less expensive, produces a more intense heat, and creates less odor.

Canned heat fits into special lamps that either come with fondue pots or can be purchased separately. The degree of heat given off by the lamp is controlled by a vented cover similar to that on the alcohol lamp. In determining how much canned heat you will need, remember that a 2 5/8 ounce can burns for 50 to 60 minutes while a 7-ounce can burns for 4 hours.

Electric fondue pots are also available and are increasing in popularity. To use, simply follow the instructions.

In addition to pots and heat sources, you may want to invest in special forks and plates. *Fondue forks* are usually two- or three-tined metal forks with wooden ends that prevent heat conduction. You'll want forks that have their ends color-keyed: each has a different color so that when the pot is filled with cooking food your guests can easily tell which fork is theirs. Fondue forks are handy but not absolutely necessary – skewers, bamboo sticks, chopsticks, or even metal knitting needles will serve the same pur-

pose. But a word of warning – if you attempt to use an all-metal object as a fondue fork, you will run the risk of possible burns.

Fondue plates are metal, plastic, or china plates divided into several compartments. They are most frequently used to serve a fondue, such as Bourguignonne, that is accompanied by several sharply different sauces. The divided plates allow your guests to serve themselves with their favorite sauces and keep those sauces from blending together into one mass.

FONDUE VARIETY

In the section that follows this information, recipes for many different kinds of fondue have been assembled. The classic traditional fondue is, of course, *cheese.* The basic cheese fondue is made with two types of Swiss cheeses: Emmentaler, a mild cheese, and the stronger Gruyere. The very mildest fondue is made wholly of Emmentaler while the very strongest is made entirely of Gruyere. There is a complete flavor spectrum awaiting your pleasure when you mix the two cheeses in different proportions. Allow about one-third of a pound of cheese per person.

Cheese for a fondue should be diced or shredded but never grated as grating will make the cheese lump. Toss your bits of cheese with the amount of flour called for in the recipe, usually a couple of tablespoons per pound of cheese. Use the cheese specified in the recipe you are following as not all cheeses are suitable for fondue.

To heighten flavor, rub the fondue pot lightly with half a garlic clove, then add the required amount of liquid. The liquid is heated until bubbles form around the edges and on the bottom of the pot. Add the cheese, a handful at a time, stirring the entire cheese mixture constantly with a wooden spoon. When all the cheese has been added, flavor with nutmeg, pepper, or other seasonings.

Your guests spear pieces of crusty French or Italian bread and use the bread to scoop up cheese fondue. (In cutting the bread, be certain that each piece has a crust with it, as it is this crust the fondue adheres to.) The mixture should be kept in constant motion by the action of the guests' swirling. The prize of the evening is the cheese crust left on the bottom of the pot; traditionally, this goes to the person who has not dropped his bread in the pot during the meal!

Fondue Bourguignonne consists of pieces of meat or seafood speared on a fork and cooked in a pot of hot oil. Some cooks prefer to use a mixture of peanut oil and butter, while others use coconut, salad, or olive oil. The latter will smoke quickly and is not preferred for fondues. Some mixtures of oil may spatter during the cooking process, particularly when foods are put into the oil to cook. A bread cube added to the hot oil helps keep down the number of these spatters.

The meat for fondue Bourgoignonne is most often beef. Tenderloin, sirloin, or porterhouse are the preferred cuts although other beef cuts may be used if they are first tenderized. Veal is apt to become tough unless you use tenderloin. If you are featuring pork, caution your guests that it must be thoroughly cooked. In planning your menu and shopping, allow five to seven ounces of meat per person. Cut the meat into 3/4-inch cubes and to reduce the eventual cooking time, leave it at room temperature for one hour.

Each place setting for fondue Bourgoignonne should have the meat or seafood that is to be cooked served in individual bowls — the small Chinese or Japanese bowls available inexpensively at many stores are ideal for this purpose. Line each bowl with fresh greens before filling it with pieces of meat or seafood. Each individual place setting should include a dinner plate, a salad fork and a dinner fork as well as an individual's fondue fork. (Because the tines of fondue forks are used for cooking, they become too hot to eat with.)

Don't forget to include at least four and preferably six sauces. Among the best ones for meat fondue are Bearnaise, Cumberland, horseradish, chili, bottled steak sauce, and barbecue. Use the same basic sauce list for seafood fondues, substituting lemon butter and tartar sauce for the steak sauces.

Serve your meat or seafood the Swiss way with an appropriate beverage, a green salad complemented by a sharply flavored dressing, and your own delicious home-fried potatoes. Add a fruit compote for dessert, and you'll have a memorable, unusual fondue meal.

BEEF

KOREAN STEAK FONDUE

3 lb. flank or chuck steak
3 tbsp. sesame seed
1/4 c. salad oil
1/2 c. soy sauce
2 cloves of garlic, crushed
1/2 tsp. pepper
1/2 tsp. ginger
1/4 c. (packed) brown sugar
2 green onions, sliced
1 1/2 qt. vegetable oil

Cut steak into 1-inch cubes. Combine sesame seed, salad oil, soy sauce, garlic, pepper, ginger, brown sugar, and onions. Place steak in glass dish; pour marinade over steak. Let stand overnight. Fill fondue pot 3/4 full of vegetable oil. Heat until sizzling hot. Dip steak into hot oil with fondue forks; cook to desired doneness. Yield: 6-8 servings.

Mrs. Marlene Osgood, Treas., Beta Alpha No. 2379
Elma, Washington

FONDUE BOURGUIGNON SUPREME

Beef tenderloin
Salad oil

Cut beef tenderloin into 3/4-inch cubes, allowing 6 to 8 ounces for each person; place cubes on platter. Fill metal fondue pot 1/4 to 1/3 full with salad oil; heat to 375 degrees. Place fondue pot over fuel in center of table; keep oil sizzling hot. Spear beef cube on fondue fork or long wooden skewer; hold in oil for about 10 seconds for rare or to desired degree of doneness. Transfer cooked beef to fork; dip in desired sauce.

Onion-Horseradish Sauce

1/4 c. chopped onion
1 tbsp. horseradish

1 tbsp. water
1/4 tsp. hot sauce

Combine all ingredients.

Mustard Sauce

1/4 c. prepared mustard
1/4 c. mayonnaise
1 clove of garlic, crushed
1/4 tsp. hot sauce

Combine all ingredients; refrigerate until ready to serve.

Curry Sauce

1/2 c. mayonnaise
2 tbsp. milk
1 tbsp. curry powder
1/4 tsp. hot sauce

Combine all ingredients; refrigerate until ready to serve.

Tomato-Mushroom Sauce

2/3 c. catsup
2 tbsp. chopped cooked mushrooms
1/4 tsp. hot sauce

Combine all ingredients; refrigerate until ready to serve. Canned mushrooms may be substituted for fresh mushrooms.

BEEF FONDUE WITH SOUR CREAM-CURRY SAUCE

2 lb. beef chuck or sirloin steak
1 c. butter
2 c. salad oil
Sauce

Cut beef into 3/4-inch cubes, trimming excess fat. Chill. Heat butter and salad oil together in saucepan until mixture bubbles and begins to brown. Pour oil mixture into fondue dish 2 inches deep. Place on stand over heat until oil begins to bubble. Cook beef for 2 to 3 minutes on fondue forks. Dip in Sauce.

Sauce

1 c. sour cream
1/2 to 1 tsp. curry powder
1 tsp. prepared horseradish
1/2 tsp. sugar
1/8 tsp. salt
Paprika

Mix all ingredients together except paprika; chill well. Place in serving bowl; sprinkle lightly with paprika. Yield: 4-6 servings.

Shirley Ward, VP, Beta Theta No. 4353
E. Gadsden, Alabama

FONDUE BOURGUIGNON AND SAUCES

3 lb. beef tenderloin
3 c. salad oil
Mild Mustard Sauce
Spicy Steak Sauce

Trim excess fat from beef; cut into bite-sized cubes. Chill. Fill fondue pot 1 1/2 inches deep with oil; heat until slice of bread browns in about 1 minute. Spear beef on fondue forks; cook to desired doneness in oil. Dip into desired sauce.

Mild Mustard Sauce

2 tbsp. prepared mustard
1/2 c. bottled coleslaw dressing

Combine mustard and coleslaw dressing. Chill.

Spicy Steak Sauce

1/3 c. mayonnaise
3 tbsp. chili sauce
2 tsp. Worcestershire sauce
1 tsp. bottled thick meat sauce
Hot sauce to taste

Combine mayonnaise with remaining ingredients. Chill.

Edna N. Newhall, Pres., Xi Chi X3079
Danville, Kentucky

FONDUE DELIGHT

1 3/4 c. milk
2 8-oz. package cream cheese, cubed
2 tsp. dry mustard
1/4 c. chopped green onions
1 2 3/4-oz. jar sliced dried beef, shredded
French bread, cut in bite-sized pieces

Heat milk. Add cream cheese; stir until cream cheese is melted. Add mustard, onions, and dried beef; cook over low heat for 5 minutes longer, stirring constantly. Serve in fondue pot. Serve with bread. Yield: 10-12 servings.

Alyce D. Vanek
International Honorary Member, BSP
Menomonie, Wisconsin

MARINATED BEEF FONDUE

2 lb. beef tenderloin
1 sm. bottle Italian salad dressing
2 c. salad oil

Marinate beef in salad dressing for 4 hours or overnight. Bring oil to a boil; fill fondue pot 1/2 full. Place beef on serving dish next to pot. Spear beef with fondue forks. Cook to desired doneness. Yield: 4-6 servings.

Hele M. Montgomery, Alpha Sigma No. 5888
Whitewood, South Dakota

FONDUE MANDARIN

1   2-lb. flank steak, trimmed
1 1/4 c. Hawaiian-style dressing
2 tbsp. soy sauce
1 clove of garlic, chopped
1 tbsp. sherry
2 tbsp. toasted sesame seed
Oil

Cut steak into bite-sized pieces. Combine dressing, soy sauce, garlic, sherry and sesame seed; marinate steak for several hours. Heat oil in fondue pot on stove until bubbling; transfer pot to fondue burner. Spear steak with fondue forks; dip into hot oil. Cook to desired doneness. Suggested accompaniments: hot mustard sauce or horseradish sauce. Yield: 4 servings.

Myrtle Miller, Preceptor Chi XP772
Sarnia, Ontario, Canada

BEEF FONDUE WITH SWEET AND SOUR SAUCE

Salad oil
1 1/2 lb. beef, cubed

Pour salad oil 2 inches deep in fondue pot. Heat to just below smoking point. Spear beef cubes with fondue forks; cook in hot oil to desired doneness.

Sweet and Sour Sauce

2 tbsp. soy sauce
1/2 c. (packed) brown sugar
1/4 c. vinegar
1/2 c. apricot nectar
1 tbsp. catsup
1/4 tsp. dry mustard
1/4 tsp. ground ginger
1/4 tsp. salt
Dash of hot sauce

Combine all ingredients in saucepan; bring to a boil. Cook until sugar is dissolved. Serve with beef fondue. Yield: 6-8 servings.

Mildred L. Smith, Prog. Chm.
Xi Alpha Delta X666, Austin, Texas

ORIENTAL FONDUE

1 sirloin steak
1 1/2 c. burgundy
1   10 1/2-oz. can beef broth
1 sm. onion, thinly sliced
1 tbsp. parsley flakes
1 tsp. salt
1 tsp. pepper
1 tsp. garlic powder
1/2 bay leaf

Trim excess fat from steak; cut into 1-inch cubes. Combine burgundy and remaining ingredients in saucepan; simmer for 5 minutes. Pour broth mixture into fondue pot; heat to boiling point. Spear beef with forks; cook in broth mixture to desired degree of doneness.

Hot-Sweet Sauce

1 tbsp. lemon juice
1 tbsp. dry mustard
1/2 tsp. salt
1/4 c. honey
1/4 c. apricot preserves

Add lemon juice to mustard and salt; mix until smooth. Add honey and apricot preserves; mix well. Serve sauce with fondue.

Marilyn Grimm, Beta Upsilon No. 4842
Medford, Oregon

FONDUE INTERNATIONAL

Beef tenderloin or sirloin
Leg of lamb
Chicken breasts
Spareribs
4 c. corn oil
English Mustard Sauce
Basic French Salad Dressing
All-American Fondue Sauce
Chinese Plum Sauce
Sesame Curry Sauce
Oriental Sauce

Cut beef and lamb into 3/4-inch cubes. Skin chicken breasts; remove bones. Cut chicken meat into cubes. Cut spareribs into 1 1/2-inch single-rib pieces. Boil spareribs for about 20 minutes in salted water; drain. Arrange meats on large serving platter next to fondue pot. Pour oil into fondue pot; place over heating unit. Bring oil to 375 degrees. Spear desired meat with fondue forks; dip into hot oil. Cook to desired doneness. Dip meat into desired sauce with dinner forks.

English Mustard Sauce

1/4 c. dry mustard
1/4 c. white vinegar
1/4 c. sugar
1/8 tsp. salt
1 egg, beaten
1/2 c. real mayonnaise

Shake mustard and vinegar together in small jar; let stand for 1 hour. Combine mustard mixture, sugar, salt and egg in small saucepan. Cook over medium heat for about 5 minutes, stirring constantly until slightly thickened and almost boiling. Cool. Stir in mayonnaise until smooth.

Basic French Salad Dressing

1 c. corn oil
1/3 to 1/2 c. white wine vinegar
1 to 3 tbsp. sugar
1 1/2 tsp. salt
1/2 tsp. paprika
1/2 tsp. dry mustard
1 clove of garlic

Combine all ingredients in bottle or jar; cover tightly. Shake well. Chill for several hours; remove garlic. Shake thoroughly before serving.

All-American Fondue Sauce

2 tbsp. corn oil
1 clove of garlic, minced
1/2 c. catsup
1/2 c. minced onion
2 tbsp. cider vinegar
1 tsp. salt
1 tsp. dry mustard
1 tsp. brown sugar
1/2 tsp. hot sauce

Mix all ingredients together in small saucepan; bring to a boil over medium heat.

Chinese Plum Sauce

1 c. plum preserves or jam
1/4 c. red wine vinegar
2 tbsp. corn oil
1 tbsp. dry mustard
1/2 sm. clove of garlic, crushed

Stir all ingredients together; mix well.

Sesame Curry Sauce

1/3 c. milk
1 c. real mayonnaise
1 to 3 tsp. curry powder
1 tsp. toasted sesame seed

Stir milk into mayonnaise gradually until blended. Stir in curry and sesame seed. Chill.

Oriental Sauce

1/2 c. real mayonnaise
1/4 c. sour cream
1/4 c. chopped green onions
1 tbsp. soy sauce
1 tsp. ground ginger

Mix all ingredients together.

TERIYAKI BEEF-VEGETABLE PLATTER

2 lb. boneless steak
5/8 c. soy sauce
1 7/8 c. water
1/2 c. sugar
3 tbsp. minced garlic
3 tbsp. ground ginger
2 tbsp. liquid smoke
Oil
Onion rings
Cauliflowerets
Cucumber cubes
Eggplant cubes
Red pepper squares
Green pepper squares
Zucchini slices
1 recipe thin pancake batter

Cut steak into 1-inch cubes. Combine soy sauce, water, sugar, garlic, ginger, and liquid smoke. Marinate steak in garlic mixture for 4 to 6 hours. Heat oil in fondue pot over fondue burner until sizzling. Arrange vegetables, steak and pancake batter around fondue cooker. Dip vegetables and steak into batter; fry in hot oil on bamboo skewers until done.

Janet A. Guinn, Pres., Omega No. 7969
Anchorage, Alaska

FONDUE BACCHUS

2 c. strong chicken broth
2 c. white wine
1 med. onion, thinly sliced
3 stalks celery with leaves,
  chopped
1 garlic clove, chopped
8 juniper berries, crushed
10 peppercorns, crushed
1/2 tsp. salt
1 tbsp. fresh tarragon
2 sprigs of fresh thyme
2 sprigs of parsley
1 bay leaf
3 lb. prime beefsteak, cubed

Combine chicken broth and wine in saucepan; bring to a boil. Add onion, celery, garlic, juniper berries, peppercorns, salt, tarragon, thyme, parsley, and bay leaf. Bring to a boil again. Let stand in refrigerator for 3 days. Strain into fondue pot; bring to a boil. Spear beef with fondue forks; cook to desired doneness in broth mixture. Broth mixture may now be served as separate course, if desired.

Nancy Leubner, Pres., Pi Beta No. 7513
Aurora, Illinois

EASY PIZZA FONDUE

1/2 lb. ground beef
1/2 env. spaghetti sauce mix
1 15-oz. can tomato sauce
3 c. shredded natural Cheddar
  cheese
1 c. shredded mozzarella cheese
1 tbsp. cornstarch
1/2 c. wine

Brown ground beef in skillet; drain off excess fat. Stir in spaghetti sauce mix and tomato sauce; blend well. Combine cheeses with cornstarch; stir into ground beef mixture gradually. Add wine. Cook, stirring constantly, until cheese is melted and fondue is thickened. Pour into fondue pot; place pot over fondue burner. Adjust heat to keep fondue just warm. Serve with French bread cubes, cut with crust on one side of each cube.

Kathie Brittain, Zeta Delta
Spokane, Washington

GOLD NUGGET FONDUE

1 lb. ground beef
1/4 c. milk
1/4 c. soft bread crumbs
1/2 tsp. seasoned salt
48 Cheddar cheese 1/2-inch cubes
1 1/2 c. salad oil
1/2 c. clarified butter
1 tsp. salt
South-Of-The-Border Dip
Sour Cream Supreme

Combine ground beef, milk, bread crumbs, and seasoned salt. Shape into an 8 x 6-inch rectangle; divide into forty-eight 1-inch squares. Place a cheese cube in center of each square; form beef mixture around each cube of cheese to make a ball, covering cheese completely. Let stand at room temperature for 30 minutes. Combine oil and butter in fondue pot; heat on top of stove to 375 degrees. Add salt; transfer to fondue burner over high heat. Spear meatballs with fondue forks; cook in oil mixture until of desired doneness. Serve with South-Of-The-Border Dip or Sour Cream Supreme. To clarify butter, melt over low heat; cool. Pour off top layer; discard sediment.

South-Of-The-Border Dip

1/2 c. sour cream
1/3 c. chili sauce
2 tbsp. sweet pickle relish
1 tbsp. prepared horseradish
1 tsp. Worcestershire sauce
1/2 tsp. salt

Combine sour cream, chili sauce, relish, horseradish, Worcestershire sauce, and salt.

Sour Cream Supreme

1 c. sour cream
1 tbsp. prepared mustard
1 tbsp. prepared horseradish
1/2 tsp. salt

Combine sour cream, mustard, horseradish, and salt.

Helen Zigich, Gamma Gamma No. 6429
Duluth, Minnesota

MEATBALL FONDUE WITH MUSTARD SAUCE

1 tbsp. soy sauce
Sugar
1/4 tsp. minced onion
1/8 tsp. garlic salt
1/8 tsp. ground ginger
1/2 lb. ground beef

1/2 c. soft bread crumbs
1 c. vinegar
1 c. dry mustard
1/8 tsp. salt
2 beaten eggs
Salad oil

Combine soy sauce, 2 teaspoons sugar, onion, garlic salt, ginger, and 1 tablespoon water; mix well. Add soy sauce mixture to ground beef; blend well. Add bread crumbs to ground beef mixture; blend thoroughly. Shape into walnut-sized balls; refrigerate until ready to serve. Combine vinegar, mustard, 1 cup sugar, and salt; refrigerate overnight. Combine vinegar mixture with eggs in saucepan; bring to a boil, stirring until thickened. Remove from heat; cool. Refrigerate until serving time. Pour oil into electric metal fondue pot; adjust temperature to 375 degrees. Dip meatballs into hot oil with fondue fork; cook to desired doneness. Serve with sauce.

Waldine Garrett, Publ. Chm.
Preceptor Alpha Zeta XP674
North Kansas City, Missouri

ORIENTAL MEATBALLS

1 tbsp. soy sauce
1 tbsp. water
2 tbsp. sugar
1/4 tsp. instant minced onion
1/8 tsp. garlic salt
1/8 tsp. monosodium glutamate
1/8 tsp. ground ginger
1/2 lb. lean ground beef
1/2 c. fine soft bread crumbs
Salad oil

Combine soy sauce, water, sugar, onion, garlic salt, monosodium glutamate, and ginger; let stand for 10 minutes. Combine beef and crumbs; stir in soy sauce mixture. Shape into 3/4-inch meatballs. Heat oil in fondue pot to 375 degrees. Dip meatballs in hot oil; cook to desired degree of doneness. Transfer to dinner fork; dip into desired sauce.

Dorothy B. Thetford, Rec. Sec.
Xi Nu Kappa No. 3862, Denton, Texas

MEATBALLS WITH SWEET AND SOUR MUSTARD SAUCE

3 eggs
1/2 onion, quartered
1/2 c. tomato juice
1 stalk of celery, chopped
1/2 tsp. salt
1/2 tsp. Worcestershire sauce
1/2 tsp. oregano
1 1/2 lb. ground beef
1 c. bread crumbs
1/2 c. (packed) brown sugar
3 tbsp. sugar
2 tbsp. prepared mustard
1/2 c. vinegar
1 tbsp. butter
2 c. salad oil

Combine 2 eggs, onion, tomato juice, celery, salt, Worcestershire sauce and oregano in blender container; blend well. Combine ground beef, bread crumbs, and egg mixture; blend well. Form into 1-inch meatballs. Refrigerate until ready to serve. Combine remaining egg, brown sugar, sugar, and mustard in saucepan; stir in vinegar and butter. Simmer, stirring constantly, until smooth and thickened. Pour oil into fondue pot; bring to a boil. Spear meatball with fondue fork; dip into hot oil. Cook to desired degree of doneness; dip into sauce.

Mrs. Sharon Brown, Rec. Sec.
Delta Beta Tau No. 7094, Arcata, California

MEXI-MEATBALL FONDUE

3/4 c. bread crumbs
1/4 c. chili sauce
1 egg, beaten
1 3/4 tsp. salt
1 tsp. minced onion
1/8 tsp. garlic powder
3/4 lb. ground beef
1 c. mashed avocado
1/2 c. sour cream
2 tsp. lemon juice
1/4 tsp. chili powder
3 slices bacon
Salad oil

Combine crumbs, chili sauce, egg, 1/2 teaspoon salt, 1/2 teaspoon onion and garlic powder; mix well. Add ground beef; mix thoroughly. Shape beef mixture into 30 meatballs. Combine avocado, sour cream, lemon juice, chili powder, remaining onion and 1/4 teaspoon salt. Cook bacon until crisp; drain well. Crumble bacon over avocado sauce; fold in gently. Fill fondue pot 1/2 full with salad oil; adjust heat to keep oil hot. Add remaining salt. Have meatballs at room temperature. Spear with fondue forks; dip into hot oil until of desired degree of doneness. Dip into sauce.

Margaret Neff, Past Pres., Xi Lambda X1220
Rogers, Arkansas

PEPPERONI-PIZZA FONDUE

1/4 lb. mozzarella cheese
1 lb. ground beef
1/2 tsp. salt
1 egg, slightly beaten
1/4 c. finely chopped pepperoni
   sausage
1 lg. can tomato sauce
2 tbsp. chopped onion
1 clove of garlic, minced
1 tsp. dried oregano

Cut cheese into 1/2-inch cubes. Combine ground beef, salt, egg and pepperoni sausage; shape into 1-inch meatballs. Place on foil-lined baking sheet. Bake at 350 degrees for 25 minutes. Combine tomato sauce, onion, garlic and oregano in fondue pot. Place over fondue burner; cover. Adjust heat just to keep warm; simmer for 10 minutes. Remove cover; spear cheese cubes and meatballs with fondue forks. Dip into sauce until cooked to desired degree of doneness.

J. Andrea Alstrup, Pres., Alpha Omega No. 3780
North Brunswick, New Jersey

PARTY PIZZA FONDUE

1 onion, chopped
1/2 lb. ground beef
2 tbsp. shortening
2   10 1/2-oz. cans pizza sauce

1 tbsp. cornstarch
1 1/2 tsp. oregano
1/4 tsp. garlic powder
1 1/4 c. grated Cheddar cheese
1 1/2 tsp. fennel seed
1 c. grated mozzarella cheese

Brown onion and beef in shortening in fondue pot on high heat; reduce heat to medium. Stir in pizza sauce, cornstarch, oregano, garlic powder, and half the Cheddar cheese. Add remaining Cheddar cheese, stirring until cheese is melted. Add fennel seed and mozzarella cheese; stir until cheese is melted and sauce is smooth. Adjust heat to keep fondue just bubbly. Serve with garlic bread cubes or toasted English muffin cubes. Yield: 10-12 servings.

Colleen Hines, Rec. Sec., Xi Nu Iota No. 3893
Sulphur Springs, Texas

TERIYAKI MEATBALLS

1 c. soy sauce
2 tsp. ginger
2 cloves of garlic, minced
2 lb. ground beef

Combine soy sauce, ginger, and garlic with 1/2 cup water; mix well. Shape ground beef into 60 meatballs; place in shallow baking pan. Pour soy sauce mixture over meatballs. Bake at 275 degrees for 1 hour. May be served with cheese fondue.

Merry Dee Hornbuckle, Omega No. 3029
Ottawa, Kansas

MEATBALL FONDUE WITH SWEET AND SOUR SAUCE

2 lb. ground round steak
1 pkg. onion soup mix
1 egg
2 tsp. salt
1/4 c. dried bread crumbs
2   14-oz. bottles catsup
1/2 c. chili sauce
1   10-oz. jar apple jelly
Oil

Mix steak, soup mix, egg, salt, and bread crumbs thoroughly; form into 1-inch meatballs. Combine catsup, chili sauce and jelly in saucepan. Simmer, stirring, for 20 minutes or until sauce is well blended. Pour oil into fondue pot; adjust heat to keep oil hot. Dip meatballs into hot oil with fondue forks until well browned. Remove to dinner fork; dip into sauce.

Patricia Coderre, Treas., Omega No. 2086
London, Ontario, Canada

SPICY BEEF EMPAÑADAS

1 tsp. butter or margarine
1/2 lb. lean ground beef
1/2 c. chopped onion
1/2 c. chopped tomatoes
1/4 c. chopped ripe olives
1 tbsp. flour
1/4 c. catsup or chili sauce
1/2 tsp. oregano
1/2 tsp. chili powder
1/4 tsp. salt
1/4 tsp. garlic salt
1/4 tsp. hot sauce
2 pkg. pie crust mix
2 c. peanut oil

Melt butter in heavy skillet. Add beef and onion; cook, stirring, until beef is lightly browned and onion is transparent. Stir in tomatoes, olives, flour, catsup, oregano, chili powder, salt, garlic salt, and hot sauce. Simmer, stirring frequently, for 10 minutes. Remove from heat; cool thoroughly. Prepare pie crust mix according to package directions; shape into rectangle. Let stand for 15 minutes. Roll out on lightly floured board; cut into 3-inch circles. Place 1 teaspoon beef mixture on side of each circle. Moisten edge of pastry; fold over filling and seal. Chill until ready to serve. Pour oil into metal fondue pot; heat to 350 degrees. Adjust heat to maintain temperature. Spear empanadas with fondue forks; cook in hot oil until golden.

Sharon Kaminskas, Rec. Sec., Pi Tau No. 4725
Fremont, California

SLOPPY JOE FONDUE

1 lb. ground beef
1 pkg. Sloppy Joe seasoning mix
1   6-oz. can tomato paste
1/3 c. chopped celery
1/4 c. chopped green pepper
French bread, cut into cubes

Brown ground beef in skillet; stir in seasoning mix. Blend in tomato paste and water according to package directions. Stir in celery and green pepper; bring mixture to a boil. Reduce heat; simmer for 10 minutes, stirring occasionally. Pour into fondue pot. Adjust heat to keep mixture just warm. Serve with cubes of French bread.

Betty Bradbury, Pres., Nu Gamma No. 6222
Lorain, Ohio

BRANDIED PLUM SAUCE FOR BEEF

1 c. plum preserves
1/2 tsp. cinnamon
1/4 tsp. cloves
1/4 tsp. nutmeg
2 tbsp. brandy
2 tbsp. whiskey

Combine preserves, spices, brandy, and whiskey in blender container. Blend until well mixed. Serve with beef fondue.

Norma Lukasiewicz, Xi Alpha Eta
Grand Island, Nebraska

FABULOUS FRANKS FONDUE

1/2 c. sifted flour
1 1/2 tsp. sugar
3/4 tsp. baking powder
1/4 tsp. salt
1/3 c. milk
1 egg
1 tbsp. chili powder
Cooking oil
1 lb. frankfurters, quartered

Sift dry ingredients together into bowl. Combine milk, egg, and chili powder. Add to dry mixture, beating until smooth. Heat oil in fondue pot until sizzling hot. Coat frankfurters with batter; dip into hot oil with fondue forks. Cook until lightly browned.

Aurora Sauce

1 c. mayonnaise
1/2 c. catsup
1/2 c. prepared mustard
Dash of Worcestershire sauce

Combine all ingredients in small bowl. Serve with hot frankfurters.

Darlene Entringer, Gamma Sigma
Mason City, Iowa

CHICKEN

CHICKEN-CURRY FONDUE

2 whole chicken breasts
3/4 c. milk
1 egg
1 c. buttermilk biscuit mix
1 tsp. curry powder
3 c. cooking oil
Chutney

Skin and bone chicken; cut into 1-inch pieces. Combine milk, egg, biscuit mix, and curry powder in blender container; blend thoroughly. Pour into small bowl. Heat oil in fondue pot to 360 degrees. Spear chicken pieces on fondue forks; dip into batter. Cook in hot oil until golden brown. Remove from forks; serve with chutney. Yield: 4 servings.

Linda L. Hailey, Iota Tau No. 3256
Fort Worth, Texas

CHINESE HOT POT FONDUE

2 chicken breasts, skinned
   and boned
1/2 lb. beef sirloin
1/2 head cauliflower
1 1/2 c. shrimp

2 c. fresh spinach
6 c. chicken broth
2 tsp. salt

Cut chicken and beef into thin strips. Break cauliflower into flowerets. Arrange chicken, beef, flowerets, shrimp, and spinach leaves on serving tray. Refrigerate, covered, until ready to serve. Pour broth into saucepan; add salt. Bring to a boil. Pour broth into fondue pot; place over burner. Spear chicken, beef, shrimp, and vegetables with fork. Dip into boiling broth; cook until done. Serve with various sauces and rice, if desired.

Sheila S. Cohen, Publ. Chm.
Xi Eta Delta X3830, Jacksonville, Florida

CHICKEN LIVER FONDUE

1/2 pt. sour cream
1/2 tsp. salt
Dash of pepper
1 lb. chicken livers
20 saltine crackers, crushed
2 c. peanut oil

Season sour cream with salt and pepper. Marinate livers in sour cream mixture for 2 hours. Roll livers in crushed crackers. Fill fondue pot 3/4 full of oil; place on fondue burner. Heat oil until bubbling. Spear livers with fondue forks. Dip in hot oil; cook until done. Yield: 4-6 servings.

Vera Holding
International Honorary Member, BSP
Norman, Oklahoma

LAMB

LAMB FONDUE WITH BEARNAISE SAUCE

1 1/2 lb. boneless leg of lamb
Salad oil

Trim lamb; cut into 3/4-inch cubes. Let stand at room temperature for 15 to 20 min-utes. Pour salad oil to depth of 2 to 3 inches in fondue pot; heat to 425 degrees or just below smoking point. Place on table over burner. Spear lamb on fondue forks; cook in oil for 1 to 2 minutes or until of desired doneness. Place lamb on plate.

Bearnaise Sauce

2 tbsp. dry white wine
1 tbsp. vinegar
2 tsp. chopped onion
1/4 tsp. tarragon leaves
1/2 c. butter
3 egg yolks
1/4 tsp. salt
Dash of cayenne pepper

Combine wine, vinegar, onion, and tarragon leaves in saucepan; simmer until liquid is reduced to 1 tablespoon. Add butter; heat until melted. Blend egg yolks, 2 tablespoons water, salt, and cayenne pepper in electric blender until thick; add hot butter mixture through hole in top of blender cover gradually, blending on low speed. Pour into heatproof dish; keep warm over hot water, stirring occasionally. Serve with lamb.

FILLED LAMB BALLS

1/2 lb. ground lamb
1 tsp. minced green onion tops
1 tsp. fine dry bread crumbs
1 1/4 tsp. salt
Curry powder to taste
2 to 3 oz. Swiss cheese, cubed
Salad oil

Combine lamb, green onion, crumbs, 1/4 teaspoon salt, and curry powder in small mixing bowl. Mix, blending well. Shape 1 teaspoon mixture around cheese cube, forming 1-inch ball. Let stand at room temperature. Fill fondue pot 1/2 full with salad oil. Add remaining salt. Heat to 375 degrees. Cook balls in oil for 2 minutes or until browned. Yield: 32 balls.

Donna Marie Sullivan, Pres.
Alpha Lambda No. 7097, Billings, Montana

LAMB FONDUE SUPREME

1 c. medium dry red wine
1/2 c. cooking oil
1/2 c. chopped onions
1/2 tsp. thick steak sauce
1 tsp. salt
Pepper
Thyme and marjoram to taste
Oregano to taste
3 lb. lamb, cut in 3/4-in. pieces
1/4 c. butter
6 tbsp. flour
2 c. light cream
3/8 c. sherry
1/2 c. shredded Cheddar cheese
2 tbsp. parsley
1/2 tsp. curry powder
1/2 tsp. sweet basil

Combine wine, oil, onions, steak sauce, 1/2 teaspoon salt, pepper to taste, and herbs in bowl, blending well. Pour marinade over lamb. Refrigerate, covered, for several hours, stirring occasionally. Melt butter in saucepan. Blend in flour and remaining salt; season with pepper. Place over low heat, stirring constantly until bubbly. Remove from heat.

Stir in cream and sherry. Cook over medium heat, stirring constantly, until thickened. Divide sauce into 2 parts. Add cheese to half the sauce, stirring until melted. Add parsley, curry powder, and basil to remaining white sauce. Stir over low heat for 5 minutes. Drain lamb; cook on fondue fork in deep fat in fondue pot until done. Serve with sauces.

Gillian White, Kappa No. 6513
Bathurst, New Brunswick, Canada

OLD WORLD-NEW WORLD LAMB FONDUE

5 lb. boneless lamb leg or
    shoulder
Dry sherry
Olive oil
Creamy Garlic Sauce
Avocado Sauce
Spanish Filbert Hot Pepper Sauce

Cut lamb into 3/4-inch cubes; marinate in sherry in refrigerator for several hours, turning frequently. Remove from refrigerator; let stand to room temperature. Drain off sherry; blot lamb cubes well on paper toweling. Fill fondue pot about 1/2 full with oil. Heat on range to 375 degrees or until oil bubbles. Reheat oil on range as necessary to maintain temperature. Set fondue pot on stand over moderately high flame. Spear lamb cubes with fondue forks; cook to desired doneness. Transfer lamb to dinner forks; dip into desired sauce.

Creamy Garlic Sauce

6 cloves of garlic, peeled
1/4 tsp. salt
1/4 tsp. white pepper
1 tbsp. lemon juice
3 egg yolks
1 c. olive oil

Combine garlic, salt, pepper, lemon juice and 1 egg yolk in blender container; blend until smooth. Add remaining egg yolks, one at a time, beating until smooth and thick. Add oil, 1/2 teaspoon at a time, blending well.

Sauce will be thick after 1/2 cup oil has been added. Add remaining oil in steady stream, blending only until thick and smooth.

Avocado Sauce

1 lg. ripe avocado
2 tbsp. lemon juice
1 sm. tomato
1/4 c. finely chopped green pepper
1/4 c. finely chopped onion
1/4 tsp. coriander
Salt and pepper to taste

Peel avocado; cut into quarters. Mash avocado with fork until smooth; stir in lemon juice until blended. Peel tomato; cut into fine pieces. Add tomato, green pepper, onion, and seasonings to avocado mixture. Chill; serve cold. Garnish with additional avocado slice if desired.

Spanish Filbert Hot Pepper Sauce

1/2 c. shelled filberts
1 sm. tomato
1/4 c. red wine vinegar
1 clove of garlic
1 tsp. salt

1/2 tsp. cayenne pepper
3/4 c. olive oil

Place filberts on baking sheet. Bake at 400 degrees for 8 to 10 minutes. Combine filberts, tomato, vinegar, garlic, salt and cayenne pepper in blender container. Blend to smooth paste. Add 1/2 cup olive oil, one teaspoon at a time, blending on medium speed. Sauce should be thick and creamy. Add remaining oil in steady stream. Chill; serve cold with lamb fondue. Additional chopped filberts may be sprinkled over sauce if desired.

SEAFOOD

WEST COAST PRAWN TEMPURA

Prawns or shrimp, cleaned
Sole, cut in sm. squares
Fresh mushrooms
Sweet potatoes, sliced thin
Sweet onions, cut in sm. wedges
Cauliflowerets
Zucchini, sliced
Green beans
2 egg yolks
1 c. water
1 c. flour
1 tsp. salt
2 1/2 c. oil
Soy sauce
Grated ginger
Lemon wedges

Arrange first 8 ingredients on large platter. Cover with plastic wrap; place in refrigerator. Beat egg yolks and water with electric mixer until frothy. Add flour and salt gradually; beat until smooth. Heat oil in fondue pot; place over burner. Place batter in 6 individual bowls; place on table. Place platter in center of table. Place vegetables and seafood on fondue forks; dip into batter. Fry in oil until golden. Serve with soy sauce, ginger, and lemon wedges.

Carol Walster, Rec. Sec., Xi Beta Lambda X2523
Moses Lake, Washington

DEEP-SEA FONDUE

4 c. bottled clam juice
2 c. dry white wine
2 c. water
1 lg. onion, finely chopped
1 lg. carrot, finely chopped
1 stalk celery, finely chopped
4 peppercorns
1 bay leaf
1/2 tsp. salt
1 lb. fillets of sole
12 lg. scallops
4 lg. lobster-tails
Lemon wedges

Mix first nine ingredients; bring to a boil. Cook over moderate heat for 30 minutes. Strain; reserve liquid. Discard solids. Cut sole in 2-inch lengths; slice each scallop into 3 pieces. Cut lobster-tails in bite-sized pieces. Heat reserved bouillon in fondue pot; keep at simmering over burner at table. Spear sole, scallops and lobster-tail chunks separately on fondue forks; cook in bouillon to desired doneness. Serve with lemon wedges and desired sauces.

Connie Lee, Recording Sec., Honolulu Alpha 885
Honolulu, Hawaii

SATURDAY NIGHT FISH FONDUE

Shrimp
Fish
Oysters
Flour
Sliced bacon
1 qt. (about) cooking oil
1 tsp. salt
Herbed butter
Caper sauce

Allow 1/3 to 1/2 pound combination of shrimp, fish, and oysters per person. Peel shrimp, leaving last shell segment and tail intact. Cut fish into strips or bite-sized pieces. Drain oysters well; roll in flour. Wrap each oyster in 1/3 slice bacon; secure with wooden pick. Refrigerate all seafood until 30 minutes before serving time. Drain well

or pat dry with paper towel. Pour oil into fondue cooker to 2-inch depth or no more than 1/2 full; heat to 375 degrees. Add salt. Spear fish, shrimp, and oyster with fondue fork; fry in oil until lightly browned. Transfer to dinner fork; dip in herbed butter or caper sauce.

Lydia McMullen, Pichi No. 4615
Harlingen, Texas

ELEGANT LOBSTER FONDUE

1/2 c. cooked or canned lobster
1   10-oz. can frozen cream of
    shrimp soup
1/2 soup can milk
1/2 c. shredded sharp cheese
Dash of paprika
Dash of cayenne pepper
2 tbsp. sherry (opt.)
Large bread cubes

Cut lobster into small pieces. Combine soup and milk in fondue pot; cook over low heat until soup is thawed. Add cheese, lobster, paprika, and cayenne pepper; heat, stirring frequently, until cheese melts. Add sherry. Serve with bread cubes. Yield: 2 to 3 servings.

Mrs. Millie Von Konsky
International Honorary Member BSP
Dublin, California

SHERRIED SEAFOOD FONDUE

2 c. lobster chunks
2 tbsp. butter
3 egg yolks
1 c. light cream
1/4 tsp. salt
3 tbsp. sherry
1/4 tsp. cayenne pepper
1 tsp. flour

Heat lobster in butter; place on platter. Keep warm. Beat egg yolks slightly; mix with cream. Add salt, sherry, cayenne pepper, and flour; cook over low heat until thickened, stirring constantly. Do not boil. Pour into fondue pot; place over low heat. Spear lobster with fondue fork; dip into sauce. Shrimp may be substituted for lobster. Yield: 4 servings.

Linda Hinkle, 1st VP, Beta Nu No. 1620
St. Joseph, Missouri

CANTONESE BATTER-FRIED SHRIMP

2 lb. large fresh shrimp
3/4 c. unsifted flour
3/4 c. water
1 egg, slightly beaten
1 tbsp. sugar
1/2 tsp. salt
Peanut oil

Peel shrimp, leaving tails intact; devein. Split shrimp halfway through lengthwise; flatten butterfly fashion. Combine flour, water, egg, sugar, and salt; beat until smooth. Fill fondue pot 1/2 full with oil; heat to 375 degrees. Place shrimp on fondue fork; dip into batter. Fry in oil until golden brown.

Mrs. Don Schooler, VP, Xi Psi
Brookfield, Missouri

SALMON FONDUE DELIGHT

2 tbsp. butter
3 tbsp. flour
1   7 3/4-oz. can salmon
Chicken broth or milk
1 c. milk
Dash of hot sauce
1 1/2 c. grated Swiss cheese
French bread, cut in bite-sized
    pieces

Melt butter in top of double boiler; stir in flour. Drain salmon; reserve liquid. Add enough chicken broth to reserved liquid to make 1/2 cup liquid; stir into flour mixture. Stir in milk; cook over simmering water until smooth and thickened, stirring constantly. Stir in hot sauce. Add cheese; stir until melted. Flake salmon; add to fondue. Cook

for 5 minutes; place in fondue pot. Serve with bread. Yield: 4 servings.

Margarete Collins, Pres., Xi Delta Xi X1635
McGregor, Texas

SALMON FONDUE

2 tbsp. butter or margarine
3 tbsp. flour
1   7 3/4-oz. can salmon
Bottled clam juice
1 c. milk
1 1/2 c. grated Swiss cheese
Dash of hot sauce
French bread, cut in chunks
Lobster chunks

Melt butter in fondue pot over burner; stir in the flour. Drain salmon; reserve liquid. Add enough clam juice to reserved liquid to make 1/2 cup liquid. Stir into flour mixture. Add milk; cook until smooth and thickened, stirring constantly. Add cheese; stir until cheese is melted. Flake salmon; add to sauce. Stir in the hot sauce; cook for five minutes. Turn flame to low. Serve fondue with French bread and lobster chunks.

HOT CRAB FONDUE

1   5-oz. jar sharp American cheese
1   8-oz. package cream cheese
1   7 1/2-oz. can Alaskan King crab
1/2 tsp. Worcestershire sauce
1/4 c. cream
1/4 tsp. garlic
1/2 tsp. cayenne pepper

Combine cheeses in top of double boiler; place over boiling water. Stir until blended. Drain crab; flake. Add to cheese; add remaining ingredients. Cook, stirring, until smooth and bubbly. Place in fondue pot; keep hot. Add more cream if fondue becomes too thick; serve with French bread cubes, melba toast rounds, or toast points.

Joann Hunter, Pres., Iota Tau No. 6795
Centerview, Missouri

MICHIGAN CRAB MEAT FONDUE

1   6-oz. can crab meat
1   10-oz. package sharp Cheddar
    cheese
1   8-oz. package sliced process
    Cheddar cheese
1/4 c. butter
1/2 c. sauterne or dry sherry
French bread cubes or crackers

Flake crab meat; remove cartilage. Cut cheeses into small pieces; place in fondue pot. Add butter and sauterne; place over low heat. Stir until cheese melts. Stir in crab meat; keep warm, stirring frequently. Serve with bread cubes. Yield: 10 servings.

Audra E. Francis
International Honorary Member, BSP
Saginaw, Michigan

CHEESE-CRAB FONDUE

1   7 1/2-oz. can crab meat
2 c. shredded process American
    cheese
2 c. shredded natural Cheddar
    cheese
3/4 c. milk
2 tsp. lemon juice

Drain and flake crab meat; remove cartilage. Combine cheeses with milk in saucepan; cook, stirring constantly, until mixture is smooth and cheese is melted. Stir in lemon juice and crab; heat through. Transfer to fondue pot; place over fondue burner. Adjust heat so mixture is just warm. Spear dipper on fondue fork; dip in fondue, swirling to coat. Suggested dippers: French bread, cherry tomatoes or cooked artichokes. Yield: 8-10 servings.

Barbara Kearns, Pres., St. Louis City Coun.
Epsilon Lambda No. 3875, Creve Coeur, Missouri

CLAMS À LA MARINARA

1 can pimentos
1 garlic clove, minced
1 sm. onion, minced
1/4 c. olive oil
1   8-oz. can tomato sauce
2 tbsp. sherry
1   10-oz. can clams
1/4 c. minced parsley
Sourdough bread cubes

Drain pimentos; mince. Saute garlic, pimentos, and onion in olive oil until onion is tender. Add tomato sauce and sherry. Drain clams; pour liquid into onion mixture. Cook until liquid is reduced and mixture is thickened. Add clams; cook for 3 to 4 minutes. Add parsley; cook for 1 minute longer. Place in fondue pot. Dip bread cubes into fondue to serve. Yield: 6-8 servings.

Doris Matthews, Treas., Xi Mu Tau X2984
Rancho Cordova, California

SEAFOOD FONDUE

Chunks of cooked halibut
Chunks of cooked salmon
Chunks of cooked red snapper
Cooked shrimp
Chunks of cooked lobster-tails
Dilled mayonnaise
Tartar sauce
Sweet-Sour Sauce
Swedish Cream Sauce
Louis Sauce

Place fish and shellfish on tray or platter; garnish with lemon. Dip into desired sauce.

Sweet-Sour Sauce

1/2 c. pickle relish
1/2 c. chili sauce

Mix relish and chili sauce; chill.

Swedish Cream Sauce

1 c. sour cream
1/4 c. grated cucumber
2 tbsp. frozen chopped chives
Salt to taste

Combine all ingredients; chill.

Louis Sauce

1 c. mayonnaise
1/4 c. French dressing
1/4 c. catsup
1 tsp. prepared horseradish
1 tsp. Worcestershire sauce
Salt to taste
Coarsely ground pepper to taste

Mix all ingredients; chill.

Photograph for this recipe on page 6.

GLORIA'S SHRIMP DIP

1 can frozen shrimp soup
1 8-oz. package Cheddar cheese, cubed
1 4-oz. can mushroom pieces
1/4 tsp. Worcestershire sauce

Combine shrimp soup and cheese in top of double boiler; place over boiling water until cheese is melted, stirring constantly. Add mushrooms and Worcestershire sauce; blend well. Transfer to fondue pot; keep warm. Serve with cauliflowerets, thin carrot sticks, celery sticks, chips, and crackers.

Gloria Yokiel, Xi Theta Alpha
Maple Heights, Ohio

LYNETTE'S SHRIMP FONDUE

2 lb. fresh or frozen shrimp
2 tsp. grated nutmeg

2 c. white wine
1 clove of garlic
1 lb. Swiss cheese, cubed
3 tbsp. cornstarch
1 tsp. salt
1/2 tsp. Worcestershire sauce
1/4 tsp. white pepper

Clean shrimp; place in saucepan. Cover with boiling water; add nutmeg. Bring to a boil; cook for 3 minutes. Drain. Place 1 3/4 cups wine and garlic in top of double boiler. Place over boiling water; heat through. Remove garlic. Add cheese; stir constantly until melted. Combine cornstarch, salt, Worcestershire sauce, pepper, and remaining wine; stir into cheese mixture. Cook, stirring, until smooth; pour into fondue pot. Keep warm. Place shrimp on fondue fork; dip into cheese mixture. Yield: 6-8 servings.

Lynette Smeby, VP, Delta Tau No. 5364
Oak Harbor, Washington

SHRIMP WITH AVOCADO FONDUE

1/2 c. butter
1 med. onion, finely chopped
1/2 c. flour
1 c. milk
1/2 c. cream
Salt and pepper to taste
4 tbsp. lemon juice
1 c. mashed avocado
1/2 c. grated Parmesan cheese
Brandy to taste
1 lb. cleaned cooked shrimp
Thin slices brown bread

Melt butter in fondue pot. Add onion; cook over low heat until soft. Stir in flour; cook for 2 to 3 minutes. Remove from heat. Add milk, cream, salt, pepper, lemon juice, and avocado; stir well. Cook for 5 minutes, stirring constantly; do not boil. Add cheese; stir until melted. Blend in brandy. Place shrimp on fondue fork; dip into fondue. Serve with bread and additional butter. Yield: 4-6 servings.

Mrs. Kaye Hummel, Past Pres.
Preceptor Eta XP693, McLean, Virginia

SEAFOOD FONDUE WITH SAUCES

Fish fillets
Fish sticks
Rock lobster-tails
Fresh shrimp
Fresh scallops
2 to 2 1/2 c. peanut oil
Louis Sauce
Sauce Remoulade
Swedish Cream Sauce
Sweet-Sour Sauce
Zippy Tomato Sauce

Cut fish fillets into 3-inch pieces; cut each fish stick into 3 pieces. Remove meat from lobster-tails; cut into 1/2-inch pieces. Peel shrimp; devein. Combine seafood on large platter; place next to fondue pot. Pour oil into fondue pot. Heat on stove to 375 degrees. Place fondue pot on fondue burner over direct heat. Spear desired seafood pieces with fondue forks; dip into hot oil. Cook to desired doneness. Transfer to plate; dip into desired sauce with dinner forks.

Louis Sauce

1 c. mayonnaise
1/4 c. French dressing

1/4 c. catsup
1 tsp. prepared horseradish
1 tsp. Worcestershire sauce
Salt and coarsely ground pepper
    to taste

Combine all ingredients, mixing well. Chill.

Sauce Remoulade

1 c. mayonnaise
2 tsp. prepared mustard
1 tsp. chopped pickle
2 tsp. drained chopped capers
1 tsp. minced parsley
1 tsp. chervil
1 tsp. tarragon
Anchovy paste to taste

Combine all ingredients; mix well. Chill.

Swedish Cream Sauce

1 c. sour cream
1/4 c. grated cucumber
2 tbsp. frozen chopped chives
Salt to taste

Combine all ingredients; chill well.

Sweet-Sour Sauce

1/2 c. pickle relish
1/2 c. chili sauce

Combine relish and chili sauce; chill.

Zippy Tomato Sauce

1/4 tsp. liquid pepper sauce
2 8-oz. cans tomato sauce
    with cheese

Combine pepper sauce and tomato sauce; chill.

TEXAS SEAFOOD FONDUE

1 5/8 c. catsup
3 tbsp. horseradish
1 c. salad dressing

2 tbsp. sweet pickle relish
1 c. butter
1 c. oil
1 1/2 lb. medium shrimp, cleaned
1 lb. scallops
1 lb. lobster chunks

Mix 1 1/2 cups catsup and horseradish; chill. Mix salad dressing, relish, and remaining catsup; chill. Place in individual sauce dishes. Melt butter with oil in fondue pot; bring to a boil. Place over burner; keep bubbling. Place shrimp, scallops, and lobster separately on fondue forks; cook in oil to desired doneness. Dip in desired sauce.

Bonnibeth Foltz, Pres., Xi No. 7419
Houston, Texas

TUNA-CHEESE FONDUE

1 clove of garlic, halved
2 c. dry white wine
1/2 lb. Swiss cheese, diced
1/2 lb. Gruyere cheese, diced
1 1/2 tbsp. cornstarch
2 tbsp. kirsch or brandy
Dash of nutmeg
1 6 1/2 or 7-oz. can tuna
French or Italian bread cubes

Rub inside of fondue pot with garlic. Add wine to fondue pot; warm over medium heat. Do not boil. Add cheeses gradually; stir until cheeses melt and mixture comes to a boil. Blend cornstarch, kirsch, and nutmeg; stir into cheese mixture. Drain tuna; flake. Add to cheese mixture; cook, stirring constantly, for 1 minute. Place over heating unit; serve with bread cubes. Yield: 4 servings.

Photograph for this recipe on page 1.

CHEESE

APPLE SWISS FONDUE

1 clove of garlic, halved
2 c. apple juice

1/2 lb. imported Swiss cheese, grated
1/2 lb. Gruyere cheese, grated
1 tbsp. cornstarch
2 tbsp. lemon juice
Nutmeg or pepper to taste
French bread cubes

Rub inside of fondue pot with garlic. Pour apple juice into fondue pot; place over low heat until bubbles rise to surface. Add cheeses, 1 spoonful at a time, stirring with wooden spoon after each addition until cheese is melted. Mix cornstarch and lemon juice; stir into fondue. Add nutmeg; stir until smooth and thickened. Serve hot with bread cubes. Swiss cheese may be used in place of Gruyere cheese. Yield: 4 servings.

Joan Miller, W and M Chm.
Preceptor Kappa XP466
North Vancouver, British Columbia, Canada

CHAMPAGNE SWISS FONDUE

1 lb. Swiss cheese, shredded
3 tbsp. flour
1 clove of garlic, cut
1 c. champagne
1 c. dry white wine
1 tbsp. lemon juice
3 tbsp. kirsch or brandy
1/8 tsp. ground nutmeg
1/8 tsp. pepper
1/8 tsp. paprika
2 loaves Italian or French bread,
    cubed

Dredge cheese lightly in flour. Rub inside of fondue pot completely with garlic; pour in champagne and wine. Bring champagne mixture just to a boil; add lemon juice. Stir in cheese gradually. Cook, stirring constantly with a wooden spoon, until cheese is melted and fondue is smooth. Bring to a rolling boil; add kirsch and spices. Reduce heat; cook, stirring constantly, until blended. Spear bread cubes through soft side into crust with fondue forks; swirl in fondue. Yield: 10-12 servings.

Linda Singer, Beta Phi No. 3154
Clearwater, Florida

CHAMPAGNE PARTY FONDUE

1 lb. Swiss cheese, diced
2 tsp. cornstarch
2 c. champagne
1 tbsp. lemon juice
1/8 tsp. white pepper
Salt

Mix cheese with cornstarch until well coated. Pour champagne into fondue pot; heat not quite to boiling. Add lemon juice; stir in cheese, small amount at a time. Cook, stirring, until cheese is melted and fondue is smooth and well blended. Add pepper and salt, if needed. Serve with desired accompaniments. Yield: 4 servings.

Mrs. Donald Blohm, Xi Delta Sigma X1856
Monroe, Michigan

CHEESE FONDUE FOR FOUR

1 clove of garlic, cut
3/4 c. dry white wine
1/2 lb. Gruyere cheese
1/2 lb. Swiss cheese
1 1/2 tsp. cornstarch
2 tbsp. kirsch
1/8 tsp. nutmeg
1/8 tsp. salt
1/8 tsp. pepper

Rub inside of fondue pot with garlic; pour wine into pot. Bring just to a boil over medium heat. Add cheeses gradually, stirring constantly until cheeses are melted and fondue is smooth. Blend cornstarch with kirsch; add to cheese mixture. Bring to a boil; add nutmeg, salt and pepper. Thin fondue with additional wine or kirsch, if needed.

Marguerite Peyton Thompson
International Honorary Member, BSP
Boulder, Colorado

BRANDIED SWISS FONDUE

2 lb. Swiss cheese, grated
6 tbsp. flour
1 garlic clove, cut in half
4 c. dry white wine

6 tbsp. brandy
Dash of ground nutmeg
1 tsp. salt
Freshly ground pepper to taste
French bread, cut in pieces

Mix Swiss cheese with flour until cheese is coated. Rub inside of fondue pot with garlic. Pour wine into fondue pot; place over low heat until bubbles rise to surface. Add cheese, several spoons at a time, stirring until cheese is thoroughly melted and mixture is bubbling. Add brandy, nutmeg, salt, and pepper; keep hot. Dip bread into fondue. Yield: 6 servings.

Pam McCartney, Rec. Sec., Omicron Pi No. 7342
Lorain, Ohio

SWISS CHEESE FONDUE

1 clove of garlic
2 c. dry white wine
1 lb. imported Swiss
   cheese, grated
1 tbsp. cornstarch
2 tbsp. kirsch
Dash of pepper
Dash of nutmeg

Rub bottom and side of fondue pot with garlic; add wine. Heat to boiling point on

stove. Add cheese gradually, stirring constantly with wooden spoon until cheese melts. Cheese and wine will not be blended. Mix cornstarch and kirsch together; add to cheese mixture. Cook for several minutes, stirring constantly, until thickened and blended. Stir in pepper; sprinkle with nutmeg. Place fondue pot over direct flame.

Waffles

1 c. buttermilk pancake mix
1 c. milk
1 egg
2 tbsp. melted shortening

Combine all ingredients in mixing bowl; beat with rotary beater until batter is smooth. Bake in hot waffle iron until steaming stops. Cut each waffle section into small pieces; dip into hot fondue with fondue forks.

CLASSIC CHEESE FONDUE

3 c. shredded natural Swiss cheese
1 c. shredded Gruyere cheese
1 1/2 tsp. cornstarch
1 clove of garlic, halved
1 c. sauterne
1 tbsp. lemon juice
Dash of pepper
French or Italian bread cubes

Combine cheeses and cornstarch. Rub inside of heavy saucepan with garlic; discard garlic. Pour sauterne and lemon juice into saucepan; place over medium heat until bubbles cover surface. Do not cover; do not boil. Add cheese, handful at a time, stirring constantly after each addition until cheese is melted. Stir in pepper; pour into fondue pot. Keep warm over low flame; add more sauterne if fondue becomes too thick. Spear bread cubes with fondue fork, piercing crust last. Dip into fondue; swirl to coat bread. Hard roll cubes or boiled potato cubes may be substituted for French bread. Yield: 10 servings.

June Morgan, Xi Omega No. 827
Sedalia, Missouri

CHEESE-TOMATO FONDUE

1   1 3/8-oz. package onion soup mix
2 c. thick tomato juice
1 tbsp. lemon juice
4 c. shredded American or sharp
    Cheddar cheese
1 tbsp. parsley flakes
French or rye bread cubes
1 sm. can whole mushrooms,
    drained

Combine soup mix, tomato juice, and lemon juice in fondue pot; bring to a simmer. Add cheese, 1/4 cup at a time; stir until melted after each addition. Add parsley flakes; stir gently. Spear bread cubes and mushrooms with fondue fork; dip into cheese mixture. Fresh mushrooms may be substituted for canned mushrooms.

Mrs. Rae Shaw
International Honorary Member, BSP
Mattoon, Illinois

FRIED CHEESE PASTRIES

1 c. all-purpose flour
1/2 tsp. salt
1 1/2 c. grated sharp Cheddar
    cheese
1/4 c. soft butter
1 tbsp. Worcestershire sauce
1 tbsp. milk
Small canned shrimp or stuffed
    olives

Sift flour with salt; cut in cheese and butter with 2 knives or pastry blender until mixture is consistency of cornmeal. Add Worcestershire sauce and milk; stir until dough cleans bowl. Chill. Roll out on lightly floured board to 1/8-inch thickness; cut into 2-inch squares. Place 1 shrimp on each square. Moisten edges; fold into triangle. Press edges together with fork. Heat deep fat in fondue pot to 380 degrees. Fry pastries in fat for 2 to 3 minutes or until brown and crisp. Drain; serve hot. Yield: 2 dozen.

Betty Bayless, Pres., Alpha Nu No. 787
Stillwater, Oklahoma

PETITE FONDUE

1 clove of garlic, peeled
1/2 lb. Swiss cheese, diced
1/2 lb. Italian cheese, diced
3/4 c. dry white wine
2 tbsp. brandy
Salt and pepper to taste

Rub inside of fondue pot with garlic. Place cheeses in fondue pot; add wine. Let stand for 5 hours. Heat over low flame, stirring constantly until cheese is melted. Add brandy, salt, and pepper; blend.

Claudia Kiker, Pres., Delta Omega
Shawnee, Oklahoma

VEGETABLES

BREADED CAULIFLOWER

1 med. cauliflower
2 eggs
Salt to taste
Pepper to taste
1/4 c. milk
1 c. flour
Bread crumbs
3 to 4 c. oil

Cut cauliflower into flowerets. Boil for 4 to 5 minutes in salted water. Strain well; cool. Beat eggs; season with salt and pepper. Beat in milk with fork. Coat cauliflower with flour; dip into milk mixture. Roll in bread crumbs. Dip cauliflower into hot oil with fondue forks; cook until golden. Breading may be done several hours ahead.

Jolana Tamajka, Pres., Xi Sigma X1618
Kamloops, British Columbia, Canada

GREEN CHILIES DIP

1 onion, chopped
2 tbsp. oil
1 lg. can tomatoes, chopped
1 can tomato paste
1 can green chilies, chopped
1   10-oz. package Cheddar cheese, grated
1/2 tsp. cumin
1/4 tsp. salt
1/4 tsp. pepper

Saute onion in oil in saucepan until tender. Add tomatoes, tomato paste, green chilies, cheese, and seasonings. Heat, stirring, until cheese melts. Spoon into fondue pot; place on fondue burner over low heat.

Eleanor Wood, Corr. Sec.
Lambda Kappa No. 7828, Enon, Ohio

ARTICHOKES WITH SWISS FONDUE

4 lg. artichokes
Salt

32

3/4 c. dry white wine
1/2 lb. Swiss or Gruyere
  cheese, grated
1 1/2 tsp. flour
1/8 tsp. salt
Dash of dry mustard
Dash of nutmeg

Wash artichokes; cut off stems at base. Remove small bottom leaves. Trim tips of leaves; cut off about 1 inch from top of artichokes. Stand artichokes upright in deep saucepan large enough to hold snugly. Add 1/4 teaspoon salt for each artichoke and 2 to 3 inches boiling water. Cover; simmer for 35 to 45 minutes or until base can be easily pierced with fork. Turn artichokes upside down to drain. Place on serving plate. Heat wine to boiling in lined copper fondue pot on stove. Toss cheese with remaining ingredients. Stir vigorously into bubbling wine; stir over medium heat until smooth and thickened. Place fondue pot on burner over low heat. Dip artichoke leaves into hot fondue.

SAUERKRAUT BALLS

8 oz. pork sausage, crumbled
1/4 c. finely chopped onion
1 14-oz. can drained sauerkraut,
  snipped
Fine dry bread crumbs
1 3-oz. package cream cheese,
  softened
2 tbsp. snipped parsley
1 tsp. prepared mustard
1/4 tsp. garlic
1/8 tsp. pepper
1/4 c. flour
2 eggs, beaten
1/4 c. milk
Oil

Saute sausage and onion in skillet until sausage is browned; drain. Add sauerkraut and 2 tablespoons bread crumbs. Combine cream cheese, parsley, mustard, garlic, and pepper; stir into sauerkraut mixture. Chill. Shape into 3/4-inch balls. Coat balls with flour. Combine eggs and milk. Dip balls in egg mixture; roll in 3/4 cup bread crumbs. Bring meatballs to room temperature. Heat oil in

fondue pot to 375 degrees over fondue burner. Spear meatballs with fondue forks; fry in hot oil until golden brown. Dip into desired sauces. Yield: 25 meatballs.

Joanne Carr, Pres., Xi Kappa Tau X2668
San Jose, California

CRUSTY VEGETABLE BITES

1 c. fine dry bread crumbs
1/4 c. grated Parmesan cheese
1 tsp. paprika
1 tsp. salt
2 eggs, slightly beaten
1 c. bite-sized fresh cauliflowerets
1 c. sliced carrots
1 c. 1-in. eggplant cubes
Salad oil

Combine bread crumbs, cheese, paprika, and 1/2 teaspoon salt. Blend eggs, 1 tablespoon water and remaining salt together, beating well. Dip vegetables into egg mixture; roll in crumb mixture. Dip into egg mixture again; roll in crumb mixture. Let vegetables stand at room temperature in serving bowl. Spear with fondue forks; fry in hot oil in fondue pot for 2 to 3 minutes or until browned.

Jacquline Smith, City Coun. Pres.
Delta Theta No. 3974, Great Bend, Kansas

TOMATO FONDUE

3 tbsp. butter
1 sliced onion
1 crushed garlic clove
1/4 tsp. thyme leaves
2 med. tomatoes, chopped
Salt and pepper to taste
3 tbsp. chopped parsley
3 tbsp. grated Parmesan cheese

Melt butter in fondue pot over fondue burner. Saute onion for 5 minutes. Add garlic, thyme, tomatoes, and seasonings. Cook, stirring frequently, for 30 minutes over low heat. Add parsley and cheese; stir until thick and smooth.

Patricia Windelborn, Pres.
Eta Lambda No. 3413, Elgin, Illinois

FONDUE MUSHROOMS

Fresh mushroom caps
4 eggs, beaten
1 c. cracker crumbs
2 c. oil

Spear mushrooms on fondue forks; dip into eggs. Twirl in cracker crumbs. Dip into hot oil in fondue pot. Cook until golden brown.

Jeannie Russ, Pres., Rho No. 7692
Gibsonia, Pennsylvania

HOT ANCHOVY AND GARLIC FONDUE

1 cucumber
2 carrots
1 sweet red pepper
1 green pepper
4 celery stalks
12 cherry tomatoes
Radishes
Cauliflowerets
1/4 lb. fresh mushroom caps
2 c. heavy cream
1 can drained anchovy fillets,
    rinsed
1 tsp. garlic, chopped
4 tbsp. butter
Bread sticks

Peel and seed cucumber; cut into 2 x 1/2-inch strips. Pare carrots; cut into 2 x 1/2-inch strips. Seed red and green peppers; cut into 2 x 2 1/2-inch strips. Cut celery into 2 x 1/2-inch pieces. Soak vegetables and mushrooms in ice water for 1 hour; pat dry. Arrange on large serving platter. Chill until serving time. Bring cream to a boil, stirring constantly. Reduce heat; simmer, stirring, until reduced to about 1 cup. Add anchovies and garlic. Place cream mixture in blender container; blend until well mixed. Melt butter in earthen fondue pot over fondue burner. Add cream mixture; bring to simmering point over low heat. Serve with vegetables, mushrooms, and bread sticks.

Dianne Grabatin, Alpha Chap.
Calgary, Alberta, Canada

VEGETABLE CURRY DIP

1 c. mayonnaise
3 tbsp. catsup
3 tsp. curry powder
1 tsp. onion juice
1 tsp. garlic juice
Salt and pepper to taste

Combine all ingredients; mix well. Chill well. Serve with fresh cauliflowerets, carrot pieces, and celery.

Patricia Harms, Pres., Omicron No. 8004
Norfolk, Nebraska

VEGETABLE FONDUE CURRY

Cherry tomatoes
Cauliflowerets
Broccoli flowerets
Green pepper strips
Peeled cucumber slices
Zucchini fingers
Sliced celery
1/4 c. butter
1 green onion, minced
2 tbsp. flour
1 tsp. minced gingerroot
1/2 c. chopped apple

1 to 2 tsp. curry powder
1 tsp. salt
1 tsp. sugar
4 whole cloves
Dash of cayenne pepper
2 c. milk
1/2 c. moist shredded coconut
1/4 c. lemon juice
Thin cream

Arrange vegetables on large serving platter; chill until serving time. Melt butter in blazer pan of chafing dish. Saute onion until transparent, stirring occasionally. Blend in flour until bubbly; add gingerroot, apple, curry powder, salt, sugar, cloves, and cayenne pepper. Remove from heat; add milk gradually. Cook, stirring constantly, until sauce thickens. Place over pan of simmering water; cook for 30 minutes, covered. Remove whole cloves. Stir in coconut. Add lemon juice gradually. Thin with cream if necessary. Spear vegetables with fondue forks; dip into sauce.

DESSERTS

ALMOND POUND CAKE FOR FONDUE

1 c. shortening
3 c. sugar
5 eggs
3 c. sifted all-purpose flour
1 tsp. salt
1/4 tsp. soda
1 c. buttermilk
2 tbsp. almond flavoring
1 tbsp. vanilla
Chocolate or caramel sauce

Cream shortening and sugar; add eggs, one at a time, beating well after each addition. Mix flour, salt, and soda; add to creamed mixture alternately with buttermilk. Stir in flavorings; place in greased and floured tube pan. Bake at 375 degrees for 1 hour and 15 minutes. Cool in pan for 10 minutes. Remove from pan; cool completely. Cut into bite-sized pieces. Pour chocolate sauce into fondue pot; heat through. Place cake on fondue fork; dip into sauce.

Judy Holtz, Mu Lambda No. 8110
Fairfax, Missouri

THREE-CHEESE DESSERT FONDUE

1 3-oz. package cream cheese
3/4 c. grated Cheddar cheese
3/4 c. grated Swiss cheese
1 tbsp. flour
1/2 c. white wine
1/8 tsp. garlic salt
Dash of cayenne pepper
Fresh apple wedges
Fresh pear wedges

Pour 1 cup water into fondue base; position tray, rack, and bowl. Cut cream cheese into cubes; mix cheeses with flour. Plug unit into outlet. Pour wine into fondue bowl; heat until bubbles rise to surface. Stir in cheeses, small amount at a time, until melted. Beat with fork to blend smoothly; stir in garlic salt and cayenne pepper. Spear apple wedges and pear wedges on fondue forks; dip into cheese mixture.

BUTTERSCOTCH FONDUE

1 tbsp. butter
2 tbsp. brown sugar
2 tsp. cornstarch
1/2 c. half and half
1 12-oz. jar butterscotch ice
    cream topping
2 tbsp. peanut butter
Banana chunks
Apple chunks
Marshmallows
Sponge or pound cake cubes

Melt butter in saucepan. Combine brown sugar and cornstarch; stir into butter. Blend in half and half; cook over low heat, stirring constantly, until thickened. Add topping and peanut butter; cook, stirring occasionally, for 10 minutes. Place in fondue pot; keep warm over low heat, stirring occasionally. Spear banana, apple, marshmallows, or cake on fondue fork; dip into sauce. Sauce may be prepared ahead, chilled, and reheated before serving.

Susie Brewer, Alpha Nu No. 9487
South Charleston, West Virginia

CARAMEL FONDUE

1/2 c. butter or margarine
2 c. half and half or whipping
    cream
1 1/2 c. (packed) light brown sugar
1/2 c. sugar
1/8 tsp. salt
1/8 tsp. nutmeg
1/8 tsp. cinnamon
Apples
Ascorbic acid
Chopped pecans (opt.)

Place butter, half and half, brown sugar, sugar, salt, nutmeg, and cinnamon in fondue pot; heat to boiling point. Cook, without stirring, for about 15 minutes or until mixture sheets when dropped from spoon, using pastry brush dipped in hot water to brush sugar crystals from side of pot occasionally.

Cut apples into bite-sized pieces; brush with ascorbic acid to keep from turning dark. Place apple on fondue fork. Dip into caramel sauce; dip into pecans. Angel food cake pieces, doughnut pieces, or other fruits may also be used for dipping.

Hugh Ann Henson, Pres., Xi Epsilon Pi X2539
Paris, Illinois

CHOCOLATE PEACH FONDUE

1 1-lb. 13-oz. can cling peach
    slices
1 6-oz. package chocolate bits
2 tbsp. butter
1/4 c. orange juice
1 tbsp. grated orange rind

Drain peaches; place in serving bowl. Combine chocolate bits, butter, orange juice, and rind in small saucepan. Place over low heat; stir until chocolate is melted. Keep warm over warmer. Dip peaches into chocolate fondue with fondue forks.

CHOCOLATE FONDUE WITH FRUITS

1/2 c. butter or margarine
2 c. sugar
1 1/4 c. cocoa
1 tall can evaporated milk
Banana chunks
Mandarin orange slices
Pineapple chunks

Melt butter in top of double boiler. Add sugar and cocoa; mix well. Stir in milk; place over boiling water. Cook, stirring, for about 30 minutes or until thickened. Pour into fondue pot; keep warm over very low flame. Dip fruits into fondue.

Susan Jane Lacey, Rec. Sec.
Tau Epsilon No. 5199, College Station, Texas

CHOCOLATE FONDUE WITH PECAN BALLS

2 1-lb. boxes powdered sugar
2 sticks butter
1 can sweetened condensed milk
3/4 c. chopped pecans
1 can coconut (opt.)
1 12-oz. package semisweet
   chocolate pieces
1 cake paraffin

Combine sugar, butter, milk, pecans, and coconut; shape into small balls. Chill. Melt chocolate and paraffin in fondue pot. Place balls on fondue forks; dip into chocolate.

Becky Anderson, Rec. Sec., Gamma Beta No. 5858
Jackson, Mississippi

CHOCOLATE-BUTTERSCOTCH FONDUE

1/3 c. light cream or half and half
1 tbsp. sugar
1/4 tsp. salt
1 1/2 c. semisweet chocolate bits
1/2 c. butterscotch bits
1/2 tsp. vanilla
1/2 tsp. maple flavoring (opt.)

Place cream, sugar, and salt in fondue pot; place over high heat until heated through. Add chocolate and butterscotch bits; cook over low heat until melted, stirring constantly. Stir in flavorings. Serve with bite-sized chunks of angel food, pound, sponge, or chocolate cake, apple wedges, banana, cantaloupe, or doughnut chunks, marshmallows, popcorn, fresh strawberries, or pineapple. May be rolled in finely chopped nuts after dipping, if desired.

Paula Ann Stiles, Alpha Gamma Psi No. 7171
Cuero, Texas

KAHLUA CHOCOLATE FONDUE

1 tsp. butter
2 sq. semisweet chocolate
1 pt. marshmallow creme
1/2 c. kahlua

Melt butter and chocolate in fondue pot. Add marshmallow creme and kahlua; heat, stirring, until blended and smooth. Serve with apple, pear, banana, pineapple, and sponge cake chunks.

Mrs. John De Boom, VP, Theta Epsilon
Niles, Michigan

EASY CHOCOLATE FONDUE

8 sq. semisweet chocolate
1/2 c. plus 1 tbsp. milk
1/4 c. sugar
Dash of cinnamon

Combine all ingredients in saucepan. Place over low heat, stirring occasionally, until melted and smooth. Pour into fondue pot; place on stand over low heat. Add additional milk if heated over 30 minutes for proper consistency. Use as dessert or snack for dipping butter cookies, ladyfingers, slices of fresh or dried fruits, mints, marshmallows, or nuts. Recipe may be doubled or tripled. Yield: About 1 1/2 cups.

Photograph for this recipe on cover.

37

1 tsp. vanilla
Angel food cake
Banana chunks
Ladyfingers

Combine honey and cream in fondue pot over high heat; reduce heat. Stir in chocolate. Heat, stirring constantly, until chocolate is melted. Stir in almonds and vanilla. Swirl cake, bananas or ladyfingers in chocolate mixture. Cool slightly before eating.

Darinda Messer, Pres., Alpha Gamma No. 650
Lawrence, Kansas

FRUIT FRITTERS

1/2 c. sugar
2 tbsp. cornstarch
Dash of salt
1/2 tsp. grated orange peel
1/4 c. orange juice
2 tbsp. butter
1/4 tsp. grated lemon peel
1 tbsp. lemon juice

Combine sugar, cornstarch, and salt in saucepan, blending well. Stir in 3/4 cup water, mixing thoroughly. Cook, stirring constantly, until bubbly and thickened. Cook for 3 minutes longer, stirring constantly. Remove from heat. Stir in orange peel and juice, butter, lemon peel and juice. Keep warm.

Fritters

2 tbsp. orange juice
1 tbsp. sugar
2 firm bananas
1 med. apple
1 sm. fresh pineapple
1   4-oz. jar maraschino cherries
1 c. sifted flour
1/2 tsp. baking powder
1 1/2 tsp. salt
2/3 c. milk
1 egg, slightly beaten
2 tbsp. melted butter
1/4 tsp. lemon extract
Salad oil

CHOCOLATE FONDUE

2   6-oz. packages semisweet
   chocolate morsels
1/2 c. sugar
1 tsp. vanilla
1/2 c. light cream
Orange sections
Sliced bananas
Whole strawberries
Apple slices
Seedless grapes

Combine chocolate, sugar, vanilla, and cream in fondue pot. Place directly over flame; stir until chocolate is melted and mixture is smooth. Reduce flame to just keep warm. Arrange fruits on serving tray next to fondue pot. Spear fruits with fondue forks; dip into warm sauce.

CREAMY CHOCOLATE FONDUE

2 tbsp. honey or light corn syrup
1/2 c. light cream
1   9-oz. bar milk chocolate,
   chopped
1/4 c. finely chopped almonds or
   pecans (opt.)

Combine orange juice and sugar in bowl; cut bananas, apple, and pineapple into bite-sized pieces. Toss fruits in orange juice mixture. Let stand until ready for use. Drain cherries. Sift flour, baking powder and 1/2 teaspoon salt into bowl. Combine milk, egg, butter, and extract in small bowl. Add to dry ingredients; beat until smooth. Pour salad oil into fondue pot to 2-inch depth. Add remaining salt. Heat to 375 degrees. Drain fruits; spear with fork. Dip into batter; fry in oil for 2 minutes or until lightly browned. Serve with warm sauce for dipping. Yield: 6-8 servings.

Connie Snoke, Sigma Lambda No. 5043
Placerville, California

PEPPERMINT FONDUE

1/2 c. milk
3 tbsp. melted butter
1 14-oz. package creamy white
    frosting mix
3/4 c. crushed peppermint candy
2 drops of red food coloring

Combine milk, butter, frosting mix, candy, and food coloring in fondue pot, blending well. Heat through, stirring occasionally. Serve with sliced apples or other fruits for dipping.

Judi Kessler, Pi No. 680
Fremont, Ohio

LEMON FONDUE

1/4 c. butter
1/2 c. confectioners' sugar
2 tbsp. cornstarch
2 2 x 1/2-in. strips lemon rind
1/4 c. frozen lemonade concentrate
1 tbsp. rum flavoring

Combine 3/4 cup water, butter, sugar, cornstarch, and rind in blender. Blend, covered, at high speed until rind is finely grated. Pour into fondue pot. Cook over medium heat, stirring constantly, until thickened and glossy. Stir in lemonade concentrate and flavoring, blending well. Reduce heat to low.

Serve with gingerbread and angel food cake cubes, orange sections, and pineapple chunks for dipping. Yield: 6 servings.

Gayle Terry, Delta Mu No. 6251
Rome, Georgia

MAPLE-ORANGE FONDUE

6 tbsp. butter
1/3 c. all-purpose flour
1 c. light cream or half and half
3/4 c. pure maple syrup
2 tbsp. light corn syrup
3/4 c. orange marmalade
1/3 c. cointreau

Melt butter in saucepan; stir in flour. Remove from heat. Stir in cream gradually, blending after each addition. Stir in syrups and marmalade; cook over medium heat, stirring constantly, until mixture comes to a boil. Cook for 2 minutes longer; stir in cointreau. Transfer to fondue pot; serve with assorted fruits. May be prepared in advance, stored in refrigerator, then reheated.

Maureen Taylor, VP, Pi Chapter No. 1488
Staunton, Virginia

MINI PASTRIES FONDUE

1 pkg. refrigerator crescent rolls
Candied cherries
Salad oil
1 tsp. salt
Sifted confectioners' sugar

Unroll dough; pinch perforations together. Cut dough into 32 squares; place 1 cherry on each square. Fold corners of dough over to cover; seal well. Fill fondue pot 1/2 full with oil; heat to 375 degrees. Add salt. Spear each pastry with fondue fork; fry in oil for about 2 minutes or until golden brown. Dip in confectioners' sugar. Candied pineapple chunks may be used instead of cherries.

Clarissa Start Davidson
International Honorary Member, BSP
High Ridge, Missouri

FRENCH TOAST

1 loaf French bread
2 eggs
1/2 c. milk
1 1/4 tsp. salt
1/2 tsp. vanilla (opt.)
Oil
Maple Sauce

Cut bread into bite-sized pieces, each piece with crust on one side. Combine eggs, milk, 1/4 teaspoon salt, and vanilla; mix well. Pour 2 inches oil into fondue pot; heat to 375 degrees. Add remaining salt. Spear bread on fondue fork through crust; dip into egg mixture. Cook in oil until golden brown; serve with Maple Sauce.

Maple Sauce

1 1/2 c. powdered sugar
1/2 c. butter
1/2 c. maple-blended syrup
1 egg white, stiffly beaten

Cream sugar, butter, and syrup; fold in egg white. Chill.

Barbara Tanner, Tau No. 7087
Worland, Wyoming

FRESH RASPBERRY FONDUE

1/2 pt. fresh raspberries
2 tbsp. sugar
1 8-oz. package cream cheese, softened
1/2 honeydew melon
1/2 fresh pineapple, peeled
2 pears
Lemon juice
1/2 pt. whole fresh strawberries

Combine raspberries and sugar. Mash through medium sieve, reserving pulp. Beat cream cheese with electric mixer at medium speed until smooth. Add reserved raspberry pulp gradually; beat until smooth. Chill. Scoop honeydew melon into balls. Cut pineapple into strips. Cut pears into thin wedges; dip

into lemon juice. Spoon fondue into serving bowl; arrange fruits around bowl. Dip fruits into fondue with cocktail forks.

Ealsa L. Rowe
International Honorary Member, BSP
Spearfish, South Dakota

CREAMY RASPBERRY FONDUE

1 4-oz. carton whipped cream cheese
2 10-oz. packages frozen raspberries, thawed
1/4 c. cornstarch
2 tbsp. sugar
1/4 c. brandy
Fruit cubes
Cake cubes

Let cream cheese come to room temperature. Crush raspberries in saucepan slightly. Blend cornstarch and 1/2 cup cold water together; add to raspberries. Cook; stirring, until thickened and bubbly. Sieve raspberries; discard seeds. Pour into fondue pot; place over fondue burner. Add cream cheese, stirring until melted. Stir in sugar; add brandy gradually. Spear fruit or cake cubes with fondue forks; dip into fondue.

Mrs. Denver Noggle, Omicron No. 679
Middletown, Ohio

ORANGE MARMALADE FONDUE

3 tbsp. butter
3 tbsp. sugar
1 tbsp. flour
1/2 c. whipping cream
1/3 c. orange marmalade
1/2 tsp. grated orange rind

Melt butter in fondue pot over low flame. Mix sugar and flour; stir into butter. Stir in cream; cook over low heat, stirring frequently, until thickened. Stir in marmalade and orange rind. Serve with pineapple chunks, banana chunks, or cake squares.

Mrs. Ronald Baughman, Xi Alpha Alpha X538
Carlisle, Pennsylvania

ANGEL FONDUE

4 c. fresh strawberries
4 to 6 slices angel food cake
2/3 c. heavy cream
1 c. miniature marshmallows
2 tbsp. powdered sugar

Wash and hull strawberries; cut cake into 1-inch cubes. Combine cream, marshmallows, and sugar in fondue pot; place over low heat. Stir until blended. Place strawberries and cake on fondue forks; dip into cream mixture. Yield: 4 servings.

Mrs. Doreen Lewis, Pres., Xi Psi X2516
North Vancouver, British Columbia, Canada

FRUIT BLUSH

1   10-oz. package frozen
     strawberries
1/2 tsp. lemon juice
1/4 c. light cream
1 tsp. cornstarch

Thaw strawberries. Place strawberries, lemon juice, cream, and cornstarch into blender. Blend, covered, at high speed until smooth. Pour into fondue pot. Cook over medium heat, stirring until slightly thickened. Reduce heat to low. Serve with cake cubes, doughnuts, watermelon balls or marshmallows for dipping. Yield: 8-10 servings.

Gail M. Bowen, Pres., Phi Nu P2340
Hartford, Connecticut

BRANDIED STRAWBERRY FONDUE

2   10-oz. packages frozen
     strawberries, thawed
1/4 c. cornstarch
2 tbsp. sugar
1/2 c. water
1   4-oz. container whipped cream
     cheese, softened
1/4 c. brandy
Pear cubes
Peach cubes
Pineapple chunks
Cake cubes
Marshmallows

Crush strawberries lightly in saucepan. Blend cornstarch with sugar and water; add to strawberries. Cook, stirring, until thickened. Pour into fondue pot; place over burner. Add cream cheese; stir until melted. Add brandy gradually. Spear pear, peach, pineapple, cake, or marshmallow with fondue fork; dip into fondue.

Mrs. Jackie Grantz, Xi Alpha Tau No. 996
Washington, Pennsylvania

CHOCOLATE FONDUE MARVEILLEUSE

1   12-oz. package semisweet
     chocolates
2 cans sweetened condensed milk
Pinch of salt
Vanilla, almond flavoring or
     brandy flavoring to taste

Mix chocolates, milk, salt, and vanilla in fondue pot; place over burner. Heat, stirring frequently, until chocolates are melted; keep warm. Place marshmallows, doughnut pieces, and banana slices on fondue forks; dip into fondue.

CHAFING DISH_____

Cooking foods in a chafing dish is one of the oldest—and most elegant ways of preparing recipes. The forerunner of today's gleaming chafing dishes was the tri-legged brazier, standard equipment in ancient homes.

One reason for the widespread popularity of chafing dish cooking—from ancient times to modern—is the graceful ease with which seemingly complicated dishes can be whipped up and served. Get acquainted with the foods you can cook in your chafing dish, and impress family and guests alike with the way you prepare appetizers, soups and chowders, omelets and other egg dishes, desserts, seafood, poultry, meat, and other foods right before their eyes. Delight yourself with the ease of preparation characteristic of chafing dish cookery. And on those occasions when you want to entertain in a style uniquely yours, call on chafing dish cooking.

One secret of successful chafing dish cookery is to have all your ingredients prepared ahead of time—minced, diced, sauteed, or prepared as your recipe designates. And another secret lies in having a tried-and-proven collection of recipes, recipes you can rely on for consistent results every time you prepare them. As you pore through the pages of this section, you'll find over a hundred recipes, each one submitted by ladies who combine home activities, community service, and even careers in their busy lives. These ladies must have recipes they can depend on. When asked to share their favorite chafing dish recipes, they submitted their most reliable—and most delicious—ones!

Prefacing these recipes are four pages of instructions on how to get the most out of your chafing dish equipment. Here you'll discover how to choose and care for a chafing dish . . . how to plan a chafing dish menu . . . how to flambé desserts for a spectacular finish to a meal . . . and much more. Enter the world of chafing dish cooking with confidence by relying on the recipes and hints assembled especially for you in this section.

chafing dish
FUNDAMENTALS___

It was a Frenchman — Alexis Soger — who in the nineteenth century streamlined the brazier, one of the most ancient of all cooking utensils, and gave it a combined double-boiler and frying pan construction. His innovation ushered in the golden age of chafing dish cookery. Victorian hostesses practiced long hours to create elegant masterpieces in front of their admiring guests. In fact, the ability to use a chafing dish with skill and ease was considered a hallmark of the past century's great hostesses. This custom of chafing dish cookery at parties has continued even into our fast-paced time. Despite the many changes between the last century and this one, nothing has replaced the chafing dish as the epitome of elegant dining.

Chafing dishes come in sizes from very small ones used to prepare dessert sauces or party appetizers to three-quart ones that hold food to serve many guests their main dish. And chafing dishes come in a variety of materials: sterling silver, copper, brass, stainless steel, and plain or color-coated aluminum. Those made of silverplate or copper plate will need replating from time to time; those made of other materials are highly durable, often cherished heirlooms passed from one generation to the next.

EQUIPMENT

The traditional chafing dish has a cover, a top pan called the blazer, a bottom pan known as the bain-marie (from the French word for water bath) that holds hot water, a stand, a burner with flame adjuster, and a heatproof tray.

The chafing dish blazer pan can be used over direct heat as a frying pan and then placed over the bain-marie to keep food warm. Such an arrangement is ideal for recipes that must be prepared over the kitchen stove and brought to the table to be kept warm in the blazer pan over the bain-marie. When you cook at the table, the same arrangement will keep your food warm while you serve it.

There are other pans that fit a chafing dish bain-marie and can be used to introduce variety into your table top cooking. Among them are the *round crepes-omelet* pan, usually thirteen to fourteen inches in diameter and one inch deep; the *skillet,* eight to ten inches in diameter and about two inches deep; the *crepes suzette* pan, similar to the skillet but only one to one and a half inches deep; the oval-shaped *omelet/fish/frying pan* that is eleven to thirteen inches long, five to seven inches wide, and one to one and a half inches deep; and the *Dutch saucepan,* a huge pan used only to keep beverages or foods warm.

Chafing dishes have their own *heat sources,* usually an alcohol lamp or burner, canned heat, or electricity. (See pages 9 to 10 for more information about all three heat sources.) Some chafing dishes use candle warmers, but such heat sources cannot provide heat intense enough for cooking — they only keep already-cooked food warm. Besides the three heat sources mentioned above, butane heaters are coming into increasing use. These must be purchased separately from the chafing dish but they do have the advantage of providing more than adequate heat for most cooking.

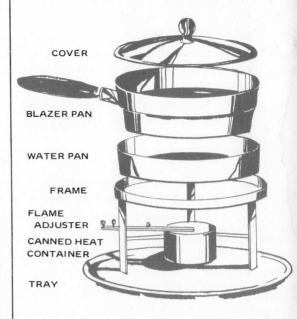

COVER

BLAZER PAN

WATER PAN

FRAME

FLAME ADJUSTER

CANNED HEAT CONTAINER

TRAY

CHAFING DISH COOKING

What can you cook in a chafing dish? Not everything. Complicated dishes, those with long cooking times, and large quantities of food are best cooked in the kitchen and served from chafing dishes. When you are looking for a recipe to be cooked in a chafing dish, choose a simple one that cooks quickly and that calls for most of the preparation to be done before the actual cooking process. Foods such as dessert sauces, party appetizers, main dishes featuring small pieces of meat, seafood, or vegetables are all well suited to chafing dish cooking.

When you have found a recipe you plan to cook in your chafing dish, you should plan to do all food preparation prior to cooking. The object of chafing dish cookery is to avoid any trip to the kitchen once you have begun cooking! If the recipe specifies foods to be chopped, diced, or mixed, do it away from the table. Each individual food or group of seasonings should be carefully measured and put into indi-

vidual dishes or containers. The dishes holding ingredients go onto an attractive serving tray along with any utensils you will need for cooking and a small, pretty towel. *Always* try to use wooden utensils for chafing dish cooking: metal ones can easily scratch and mar the surfaces of your dish.

Before cooking in the dish, remove the cover, blazer pan, and bain-marie from the frame. Place the chafing dish stand onto a tray. Set the fuel in place. If your recipe specifies that you cook over the bain-marie, set it firmly into the stand and fill it one-quarter to one-half full of hot water.

You will always do your cooking in the blazer pan that is placed either directly over the heat source or over the bain-marie. Add ingredients in small amounts and let them warm thoroughly before adding more. If you try to put all the ingredients in at once, those closest to the heat will cook while those away from it will still be at room temperature.

CHAFING DISH DESSERTS

Few foods have the eye-drawing appeal of desserts prepared in a chafing dish. Enterprising hostesses keep a store of crepes (thin dessert pancakes) in their freezers for last-minute desserts. The pancakes thaw while the main course is being consumed. Then the chafing dish comes out, a delicious but easy sauce is mixed in it, and the crepes are added. The crepes are rolled, dusted with powdered sugar, and served amidst many compliments!

Of all chafing dish cookery, no method is more spectacular than that known as "flambé." This method produces such flaming foods as cherries jubilee. To flambé, you will need a high proof liqueur: brandy, light or dark rum, or the more traditional orange, apricot, and cherry liqueurs. We specify high proof because all the alcohol burns off during the flambé process, leaving only the rich bouquet of the beverage behind.

Warm the liquid of your choice by pouring it into a deep ladle or long-handled pan and holding that utensil three to four inches above a very low flame. At the same time, be certain that the food you will flambé is in the chafing dish pan and is as hot as possible without scorching. Gently pour the heated liqueur over the hot food, and tilt your chafing dish pan to one side. With a long stemmed match, light the *fumes* that will accumulate at the tipped edge of the pan. Do not light the liquid or the food – it is the alcohol fumes you are burning off, not the flavor. Spoon the flaming liqueur over the food until the flames die, then serve each guest a portion of the flambéed food.

CHAFING DISH APPETIZERS

While chafing dishes are effectively used to cook main dishes, many hostesses also enjoy using them to hold appetizers at parties or buffets. Serve just one chafing dish appetizer at a time, as two or more may dilute the visual impact of the elegant chafing dish. If your party goes longer than an hour or so, check to be certain there is water left in the bain-marie. You may want to keep a container of water close at hand – try using a silver teapot for pouring accuracy and attractiveness!

Once you have discovered how much fun and pleasure lies in chafing dish cooking, you'll want to try it often. Each time you use your chafing dish, it should be thoroughly cleaned. Before cleaning, let the dish cool thoroughly. If still warm when it gets to the water, the dish may discolor and warp. After the dish has cooled, empty the fuel container. Then, remove all handles and knobs. If for any reason they cannot be removed, wash the dish trying to keep the handles and knobs out of the water. Wash quickly; above all, do not soak the dish as soaking will probably stain and streak the finish. After washing, pat the dish dry with a clean, lintless towel. Replace knobs and handles, and return the chafing dish to its storage place. But don't put it too far away – you'll want to use it again, very soon!

CHEESE & EGGS

CHILI-CHEESE DIP

1   15-oz. can chili with beans
1   10-oz. package frozen Welsh
    rarebit
1/4 tsp. garlic powder
1 tsp. Worcestershire sauce
Hot sauce to taste

Pour chili into skillet; mash beans with fork. Add remaining ingredients; cook, stirring, until well blended and heated through. Pour into chafing dish; adjust heat to keep dip hot. Serve with corn chips.

Audrey Ann Simmons
International Honorary Member, BSP
Saint Louis, Missouri

WELSH RAREBIT

1/4 c. butter
8 c. shredded sharp Cheddar cheese
2 tsp. Worcestershire sauce
1 tsp. dry mustard
Dash of cayenne pepper

1 c. light cream
4 eggs, slightly beaten

Melt butter in blazer pan or top of double boiler over hot water. Add cheese; heat, stirring occasionally, until cheese is melted. Stir in Worcestershire sauce, mustard, and cayenne pepper. Combine cream and eggs; stir into cheese mixture. Cook until thick, stirring frequently; keep warm. Serve over buttered English muffins or buttered toast triangles, hard-cooked egg slices, broiled mushroom caps stuffed with cooked, crumbled bacon, shrimp, crab meat, asparagus spears, and tomato slices.

CHILI CON QUESO WITH TOSTADOS

1 onion, chopped
1 tomato, chopped
6 to 8 green chilies, chopped
1 to 2 jalapenos, chopped
Garlic salt to taste
2 lb. Velveeta cheese, cubed
Corn tortillas

Combine onion, tomato, green chilies, jalapenos and garlic salt in saucepan over low heat; cook until onion is tender. Add Velveeta cheese gradually, stirring constantly until cheese is melted and mixture is smooth. Serve hot with crispy tostados. Cut tortillas into 6 wedges; deep-fat fry until crisp to make tostados.

Pat Murphy, Xi Alpha Xi X2183
Las Cruces, New Mexico

GOURMET SCRAMBLED EGGS

6 tbsp. butter
12 eggs
2 1/4 c. dry cottage cheese
2 tsp. salt
Freshly ground pepper to taste

Melt butter in chafing dish over low heat; remove from heat. Break eggs into chafing dish; beat with a fork. Stir in cottage cheese and salt. Return to heat; cook stirring constantly, until set. Sprinkle with pepper. Serve with toast, English muffins or biscuits. Yield: 6 servings.

Mona Lane, Pres., Alpha Tau No. 1019
Garden City, Kansas

HOT CHEESE DIP

2 c. cubed Tillamook cheese
2 cans cream of mushroom soup
1 lb. bacon, diced
1 bunch green onions, chopped
Dash of hot sauce
Dash of cayenne pepper

Melt cheese in chafing dish over low heat; add soup. Combine bacon and green onions in skillet; saute until onions are tender. Add to cheese mixture; stir well. Add hot sauce and cayenne pepper; blend thoroughly. Keep warm in chafing dish or fondue pot; may be used as dip or fondue.

Mary Steinbock, Dir., Gamma Alpha No. 4901
Astoria, Oregon

SPANISH OMELET

1 avocado
1 med. onion, chopped
1/2 tsp. lemon juice
2 tbsp. (rounded) sour cream
1/4 tsp. Worcestershire sauce
1/2 tsp. garlic salt
1/2 tsp. salt
1/2 tsp. pepper
1/4 lb. bacon, diced
2 sm. tomatoes, diced
1/3 can diced green chilies
8 to 10 eggs
Milk to taste
1/3 lb. Tillamook cheese, grated

Mash avocado; mix with 1/3 of the onion, lemon juice, sour cream, Worcestershire sauce, 1/4 teaspoon each garlic salt, salt, and pepper. Chill thoroughly. Saute bacon, remaining onion, tomatoes, green chilies, remaining garlic salt, salt, and pepper in chafing dish. Combine eggs and milk; blend well.

Additional salt and pepper may be used, if desired. Make 4 omelets; add cheese to each omelet after eggs have set. Spoon bacon mixture over omelets; top with avocado sauce. Yield: 4 servings.

Barbara Goetzinger, Xi Eta Zeta X1946
North Hollywood, California

SCRAMBLED EGGS AND SMOKED SALMON ON TOAST

2/3 c. shredded Swiss cheese
Butter
1/4 c. chopped chives
6 slices whole wheat toast
12 slices smoked salmon
6 eggs
2 tbsp. light cream or milk
Salt and pepper to taste

Combine Swiss cheese, 1/4 cup soft butter, and chives; spread on toast. Place 2 salmon slices on each toast slice. Keep warm. Beat eggs and cream together. Melt 1 1/2 tablespoons butter in blazer pan of chafing dish over medium flame. Scramble eggs softly; season. Spoon over toast slices; serve.

Patricia Peru, Pres., Beta Rho No. 4542
Kenosha, Wisconsin

TABLE-SCRAMBLED EGGS

1/2 c. butter
12 eggs
Hot sauce to taste
1 tsp. finely chopped tarragon
Salt and pepper to taste
1 c. button mushrooms
Chopped parsley

Melt butter in chafing dish over low heat. Beat eggs lightly, adding 1/4 cup water, hot sauce, tarragon, salt, and pepper. Cook eggs in butter, stirring frequently, until just set; fold in mushrooms. Sprinkle with parsley. Serve with toasted English muffins, sliced tomatoes, and sausage patties. Yield: 8-10 servings.

Mrs. Barbara Fagerlund, Rec. Sec.
Xi Epsilon Delta X3671, Salisbury, Missouri

NOODLE PARTY PANCAKES

Salt
3 to 4 qt. boiling water
4 c. (about) fine egg noodles
2 eggs
1/4 c. melted butter or margarine
Butter

Add 1 tablespoon salt to boiling water; add noodles gradually so that water continues to boil. Cook, stirring occasionally, until tender; drain in colander. Beat eggs with 3/4 teaspoon salt in large bowl; stir in melted butter. Add warm noodles; toss until mixed. Melt about 3 tablespoons butter in skillet over medium heat; drop noodle mixture by tablespoonfuls into skillet to make small pancakes. Saute on both sides until golden brown, adding butter to skillet as needed. Serve hot with sour cream and caviar. Yield: About 80 pancakes.

SPORTSMAN'S EGGS

1 tbsp. chopped onion
1 tsp. chopped green pepper
4 chicken livers, chopped
2 tbsp. butter
1 tbsp. tomato paste
1/4 c. white wine
4 eggs
Salt and pepper to taste
4 slices buttered toast

Saute onion, green pepper, and chicken livers in butter in blazer pan of chafing dish over medium flame. Thin tomato paste with 4 tablespoons warm water; add to chicken liver mixture. Cover; cook for 5 minutes. Stir in wine; cook for 3 minutes longer. Break eggs, one at a time, into chicken liver mixture. Cover; cook until egg whites are set. Add seasonings; serve at once on buttered toast.

Vivian Wood, Preceptor Pi XP257
Fresno, California

BEEF

BURMESE BEEF CURRY

2 lb. beef chuck
1/4 c. oil
1 c. chopped onions
1 clove of garlic, crushed
2 c. water
1/4 tsp. chili powder
2 to 3 tsp. curry powder
2 tbsp. slivered crystallized ginger
1/2 tsp. salt
1 tbsp. soy sauce
Hot cooked rice

Cut beef into 1-inch cubes; cook in oil in deep skillet or Dutch oven for about 20 minutes or until brown. Push to one side of skillet. Add onions and garlic; cook until transparent. Remove skillet from heat; add water. Stir in remaining ingredients except rice. Bring to a boil; reduce heat. Cover. Cook for about 1 hour or until beef is tender. Remove cover; simmer for about 20 minutes or until thickened. Transfer to chafing dish; serve with rice. Yield: 4 servings.

Dorothy K. Zent, Pres., Alpha No. 218
Cheyenne, Wyoming

SIRLOIN TIP WITH NOODLES

2 lb. beef sirloin tip
2 tbsp. flour
1 to 2 tsp. chili powder
1 tsp. salt
1/8 tsp. pepper
1/4 c. oil
1 6-oz. can tomato paste
2 c. water
1 med. onion, chopped
1/2 c. chopped green pepper
1 8-oz. package wide noodles

Cut beef into 2 x 1/2-inch strips. Mix flour, chili powder, salt, and pepper in bag. Add beef; toss until coated. Brown beef in oil in skillet; stir in tomato paste, water, onion, and green pepper. Cover. Simmer for about 1 hour or until beef is tender. Cook noodles according to package directions; drain. Place beef mixture in chafing dish; serve with noodles. Yield: 6 servings.

Betty Anick
International Honorary Member, BSP
West Allis, Wisconsin

BEEF WITH SNOW PEAS

3 tsp. cornstarch
1 tsp. soy sauce
2 tsp. vinegar
1/4 tsp. sugar
Oil
1/2 lb. beef, sliced thin
2 tsp. water
1/2 tsp. monosodium glutamate
Dash of pepper
1/2 tsp. salt
1 thin slice ginger, crushed
2 6-oz. packages frozen snow
    peas, thawed
1/2 c. chicken stock

Combine 1 teaspoon cornstarch, soy sauce, vinegar, sugar, and 1/4 teaspoon oil. Add beef; mix well. Set aside. Combine remaining cornstarch, water, monosodium glutamate, and pepper; set aside. Heat 1 tablespoon oil in wok or chafing dish over medium-high heat; add salt and ginger. Add snow peas; cook, stirring, for 1 minute. Add chicken stock; cover. Cook for 30 seconds. Uncover; stir. Remove peas; set aside. Place 1 tablespoon oil in wok; add beef. Cook, stirring, for 45 seconds; add snow peas. Stir in cornstarch mixture; cook until thickened.

Rebekah Kepley, Preceptor Beta Rho XP724
Lancaster, California

STEAK SAN MARCO

2 lb. chuck steak
1 env. onion soup mix
1 1-lb. can Italian peeled
    tomatoes
1 tsp. oregano
Garlic powder to taste
Freshly ground pepper to taste
2 tbsp. cooking oil
2 tbsp. wine vinegar

Cut steak into serving pieces; place in large skillet. Cover with soup mix and tomatoes; add oregano, garlic powder, pepper, oil, and vinegar. Cover. Simmer for 1 hour and 30 minutes or until steak is tender. Place in chafing dish; keep hot.

Kathaleen W. Dicken, Pres., Lambda Nu No. 5479
Columbus, Ohio

STEAK SIZZLERS

1 lb. sirloin steak
Onion salt to taste
Garlic salt to taste
1 1/2 c. salad dressing or
    mayonnaise
4 tbsp. (or more) catsup
Parsley flakes to taste

Sprinkle steak with onion salt and garlic salt; cut into 1/2-inch cubes. Place in broiling pan. Broil to desired doneness. Mix salad dressing, catsup, and parsley flakes in chafing dish; heat through. Place steak cubes on fondue forks; dip into sauce. Bread sticks may be served with steak, if desired.

Bonnie Murphy, Corr. Sec.
Illinois Kappa No. 7202, Springfield, Illinois

PINEAPPLE-BEEF TERIYAKI

2 lb. boneless sirloin steak
1 pineapple
1/4 c. (packed) brown sugar
1/4 c. soy sauce
2 tbsp. lemon juice
1 tbsp. salad oil
1/4 tsp. ginger
1 garlic clove, minced

Cut steak and pineapple into 1-inch cubes. Combine brown sugar, soy sauce, lemon juice, oil, ginger and garlic in medium bowl; stir in beef cubes. Cover; refrigerate for 1 hour, stirring several times. Drain; reserve marinade. Thread beef on skewers alternately with pineapple cubes; place in broiling pan. Broil until beef is of desired doneness, basting with reserved marinade and turning frequently. Place in chafing dish; keep warm. Yield: 6 servings.

Ivy Baker Priest
International Honorary Member, BSP
Sacramento, California

BENGAL CURRY

4 lb. beef chuck
1/4 c. shortening
1 c. sliced onions
2 tbsp. curry powder
2 tsp. salt
1/4 tsp. pepper
1/4 tsp. cloves
1/4 c. slivered crystallized ginger
2 tbsp. chopped fresh mint leaves
1/4 c. unsifted all-purpose flour
3 cans beef bouillon
1 c. canned flaked coconut
1/4 c. lime juice
1 c. light cream
Pineapple Rice

Cut beef into 1-inch cubes; cook in shortening in large Dutch oven for about 20 minutes or until brown, stirring frequently. Remove beef from Dutch oven; drain off all except 2 tablespoons drippings. Add onions, curry powder, salt, pepper, cloves, ginger, and mint; cook, stirring, for about 5 minutes or until onions are tender. Remove from heat; stir in flour. Stir in undiluted bouillon gradually. Add beef; bring to a boil. Reduce heat; cover. Simmer for 1 hour and 30 minutes or until beef is tender. Stir in coconut, lime juice, and cream; simmer for about 5 minutes. Turn into chafing dish; serve with Pineapple Rice. Serve with accompaniments of chopped cashew nuts, chopped unpared cucumbers, chutney, and preserved kumquats. May be prepared day before, refrigerated, and reheated. One teaspoon dried mint leaves may be substituted for fresh mint.

Pineapple Rice

2 1/2 c. long grain rice
2 1/2 tsp. salt
2 1/2 tbsp. butter
1 8-oz. can crushed pineapple, drained

Combine rice with 1 quart water and salt in 3-quart saucepan; bring to a boil over high heat, stirring several times with fork. Reduce heat; cover. Simmer for 12 to 14 minutes or until rice is tender and liquid has evaporated. Add butter and pineapple; mix well.

Isabella S. Jackson, Corr. Sec.
Alpha Gamma No. 6753, Stacy, Wyoming

ITALIAN BEEF

Seasoned salt to taste
1 10-lb. rolled beef rump roast
7 3/4 c. water
3 bouillon cubes
8 tbsp. Worcestershire sauce
4 tsp. oregano
2 tsp. basil
2 pkg. Italian salad dressing mix
Italian or poor boy buns

Sprinkle seasoned salt on roast; place in baking pan. Bake at 350 degrees until medium rare. Drain; reserve drippings. Cool roast; slice very thin. Place water, bouillon cubes, reserved drippings, Worcestershire sauce, oregano, basil, and Italian dressing mix in large saucepan; bring to a boil. Cook for 1 minute; remove from heat. Add sliced beef; cool. Refrigerate for 2 to 4 days, spooning liquid over beef each day. Place beef and liquid in chafing dish; heat through. Serve with buns. Yield: 30 servings.

Tina Buente, Treas., Pi Eta No. 7621
Granite City, Illinois

SAVORY BEEF STROGANOFF

1 1/2 lb. beef round
1/4 c. butter
1 c. sliced mushrooms
1/2 c. chopped onion
1 clove of garlic, minced
1 can tomato soup
Dash of pepper
1 c. sour cream

Cut beef into 3 x 1/2 x 1/8-inch strips; brown in butter in heavy skillet. Add mushrooms, onion, and garlic; cook until onions are light brown. Blend in soup and pepper; cover. Simmer for about 1 hour or until beef is tender, stirring occasionally. Blend in sour cream; heat through. Place in blazer pan; place over water pan. Keep warm. Serve with rice. Yield: 6 servings.

Mrs. Wilber M. Brucker
International Honorary Member, BSP
Grosse Pointe Farms, Michigan

HOSPITALITY PINEAPPLE MEATBALLS

1 8 3/4-oz. can pineapple tidbits
3 slices white bread
1 lb. ground lean beef
2 eggs, slightly beaten
1 tsp. onion salt
3 tbsp. butter or margarine
2 tbsp. oil
3/4 c. beef broth
2 tbsp. lemon juice
3 tbsp. catsup
2 tsp. cornstarch

Drain pineapple, reserving 1/2 cup syrup. Place pineapple on paper towels. Soak bread

in water; squeeze dry. Mix bread, beef, eggs and onion salt together well. Wrap small amount of beef mixture around each pineapple tidbit, forming small meatballs. Melt butter in skillet; add oil. Brown meatballs evenly. Drain off excess fat. Blend reserved pineapple syrup with remaining ingredients. Pour over meatballs. Cook over moderate heat for about 10 minutes or until sauce boils and thickens slightly. Serve meatballs in blazer pan of chafing dish over simmering water. Serve with pretzels, bread sticks or crackers if desired.

EASY BEEF STROGANOFF

2 to 3 lb. stew beef
1 pkg. onion soup mix
2 cans cream of mushroom soup
1 med. can mushrooms
1 c. sherry

Cut beef into bite-sized pieces. Mix all ingredients in casserole. Bake at 325 degrees for about 4 hours, stirring occasionally. Place in chafing dish; serve with noodles or rice.

Kathy Mattish, Serv. Chm., Delta Gamma Psi
San Jose, California

CURRIED MEATBALLS

1 1/2 lb. ground beef
2/3 c. quick or old-fashioned oats
1/3 onion, chopped
2 3/4 tsp. salt
1/4 tsp. garlic powder
1 egg, beaten
1/2 c. milk
Shortening
2 tbsp. cornstarch
2 c. cold water
2 tsp. sugar
1 1/2 tsp. curry powder
1/2 tsp. ground cumin
1/2 tsp. ginger
1/2 c. raisins

Combine beef, oats, onion, 1 1/4 teaspoons salt, garlic powder, egg, and milk; form into 18 meatballs. Brown in small amount of shortening in large skillet; drain off all except 2 tablespoons drippings. Combine cornstarch and water; pour over meatballs, stirring constantly. Bring to a boil. Add remaining salt and remaining ingredients; cover. Simmer for about 30 minutes. Serve from chafing dish with hot, cooked rice. Serve with accompaniments of chopped peanuts, sliced green onion, chopped tomato, and toasted flaked or shredded coconut.

Kathy Fredricks, Tau No. 2802
Caldwell, Idaho

GLAZED MEATBALLS

1 lb. ground round
1/2 c. bread crumbs
1/4 c. milk
1 tsp. garlic salt
1/2 tsp. salt
2 tbsp. cooking oil
1 sm. bottle catsup
1 sm. jar grape jelly
2 tbsp. brown sugar
1 onion, diced
2 tbsp. vinegar

Mix ground round, bread crumbs, milk, garlic salt, and salt; shape into 1-inch balls.

Brown in cooking oil. Mix remaining ingredients; bring to boiling point. Add meatballs; simmer for 2 to 3 hours or until glaze is very thick. Place in chafing dish; keep hot. Yield: 40 to 50 meatballs.

Sally Watson, Pres., Xi Beta Zeta X964
Wilmington, Ohio

EASY SWEDISH MEATBALLS

2 lb. lean hamburger
1 pkg. onion soup mix
2 eggs
1 to 1 1/2 c. oats
2 cans beef gravy
1 1/2 12-oz. cartons sour cream

Mix hamburger, soup mix, eggs, and oats; shape into bite-sized meatballs. Place on cookie sheet. Bake at 350 degrees for 45 minutes; drain off drippings. Mix gravy and sour cream; heat through. Add meatballs; place in blazer pan. Place over water pan; heat for 1 hour.

Scarlet Pagel, Epsilon Chi No. 4153
Kansas City, Missouri

MEATBALLS IN RED WINE SAUCE

1 onion, finely chopped
1 c. fine dry bread crumbs
2 lb. ground chuck
2 eggs
1 tsp. salt
1/4 tsp. pepper
1/4 tsp. curry powder
1/2 tsp. Worcestershire sauce
1/4 tsp. garlic powder
1 c. flour
2 tbsp. salad oil
1 clove of garlic, minced
1 c. burgundy or chianti
1 beef bouillon cube
1 8-oz. can tomato sauce
1 c. tomato juice
1/8 tsp. crushed oregano

Mix first 9 ingredients; form into 1-inch meatballs. Roll in flour lightly. Heat salad oil and garlic in electric skillet. Add meatballs; cook for about 8 minutes or until brown on all sides. Drain. Combine remaining ingredients in saucepan; bring to a simmer. Pour off excess oil from skillet. Return meatballs to skillet; add sauce. Simmer for 25 to 35 minutes. Place in chafing dish; keep warm. Yield: 80 meatballs.

Lynne Dunlap, Corr. Sec.
Epsilon Upsilon No. 2623, Columbus Grove, Ohio

PARTY MEATBALLS

2 lb. lean ground beef
2 eggs
1/2 tsp. salt
1/4 tsp. pepper
1   12-oz. jar chili sauce
1 tsp. lemon juice
1   10-oz. jar grape jelly

Mix ground beef, eggs, salt, and pepper; shape into miniature balls. Combine chili sauce, lemon juice, and grape jelly; place in 13 x 9 x 2-inch baking pan. Add meatballs; cover. Bake at 350 degrees for 1 hour. Remove cover; bake for 30 minutes longer. Transfer to chafing dish; serve hot with toothpicks. Yield: 30 to 40 meatballs.

Dr. Pauline Beery Mack
International Honorary Member, BSP
Denton, Texas

COCKTAIL MEATBALLS

2 lb. ground round steak
1 c. packaged corn flake crumbs
1/3 c. dried parsley flakes
2 eggs
2 tbsp. soy sauce
1/4 tsp. pepper
1/2 tsp. garlic powder
1/3 c. catsup
2 tbsp. minced onion
1   1-lb. can jellied cranberry
     sauce
1   12-oz. bottle chili sauce
2 tbsp. (packed) dark brown sugar
1 tbsp. lemon juice

Preheat oven to 350 degrees. Combine first 9 ingredients in large bowl; blend well. Form into walnut-sized meatballs; place in 15 1/2 x 10 1/2 x 1-inch pan. Combine cranberry sauce, chili sauce, brown sugar, and lemon juice in medium saucepan; cook over moderate heat, stirring occasionally, until cranberry sauce is melted. Pour over meatballs. Bake for 30 minutes. Serve in chafing dish; spear with toothpicks to serve.

Kitty Faulkner, Rec. Sec., Lambda No. 1399
Martinsville, Virginia

SWEDISH MEATBALLS IN BURGUNDY SAUCE

3 lb. ground beef, pork or veal
1 onion, chopped
Dash of allspice
3 c. light cream
3 c. dry bread crumbs
3 tsp. cornstarch
4 eggs, beaten
1 1/2 tsp. salt
3/4 c. salad oil
1 c. flour
4 bouillon cubes
2 tsp. sugar
1 c. burgundy
1/4 tsp. pepper
Gravy browning sauce

Combine ground beef, onion, allspice, cream, bread crumbs, cornstarch, eggs, and 1 teaspoon salt in mixing bowl. Blend thoroughly. Shape mixture into small balls. Pour salad oil into skillet. Fry balls, several at a time, until browned. Remove from skillet. Stir flour into remaining oil in skillet, blending well. Combine bouillon cubes, 5 cups water, remaining salt, sugar, burgundy, pepper, and browning sauce, stirring well. Add to flour mixture, stirring constantly until blended and smooth. Place meatballs in sauce. Simmer for 30 minutes, stirring occasionally. Pour meatballs and sauce into chafing dish. Serve hot.

Barbara Mueller, Xi Alpha Psi No. 1913
Ballston Lake, New York

ONE-BITE MEATBALLS IN DILL SAUCE

1 1/2 lb. ground round steak
4 tbsp. fine dry rye bread crumbs
1 tsp. salt
1/2 tsp. monosodium glutamate
2 tbsp. catsup
2 tbsp. flour
1/2 tsp. celery salt
3 tbsp. butter
1 can consomme
1 tbsp. finely chopped
    fresh dill

Mix ground steak, bread crumbs, salt, monosodium glutamate, and catsup; shape into 1-inch balls. Refrigerate until chilled. Combine flour and celery salt. Melt butter in chafing dish. Add meatballs, several at a time; brown on all sides. Remove from pan. Blend flour mixture into butter remaining in pan; cook, stirring constantly, until smooth. Stir in consomme gradually; cook for 6 to 8 minutes or until thickened. Add dill and meatballs. Serve with picks. Two teaspoons dried dill may be substituted for fresh dill.

Mrs. D. Whitehead, Pres., Xi Delta X2510
Saint John's, Newfoundland, Canada

BEEF-PORK BARBECUE

3 lb. beef chuck
1 fresh pork shoulder tip
1 c. catsup
1 bag mixed pickling spices
1 sm. head cabbage
1 sm. onion
1/2 green pepper
Vinegar
Sugar to taste
Miniature buns

Place beef and pork in kettle; cover with boiling, salted water. Cook until meats are very tender and most of the water has evaporated. Remove meats; cool. Shred; place back in kettle. Add catsup, 1 cup water, and spice bag; simmer until spiced to taste. Remove spice bag; place in chafing dish. Keep warm. Shred cabbage, onion, and green pepper; mix. Mix equal parts of vinegar and water; add sugar. Stir in cabbage mixture. Place meat mixture on buns; top with slaw. One 1-pound pork roast may be substituted for pork shoulder.

Shirley Clark, Xi Theta Gamma X3765
Trotwood, Ohio

HUNGARIAN MEATBALLS IN PAPRIKA-WINE SAUCE

1 med. onion, chopped
1 tbsp. butter
1/2 c. evaporated milk
1 slice dry bread
1 lb. ground beef
1 lb. ground pork
1 egg, slightly beaten
2 tsp. salt
1/2 tsp. pepper
2 tbsp. lemon juice
2 tbsp. chopped parsley

Saute onion in butter in skillet for 3 minutes. Pour milk over bread; let stand for 5 minutes. Mix onion, bread mixture, meats, egg, seasonings, lemon juice, and parsley; form into 1-inch balls.

Sauce

1 can beef bouillon or consomme
1 c. dry red wine
1 sm. onion, chopped
3 tbsp. butter
1 tsp. sweet paprika
3 tbsp. flour

Mix bouillon and wine in a saucepan; bring to boiling point. Add meatballs; cover. Reduce heat; cook for 40 minutes. Remove meatballs to chafing dish; keep warm over low heat. Saute onion in butter in skillet for 5 minutes; blend in paprika, then flour. Add bouillon mixture; cook, stirring constantly, until thickened. Pour over meatballs.

Hellen N. Tullis
International Honorary Member, BSP
Baltimore, Maryland

SWEET AND SOUR SURPRISES

2 tbsp. cornstarch
2 tbsp. sugar
1 chicken bouillon cube
1 c. pineapple juice
1/3 c. vinegar
2 tbsp. soy sauce
1 tbsp. butter
1/2 lb. cooked chicken livers
1/2 lb. small meatballs, cooked
1/2 lb. cooked shrimp

Combine cornstarch, sugar, and bouillon cube in chafing dish blazer pan, mixing well. Add pineapple juice, 1/2 cup water, vinegar, soy sauce, and butter. Blend thoroughly. Cook over medium heat, stirring constantly, until thickened and bubbly. Reduce heat; simmer for 5 minutes. Cut chicken livers into halves. Add meatballs, shrimp, and chicken livers to sauce. Heat through. Serve warm with wooden picks. Yield: 60-65 appetizers.

Virginia Fowler, Pres., Xi Epsilon Alpha X1729
Hereford, Texas

RAISIN-LAMB CURRY

1 tbsp. curry powder
1 tbsp. butter
1 med. onion, sliced
2 med. stalks celery, sliced
1 1/2 lb. boneless lean lamb, cubed
1   14-oz. can chicken broth
1 tsp. garlic salt
1 1/2 tbsp. cornstarch
2 tbsp. water
2/3 c. California seedless raisins

Combine curry powder, butter, onion and celery in saucepan; cover. Cook over moderate heat for several minutes, until vegetables wilt. Add lamb, broth and garlic salt. Cover tightly; simmer for 1 hour to 1 hour and 30 minutes or until lamb is tender. Combine cornstarch and water; add cornstarch mixture and raisins to curry. Cook over low heat, stirring, for about 15 minutes longer or until thickened.

Persian Rice

2 tbsp. butter
1 c. rice
1 c. orange juice
1 1/2 c. water
1 tsp. salt
1/2 c. California seedless raisins
1/4 c. slivered toasted almonds
1/4 tsp. grated orange peel
1 tbsp. chopped parsley

Combine butter and rice in skillet. Cook, stirring, over moderate heat until rice is lightly toasted. Stir in orange juice, water, salt and raisins. Cover tightly; simmer for about 15 minutes or until rice has absorbed all liquid and is tender. Stir once or twice during first 5 minutes of cooking. Remove from heat; fluff rice with fork. Add almonds, orange peel, and parsley. Spoon hot curry into blazer pan of chafing dish; place in water pan over low heat. Serve rice with curry. Serve with flaked coconut and salted peanuts if desired.

PORK

BLACK MAGIC LUNCHEON

3 c. diced cooked ham
1/2 c. chopped onion
Butter
2 tbsp. flour
2/3 c. milk
2 c. sour cream
1/2 c. sliced ripe olives
1/4 c. toasted slivered almonds
8 patty shells

Combine ham and onion with small amount of butter in blazer pan of chafing dish; cook until onion is tender. Remove from heat. Blend flour with milk; stir into sour cream. Add to ham mixture; stir in olives. Heat through, stirring constantly. Stir in almonds. Serve in patty shells. Yield: 8 servings.

Virginia Chronister, Pres.
Preceptor Phi XP934, York, Pennsylvania

HAM BITES IN CHERRY-ALMOND SAUCE

2 lb. cooked ham
2 tbsp. wine or cider vinegar
1 tsp. prepared mustard
1/4 tsp. ground cloves
1 can cherry pie filling
1 tbsp. butter or margarine
1/3 c. toasted slivered almonds

Cut ham into 3/4-inch cubes. Combine wine, 3 tablespoons water, mustard, and cloves in blazer pan of chafing dish. Stir in pie filling. Bring just to a boil, stirring carefully, over direct medium heat; reduce heat. Add ham and butter; mix gently. Place blazer pan in water jacket over heat; cover. Adjust heat to keep ham mixture warm. Sprinkle with almonds before serving. Serve with long picks or cocktail forks.

Mary Louise Eayrs, Pres.
Preceptor Epsilon XP0461, Kalispell, Montana

FLAMING POLYNESIAN HAM

1/4 c. sugar
1/4 c. cornstarch
1/4 tsp. salt
1 c. pineapple juice
1/3 c. orange marmalade
1/3 c. vinegar or lemon juice
1 lb. cooked ham, cubed
1   13 1/2-oz. can pineapple tidbits
3/4 c. seedless green grapes
3/4 c. cantaloupe chunks
1/2 c. cointreau (opt.)
6 c. cooked rice
1/2 c. toasted slivered
    almonds (opt.)

Combine sugar, cornstarch, and salt in blazer pan of chafing dish; mix well. Place over direct high flame; stir in pineapple juice, marmalade, and vinegar. Cook, stirring, until thickened. Reduce heat to low; fold in ham. Heat through; add fruits and 1/4 cup cointreau. Heat through; place blazer pan in water jacket. Pour remaining cointreau over ham mixture; ignite. Serve over rice; sprinkle with almonds. One-half teaspoon curry powder may be stirred into cooked rice, if desired. Yield: 6 servings.

Elsie M. Ainslie, Preceptor Eta XP598
Ithaca, New York

CREAMED HAM WITH MUSHROOMS AND EGGS

2   3-oz. cans sm. whole mushrooms
2 tbsp. butter or margarine
1/2 tsp. paprika
2 1/2 c. diced cooked ham
Chicken broth
2 cans cream of chicken
    soup
6 hard-cooked eggs

Drain mushrooms; reserve liquid. Saute mushrooms in butter with paprika, stirring occasionally; add ham. Saute until heated through. Combine reserved liquid with enough chicken broth to measure 1 cup. Stir soup and chicken broth mixture into ham mixture. Simmer, stirring constantly, until smooth and heated through. Separate 1 egg yolk from white; reserve for garnish. Quarter egg white and remaining eggs; fold into ham mixture. Cool; refrigerate, covered, overnight. Place in chafing dish; heat through. Adjust heat to keep mixture warm. Garnish with reserved shredded egg yolk, pimento, and parsley. Serve with rice and peas. Yield: 6 servings.

Nelda Conkwright, Pres., City Council
Xi Delta Kappa X1947, Champaign, Illinois

GLAZED HAM BALLS

2 c. ground ham
2 c. ground pork
3/4 c. milk
1 1/2 c. dry bread crumbs
1 c. (packed) brown sugar
1/2 c. vinegar
1 tsp. dry mustard

Combine ham, pork, milk, and bread crumbs; mix well. Refrigerate for 1 hour. Mix brown sugar, vinegar, 1/2 cup water and mustard in large skillet; bring to boil over medium heat. Reduce heat; simmer for 15 minutes. Shape ham mixture into balls. Add to brown sugar mixture. Simmer, stirring occasionally, until ham balls are cooked. Turn into chafing dish; keep warm over low heat.

Carol Lynne Troup, Treas.
Epsilon Beta No. 2798, Saginaw, Michigan

SWEDISH HAM BALLS

1 lb. ground ham
1/2 lb. ground pork
2 c. bread crumbs
2 eggs, well beaten
1 c. milk
1/2 c. vinegar
1/2 c. (packed) brown sugar
1 tsp. dry mustard

Combine ham, pork, bread crumbs, eggs, and milk; shape into walnut-sized balls. Place in shallow baking dish. Combine vinegar,

brown sugar, and mustard; stir until sugar is dissolved. Pour over meatballs. Bake, covered, at 275 degrees for 1 hour and 30 minutes. Transfer to chafing dish; keep warm over low heat.

Muriel Collins, Soc. Chm.
Xi Alpha Gamma X3337, Coon Rapids, Minnesota

BARBECUED COUNTRY RIBS

Spareribs
Salt
Pepper
Onion slices
Lemon slices
5 c. catsup
1 2/3 c. Worcestershire sauce
5 tsp. chili powder

Preheat oven to 450 degrees. Place ribs in baking pan. Season with salt and pepper. Place onion and lemon slices over top. Bake for 30 minutes. Combine catsup, Worcestershire sauce, chili powder, 5 teaspoons salt, and 7 cups water, blending well. Pour sauce over ribs. Reduce oven temperature to 350 degrees. Bake for 1 hour and 30 minutes or until tender, basting occasionally. Cut ribs into serving pieces. Place in chafing dish; pour sauce over ribs. Serve hot.

Sharlene A. Scott, Pres., Delta Lambda No. 8218
Vienna, West Virginia

CHINESE RIBS

1 1/2 tbsp. black beans
2 lb. sparerib tips
4 cloves of garlic, crushed
1 1/2 c. soy sauce

Soak beans in water to cover for 30 minutes. Brown ribs in small amount of fat in skillet. Add water to cover. Mash beans; combine with garlic, blending thoroughly. Combine garlic mixture and soy sauce. Pour over ribs; cook until ribs are tender and sauce is clear. Spoon into chafing dish. Serve hot.

Dixie Miller, Pres., Alpha Epsilon XP910
Overland Park, Kansas

KABOB APPETIZERS

1 5-lb. baked ham
3 No. 2 1/2 cans sliced pineapple
Bits of pickle (opt.)
Olives (opt.)
1 c. chopped onions
3 tbsp. butter, melted
1 c. chopped celery (opt.)
1 c. sugar
3/4 c. vinegar
4 tbsp. Worcestershire sauce
1 1/4 c. catsup
3 tbsp. mustard
3 tsp. paprika
1/2 tsp. oregano

Cut ham into bite-sized cubes. Drain pineapple; cut into bite-sized sections. Arrange ham, pineapple, pickles, and olives on wooden picks; place in blazer pan of chafing dish. Place blazer pan in water jacket over low heat. Brown onions in butter in saucepan; stir in celery, sugar, vinegar, Worcestershire sauce, catsup, mustard, paprika, oregano, and 1 1/4 cups water. Bring to a boil over low heat. Pour sauce over ham kabobs; adjust heat to keep sauce just simmering. Serve with cocktail forks.

Mrs. Patricia Ann Law, Pres.
Epsilon Eta No. 2239, Springfield, Ohio

ALMOND-PORK LO MEIN

1 lb. diced fresh pork
2 tbsp. oil
1/3 c. flour
2 c. beef bouillon
3 tbsp. soy sauce
3/4 c. mushrooms
1 c. chopped onions
1/2 c. bean sprouts
3 c. thinly sliced celery
1 c. slivered blanched almonds
4 c. thin egg noodles
2 tbsp. butter

Brown pork in oil in chafing dish blazer pan over direct heat. Sprinkle pork with flour, tossing to coat well. Stir in bouillon and soy sauce. Heat through. Add mushrooms, onions, bean sprouts, celery, and almonds. Simmer, covered, until celery is crisp-tender, stirring occasionally. Cook noodles according to package directions; drain. Combine butter and noodles, tossing until butter is melted. Serve hot with pork mixture.

Joan Haslam, Pres., Eta No. 1744
Nanaimo, British Columbia, Canada

ORIENTAL BANANAS AND PORK

6 pork steaks
Salt and pepper to taste
1 chicken bouillon cube
1 15-oz. can sliced peaches
2 tbsp. soy sauce
1/4 c. cornstarch
2 bananas, cut into chunks

Brown pork in small amount of fat in large skillet. Season with salt and pepper. Dissolve bouillon cube in 1 1/2 cups boiling water. Pour over pork. Simmer, covered, for 25 minutes. Drain peaches, reserving syrup. Combine soy sauce and reserved syrup. Stir cornstarch into syrup mixture, blending thoroughly. Pour over pork; stir constantly until thickened. Add peaches and bananas, mixing well. Bring to a boil. Turn into chafing dish. Serve hot with rice.

Patricia Lee Edwards, Kappa Omega No. 4893
Ashland, Ohio

SAUCY SAUSAGES

2 8-oz. packages brown and
   serve sausage links
1 env. spaghetti sauce mix
Canned tomato sauce

Cut links into thirds crosswise. Prepare sauce mix according to package directions, using tomato sauce variation and substituting 1 1/4 cups water for recommended amount. Pour sauce into chafing dish blazer pan. Add sausage. Heat through over direct heat. Place over hot water. Serve hot with picks.

Margaret Neff, Past Pres., Xi Lambda X1220
Rogers, Arkansas

CHAFING DISH QUICKIE

1 green pepper, cut in 3/4-in.
   pieces
1 can luncheon meat, cubed
Dash of pepper
2 tsp. soy sauce
1/4 c. vinegar
1/4 c. light corn syrup
1 c. chicken bouillon
3 tbsp. cornstarch
1/2 c. pineapple juice
4 slices canned pineapple, cut
   in eighths

Cook green pepper in small amount of boiling water for 2 minutes; drain. Add meat to 1 1/2 tablespoons hot fat in skillet; brown on all sides quickly. Add pepper, soy sauce, vinegar, corn syrup and bouillon, stirring well. Combine cornstarch and juice, blending well. Add to vinegar mixture, stirring to blend. Bring to a boil; cook, stirring constantly, for 5 minutes. Add pineapple and green pepper. Simmer for 1 hour. Place in chafing dish; serve over rice. Yield: 8 servings.

Reka Faye Schwarz, Adv., Phi Pi No. 700
Spokane, Washington

MACADAMIA NUT MEATBALLS

2 to 3 lb. ground meat
2 sm. jars macadamia nuts,
   chopped fine
Dash of salt and pepper
Dash of ginger
1 bottle sweet and sour sauce
Butter
1 bottle teriyaki sauce

Blend meat, nuts, salt, pepper, ginger, and 1/2 cup sweet and sour sauce; shape into tiny balls. Saute in small amount of butter until brown; drain. Mix teriyaki sauce and remaining sweet and sour sauce in chafing dish; heat through. Add meatballs; simmer for several minutes to blend flavors. Keep warm.

Mrs. Robin Felish, Pres., Lambda Pi No. 4057
Canoga Park, California

KIDNEYS WITH RICE

4 beef kidneys
1 tbsp. salt
Flour
8 bacon slices
1 lg. can mushrooms, drained

Place kidneys in 1 quart water; add salt. Soak overnight. Drain; cut into 2-inch pieces. Dredge with flour. Dice bacon; fry in skillet until crisp. Remove from skillet. Fry kidneys in pan drippings until browned. Place bacon, kidneys, and mushrooms in chafing dish with enough water to cover. Simmer for 20 minutes. Serve hot with rice. Yield: 6 servings.

Mrytle Ropert, VP, Xi Chi X2714
Bunkie, Louisiana

SWEET-SOUR BALLS

1 lb. ground meat
1 tbsp. curry powder
1 egg, beaten
1/2 c. flour
2 tbsp. oil
1 No. 303 can pineapple tidbits
1/4 c. cider vinegar
1/3 c. (packed) brown sugar
1 tbsp. soy sauce
1 tbsp. cornstarch
1 green pepper, finely chopped

Combine ground meat and curry powder, blending well. Shape into 24 small balls. Dip balls in egg; roll in flour. Heat oil in large skillet. Brown balls gradually in hot oil. Remove balls from skillet. Drain pineapple, reserving juice. Combine reserved juice, vinegar, brown sugar, and soy sauce in skillet. Stir in cornstarch, blending well. Cook, stirring constantly, for 1 minute or until transparent. Add green pepper and meatballs. Simmer, covered, for 5 minutes. Add pineapple; simmer for 5 minutes. Pour into chafing dish. Serve warm with wooden picks.

Anna H. Hayes
International Honorary Member, BSP
Twin Falls, Idaho

FANCY FRANKS

1/2 c. chili sauce
1/2 c. currant jelly
1 1/2 tbsp. lemon juice
1 1/2 tsp. prepared mustard
2 7-oz. packages cocktail franks
1 13 1/2-oz. can pineapple chunks

Combine chili sauce, jelly, juice, mustard, and franks in saucepan. Drain pineapple. Stir into chili sauce mixture, mixing well. Simmer for 15 minutes. Serve warm in chafing dish with cocktail picks.

Patricia L. Phillips, Past Pres.
Xi Gamma Alpha X2450, Mexico, Missouri

HOT APPETIZER FRANKS

1 1/2 lb. frankfurters
2 8-oz. cans tomato sauce
2 tbsp. prepared mustard
2 tbsp. (packed) brown sugar
1/4 c. Worcestershire sauce

Cut frankfurters into 1/2-inch pieces. Combine frankfurters, tomato sauce, mustard, brown sugar, and Worcestershire sauce; stir well. Place in saucepan. Simmer for 15 minutes. Serve franks and sauce in chafing dish with wooden picks. Yield: 10-15 servings.

Mrs. Donna Baily, Treas., Theta Gamma No. 5442
Hatboro, Pennsylvania

PIQUANT WIENER BITS

1 6-oz. jar prepared mustard
1 10-oz. jar currant jelly
1 lb. wieners

Combine mustard and jelly in saucepan, stirring until blended. Heat through. Cut wieners into bite-sized pieces. Place in water to cover. Simmer until tender. Combine sauce and wieners in chafing dish. Serve hot with wooden picks. Yield: 10 servings.

Lou Brown, Pres., Xi Delta Theta X1748
Cambridge, Ohio

VEAL

VALIANT VEAL

1 1/2 lb. boneless veal
1 med. onion, sliced
4 stalks celery, sliced
3 peppercorns
3 tbsp. butter
3 tbsp. flour
1/2 c. light cream
1/8 tsp. mace
1/8 tsp. cayenne pepper
4 hard-cooked eggs, cooled
2 to 3 tbsp. sherry

Simmer veal, onion, celery, and peppercorns in salted water to cover until veal is tender; cool in stock. Cut veal into 2-inch slivers; refrigerate. Boil stock until reduced to 1 1/2 cups; strain. Melt butter in saucepan; stir in flour. Add cream and stock gradually, stirring constantly; cook until sauce is smooth and thickened. Stir in mace and cayenne pepper; remove from heat. Cool; refrigerate until ready to use. Place sauce in blazer pan over water pan. Adjust heat to medium. Sieve egg yolks; stir into sauce. Cut egg whites into thin strips; combine with veal. Stir veal mixture carefully into sauce; stir in sherry. Keep warm; serve over toast points. Yield: 6 servings.

Wanda G. Chandler, Soc. Chm.
Epsilon Sigma No. 6834, Toppenish, Washington

VEAL STEAKS SUPREME

4 4-oz. thin veal steaks
Lemon juice
Salt and pepper to taste
Flour
2 tbsp. butter
2 tbsp. oil
1/2 c. marsala
1/4 c. chicken stock

Place veal steaks between pieces of plastic wrap; pound to 1/8-inch thickness. Sprinkle with lemon juice; let stand for 10 minutes. Season with salt and pepper; coat lightly with flour. Melt butter in chafing dish over direct flame, add oil. Saute veal steaks quickly until golden brown on both sides, turning once. Stir in marsala and stock. Simmer for 2 minutes. Serve veal on a heated platter; pour sauce over veal. Garnish with lemon wedges. Serve with hot buttered green noodles. Yield: 4 servings.

Tena Ladd Pipkin, Pres.
Epsilon Beta No. 952407, Durham, North Carolina

VEAL SMETANA

12 veal scallops, 8 x 4 x 1/2 in. thick
Salt
Flour
6 to 8 tbsp. butter or margarine
1 c. minced onion
1 lb. mushrooms, thinly sliced
1/4 c. brandy
1 c. sour cream

Dry scallops. Sprinkle with salt to taste; dredge with flour. Heat 2 tablespoons butter in blazer pan until bubbly. Add some of the scallops; do not crowd. Cook for 3 minutes on each side; remove to warm plate. Cook remaining scallops in same way, adding butter for each batch; remove to same warm plate. Add onion to butter remaining in blazer pan; saute for 2 to 3 minutes, stirring with wooden spoon. Add remaining butter to blazer pan. Add mushrooms; stir. Cover; cook for 5 to 8 minutes or until mushrooms are tender, stirring occasionally. Add brandy; shake blazer pan, keeping face turned away. Ignite if brandy does not flame; let flames subside. Stir in sour cream and 1/2 teaspoon salt; bring just to boiling point. Place over water pan to keep warm.

Ginger Ingram, Parliamentarian, Social Chm.
Xi Eta Delta X1938, San Bernardino, California

VEAL À LA SHERRY

3 lb. veal cutlets
1/4 c. butter or margarine

2/3 c. chopped green pepper
1/2 c. chopped onion
2 pkg. mushroom gravy mix
1 c. tomato sauce
1 tsp. minced parsley
1/2 c. cooking sherry
2 4-oz. cans sliced mushrooms

Cut veal in small pieces. Melt butter in skillet; brown veal, onion, and green pepper in butter. Prepare gravy according to package directions in saucepan; add tomato sauce, parsley, and sherry. Simmer for 10 minutes. Add veal mixture and mushrooms to sauce; simmer for 20 minutes longer. Pour into chafing dish; keep warm until ready to serve.

Judy Griesemer, Pres.
Alpha Delta No. 3203, Bel Air, Maryland

CHICKEN

CHICKEN ALBERNI

1 tbsp. cooking oil
10 chicken thighs
Poultry seasoning to taste
1/2 lb. sliced fresh mushrooms
1 10-oz. can cream of chicken soup
3/4 c. sherry
1 tbsp. soy sauce
10 pimento-stuffed olives, halved
Salt and pepper to taste

Heat oil in large deep frying pan. Place chicken in pan, skin sides down. Fry quickly over high heat until golden brown, turning to brown evenly. Sprinkle with poultry seasoning. Add mushrooms; cover. Reduce heat to medium; cook for 15 minutes, adding water if necessary. Combine soup, sherry, and soy sauce; pour over chicken. Stir in olives and seasonings. Cover; simmer over low heat until chicken is fork-tender. Spoon into blazer pan of chafing dish; place in water pan over low heat. Yield: 5 servings.

Mrs. Pauline M. Barrett
International Honorary Member, BSP
Port Alberni, British Columbia, Canada

CHICKEN IN WINE

8 chicken breasts
1 tsp. flour
1/2 c. water
1   10-oz. can cream of mushroom
       soup
1/2 tsp. paprika
1 tsp. parsley
1 tsp. salt
1/2 tsp. pepper
1/2 c. dry white wine

Remove bones from each chicken breast; cut into 2 pieces. Saute in skillet in small amount fat until brown. Pour off fat, reserving 1 tablespoon in skillet. Place chicken on heated plate; keep warm. Mix remaining ingredients in skillet in order listed. Stir until smooth over medium heat. Add 1 cup water and add chicken. Cover; cook for 20 to 30 minutes. Baste occasionally. Remove cover; cook over low heat until sauce is thick. Place chicken in blazer pan; pour sauce on top. Keep warm in water pan over low flame.

Linda Ceyanes, Corr. Sec., Pi Gamma No. 4469
Dickinson, Texas

CURRIED CHICKEN

2 tbsp. dried flaked coconut
1   3 1/2-lb. chicken, disjointed
2 tbsp. oil
2 med. onions, chopped
1 tbsp. coriander
1 tsp. cumin
1 tsp. chili powder
1/2 tsp. turmeric
Salt and pepper to taste
1 c. canned tomatoes

Pour 1 cup boiling water over coconut; let stand. Saute chicken in oil in large skillet until golden brown. Remove from skillet; drain on absorbent paper towels. Saute onions in pan drippings until golden brown. Blend spices together; add to onions. Cook for 2 minutes. Stir in coconut with liquid; bring to a boil. Return chicken to skillet; season with salt and pepper. Cover; simmer for 15 to 20 minutes. Chop tomatoes; add to curry. Cover; simmer until chicken is tender. Place in blazer pan of chafing dish over hot water in water pan. Serve with boiled rice, chutney, raisins and coconut.

Helen McClare, Pres., Epsilon Phi No. 7226
West Hill, Ontario, Canada

CHICKEN CURRY

4 whole chicken breasts
4 tbsp. butter
1 apple, chopped
1 onion, chopped
2 tbsp. curry powder
2 cans cream of chicken soup

Simmer chicken in 1 1/2 cups water in saucepan until tender. Remove meat from bones; cut into bite-sized pieces. Reserve stock. Melt butter in skillet; saute apple, onion, and curry powder for 15 minutes. Thin soup to desired consistency with reserved stock; add to apple mixture. Add chicken meat. Spoon into blazer pan of chafing dish; place in water pan over low heat. Serve with desired condiments such as chopped peanuts, chutney, raisins, chopped green onions or chopped crisp bacon.

Erin Callaghan Truesdale
Alpha Kappa No. 241118
Grand Forks AFB, North Dakota

CHICKEN AND OYSTERS A LA KING

1   10-oz. can frozen oysters
6 tbsp. butter
1/2 c. chopped onion
1/2 c. chopped celery
1/2 c. chopped green pepper
2/3 c. all-purpose flour
1 tsp. salt
1/8 tsp. pepper
3 c. milk
1   4-oz. can sliced mushrooms
1 egg, beaten
3 c. chopped cooked chicken
1 1/2 tbsp. chopped pimento
Softened butter

8 lg. English muffins, split
Grated Parmesan cheese

Thaw oysters. Drain; reserve 1/2 cup liquid. Melt butter in 3-quart saucepan. Add onion, celery, and green pepper; saute until tender. Stir in flour, salt, and pepper; remove from heat. Stir in milk and reserved oyster liquid gradually. Add oysters and mushrooms and liquid; cook over medium heat, stirring constantly, until thickened. Blend small amount of hot mixture into egg; stir back into hot mixture. Cook for 1 minute. Add chicken and pimento; cover. Cook over low heat to serving temperature; do not boil. Place in chafing dish; keep warm. Spread butter on muffins; sprinkle with Parmesan cheese. Toast under broiler. Serve chicken mixture over English muffins. One pint fresh oysters may be substituted for frozen oysters.

Photograph for this recipe on page 46.

CRÊPES À LA REINE

3 tbsp. butter
1   4-oz. can sliced mushrooms, drained
1 tsp. instant minced onion
Flour
1 2/3 c. evaporated milk
1/3 c. chicken broth
Salt
Pepper
Nutmeg
2 tsp. chopped chives
3 tbsp. dry sherry
2 c. diced cooked chicken
1/2 c. water
3 eggs, well beaten

Preheat oven to 350 degrees. Melt butter in medium saucepan; add mushrooms and onion. Saute until mushrooms are lightly browned. Blend in 3 tablespoons flour; stir in 2/3 cup evaporated milk and chicken broth gradually, keeping mixture smooth. Cook, stirring, over medium heat until thickened. Season to taste with salt, pepper, and nutmeg. Blend in chives, sherry, and chicken. Cover and chill. Mix 3/4 cup flour

with 1/2 teaspoon salt; mix remaining evaporated milk with water. Add flour mixture alternately with liquid to beaten eggs, keeping mixture smooth. Pour 1/4 cup batter onto lightly greased hot griddle. Batter will be thin. Repeat to make 12 pancakes. Brown each of the pancakes on 1 side only, removing from griddle when upper surface looks bubbly and slightly dry. Place pancakes, browned sides down, on towel to cool. Divide chilled filling mixture into 12 portions; place 1 portion on uncooked side of each pancake. Roll pancake around to secure filling. Place filled pancakes, seam sides down, in greased baking dish. Cover tightly. Bake for 20 minutes or until heated through. Transfer to chafing dish over warm water.

Sauce Supreme

2 tbsp. butter
2 tbsp. flour
1 c. evaporated milk
1/2 c. chicken broth
Salt and pepper to taste

Melt butter in small saucepan; blend in flour until bubbly. Add milk and chicken broth gradually, keeping mixture smooth. Cook, stirring, over medium heat until thickened. Season with salt and pepper. Pour sauce over pancakes in chafing dish; serve immediately.

PARTY CHICKEN LIVERS

2 lb. chicken livers
1/4 c. butter or margarine
1 1/2 tsp. salt
1/4 c. finely chopped onion
1/4 c. sherry
1/2 tsp. hot sauce

Cut chicken livers in half. Heat butter in large skillet. Add half the chicken livers; sprinkle with 3/4 teaspoon salt. Brown livers quickly on both sides. Place in chafing dish. Add remaining chicken livers; sprinkle with remaining salt. Brown livers; place in chafing dish. Add onion to skillet; cook until tender but not brown. Stir in sherry and hot sauce; heat, stirring occasionally, until brown particles are loosened from pan. Pour sherry mixture over livers in chafing dish. Cook over boiling water, stirring frequently, for about 10 minutes or until livers are done.

BLAZING CHICKEN LIVERS

2 tbsp. butter
2 tbsp. flour

1/2 tsp. salt
Dash of freshly ground pepper
1 doz. chicken livers
1/4 c. warm brandy
2 doz. toast rounds

Melt butter in blazer pan over moderate heat. Sprinkle flour, salt, and pepper over chicken livers; saute quickly on all sides. Cut chicken livers into bite-sized pieces; pour brandy over livers. Ignite. Let blaze subside. Place blazer pan over hot water in water pan. Serve on toast rounds.

Marjorie M. McRae, Preceptor Alpha XP112
Winnipeg, Manitoba, Canada

CHICKEN LIVERS IN WINE

2 lb. chicken livers
Seasoned flour
1 c. butter
3 cloves of garlic, minced
Finely chopped parsley to taste
2 c. red wine

Prick livers with fork; toss in seasoned flour. Heat butter to 380 degrees in electric skillet. Brown livers evenly in butter; sprinkle with garlic and parsley. Remove liver mixture from skillet. Pour wine into hot skillet; heat through. Place liver mixture in blazer pan of chafing dish; pour wine over livers. Serve.

Barbara L. Gallagher, Serv. Chm.
Beta Tau No. 8488, Laurel, Maryland

CHICKEN LIVERS AND MUSHROOMS

1 1/2 lb. chicken livers
Seasoned flour
1 tbsp. (heaping) shortening
1 med. onion, chopped
2 tbsp. margarine
2 tbsp. flour
Salt and pepper to taste
1 c. (about) milk
1 sm. can sliced mushrooms

Coat chicken livers with seasoned flour. Melt shortening in skillet. Cook livers and onion until livers are browned. Remove livers and onion from skillet. Add margarine to pan drippings in skillet. Add flour; cook, stirring, until bubbly. Add seasonings. Add milk gradually. Cook, stirring constantly, until slightly thickened. Return livers and onion to skillet; add mushrooms. Cover; simmer for about 10 minutes, stirring frequently, until of medium thickness. Spoon liver mixture into blazer pan of chafing dish; place in water pan over low heat.

Sandy Everhart, Corr. Sec., Eta Chap.
Florence, South Carolina

SEAFOOD

ANGELS ON HORSEBACK

12 lg. oysters, well drained
1/2 tsp. seasoned salt
Pepper to taste
12   1/4-in. thick slices
    cooked chicken
6 thin slices bacon
1 tbsp. butter or margarine
12 toast rounds

Season oysters with salt and pepper. Trim chicken to size of oysters; cut bacon slices in half. Place oysters on chicken; wrap with bacon. Skewer with wooden pick. Melt butter in blazer pan; add wrapped oyster mixture. Cook until oysters are curled and bacon is browned; turn occasionally. Serve on hot toast rounds. Yield: 4 servings.

Judi Palinkas, Soc. Chm.
Xi Gamma Omicron X3080
Grosse Pointe Park, Michigan

CREAMY CRAB

2 cans crab meat, drained
1/4 c. dry sherry (opt.)
1/4 c. butter
2 tbsp. sliced green onions
2 tbsp. chopped green pepper
1/4 c. flour

1 1/4 c. light cream
Several drops of hot sauce
1/8 tsp. pepper
1/4 c. sliced stuffed olives

Place crab meat in bowl. Sprinkle with sherry. Melt butter in saucepan; add onions and green pepper. Saute until tender. Add flour, blending until smooth. Add cream gradually, mixing well. Cook over medium heat, stirring constantly, until smooth and thickened. Remove from heat; stir in hot sauce, pepper, crab meat, and olives. Place in chafing dish; simmer for 5 minutes. Serve over toast points or saffron rice.

Jean Seymour, Gamma Nu No. 8395
Fort Nelson, British Columbia, Canada

BLUE CHEESE AND CRAB MEAT

2 tbsp. butter
2/3 c. finely chopped onion
1/2 c. chopped green pepper
1 c. diced celery
1 c. milk
1 c. light cream
2   3-oz. packages blue cheese,
    crumbled
4   6-oz. packages frozen crab
    meat, thawed and drained
1 c. sliced pitted ripe olives
1 tsp. paprika
2 tbsp. chopped parsley

Melt butter in large skillet over medium heat; saute onion, green pepper, and celery in butter, stirring constantly, until vegetables are crisp-tender. Combine milk, cream, and cheese in top of double boiler over hot water; stir until mixture is smooth and cheese is melted. Pour cheese mixture into vegetable mixture; stir in crab meat and olives. Simmer, stirring occasionally, for 20 minutes or until heated through. Pour into chafing dish; sprinkle with paprika. Arrange parsley around edge; serve with Chinese noodles. Yield: 10 servings.

Theodora Mulcahy, Pres.
Xi Alpha Lambda X1137, Windsor, New York

HOT CLAM DIP

2 cans clams, drained
1   8-oz. package cream cheese
2 1/2 tbsp. mayonnaise
Cream
1/2 tsp. chopped olives
1/2 tsp. Worcestershire sauce
1/4 tsp. mustard

Combine clams and cream cheese; blend well. Add mayonnaise, enough cream to moisten, and olives to clam mixture. Stir in Worcestershire sauce and mustard. Blend thoroughly. Place in chafing dish, stirring occasionally. Serve hot with potato chips or crackers. Yield: 10-12 servings.

Mrs. David L. Black
Honorary International Member, BSP
Daytona Beach, Florida

PEPPERED EGGS AND SALMON

1   1-lb. can salmon, drained
3 strips bacon
2 tbsp. butter
1/2 c. chopped green onions
   with tops
1 green pepper, diced
1/2 tsp. salt

1/4 tsp. cayenne pepper
6 eggs, lightly beaten
1/4 c. light cream
1 tsp. Worcestershire sauce

Flake salmon. Saute bacon in chafing dish blazer pan until crisp; drain on absorbent paper. Crumble bacon. Pour off bacon fat from blazer pan. Melt butter in blazer pan. Add onions and green pepper; saute for about 5 minutes or until onion is transparent. Add seasonings and salmon. Combine eggs, cream, and Worcestershire sauce. Add to salmon mixture; cook over moderate heat, stirring constantly, until eggs are just set but still creamy. Sprinkle with bacon.

WHITE GULL LOBSTER CANTONESE

2 baby lobsters or 4 lobster-tails
2 tbsp. olive oil
1 tsp. salt
Pepper to taste
1 clove of garlic, cut
1/2 lb. pork, chopped
1 tsp. minced scallions
1 c. chicken bouillon
1 egg, slightly beaten
2 tbsp. cornstarch
1 tsp. soy sauce

Cook lobsters in boiling water for 5 minutes; drain. Split lobsters in half lengthwise; cut crosswise into 2-inch pieces, leaving shells on. Cut claws into 3 pieces. Combine oil, salt, pepper, and garlic in heavy saucepan; simmer for 2 minutes. Remove garlic; discard. Stir pork and scallions into oil; add lobster. Cook, covered, over medium heat for 10 minutes. Add bouillon; heat through. Add small amount of bouillon to egg; return to hot mixture. Simmer, stirring constantly, for 2 minutes. Blend cornstarch, soy sauce, and 1/4 cup water; stir into lobster mixture. Cook, stirring constantly, until mixture is thickened. Transfer to chafing dish; keep warm over hot water. Yield: 4-6 servings.

Mrs. Louise E. Fraser, Pres., Rho No. 1490
Waynesboro, Virginia

CURRIED LOBSTER-TAILS

2 tbsp. butter or margarine
1 1/2 c. finely chopped pared
  tart apples
1/4 c. chopped onion
2 tbsp. flour
2 to 2 1/2 tsp. curry powder
1 tsp. turmeric
1 tsp. salt
2 c. milk
8 3-oz. packages frozen
  lobster-tails, cooked

Melt butter; add apples and onion. Simmer for 5 minutes. Combine flour, curry powder, turmeric, and salt; stir into apples. Add milk gradually; cook, stirring constantly, until mixture thickens. Dice lobster; stir into apple mixture. Pour into blazer pan of chafing dish. Serve with chopped hard-cooked egg, chutney, shredded coconut, plumped raisins, peanuts, and green onion slices.

Dottie Tomberg, Cor. Sec., Beta Eta No. 2967
Lake Park, Florida

LOBSTER NEWBURG SUPREME

6 tbsp. butter or margarine
2 tbsp. flour
2 c. light cream
3 egg yolks, slightly beaten
3 c. diced cooked lobster
1/8 tsp. nutmeg
Dash of paprika
1 tsp. salt
3 tbsp. sherry

Melt butter in blazer pan of chafing dish over direct low heat; stir in flour. Add cream to egg yolks; mix well. Stir cream mixture into flour mixture gradually; simmer, stirring constantly, until smooth and thickened. Place blazer pan in water jacket over low heat. Stir in lobster, nutmeg, paprika, salt, and sherry; heat through. Serve with toast points, patty shells or biscuits. Yield: 6 servings.

Julie Hajek, Pres., City Coun.
Bremerton, Washington

LOBSTER DIP ELEGANTE

1 5-oz. can lobster
1 8-oz. package cream cheese
1/4 c. mayonnaise or salad dressing
1 clove of garlic, crushed
1 tsp. sugar
1 tsp. prepared mustard
1 tsp. grated onion
Seasoned salt to taste
3 tbsp. sauterne

Drain lobster; flake and remove cartilage. Melt cream cheese, stirring constantly, in blazer pan of small chafing dish over direct low heat. Stir in mayonnaise, garlic, sugar, mustard, onion and seasoned salt; blend in lobster and sauterne. Place blazer pan in water jacket over low heat. Serve with melba toast and assorted crackers.

Darlene A. Garstecki, Pres.
Kappa Omicron No. 7815, Rochester, Michigan

LOBSTER APPETIZER BITS

8 4-oz. frozen lobster-tails
1 c. rhine wine
1/2 c. salad oil
1 tbsp. minced onion
1 tsp. rosemary
2 tsp. sugar
1/4 tsp. salt
Pepper to taste
1/2 c. butter or margarine, melted
2 tbsp. lemon juice

Cook lobster-tails in boiling salted water for 7 minutes; cool. Remove shells; cut crosswise into 1-inch pieces. Combine wine, salad oil, onion, rosemary, sugar, salt, and pepper; pour over lobster. Chill well, stirring occasionally. Drain, reserving marinade. Place lobster in blazer pan of chafing dish. Combine 1/2 cup marinade, butter and lemon juice; pour over lobster. Place blazer pan in water jacket over low heat. Serve with cocktail picks.

Jane E. Sweers, Pres.
Preceptor Epsilon XP243, Flint, Michigan

EASY LOBSTER NEWBURG

1   5-oz. can lobster
6 tbsp. butter or margarine
2 tbsp. all-purpose flour
1 1/2 c. light cream
3 beaten egg yolks
3 tbsp. dry white wine
2 tsp. lemon juice
1/4 tsp. salt
Paprika
Toast cups

Drain lobster; break into large pieces and remove cartilage. Melt butter in blazer pan of chafing dish over direct heat; blend in flour. Add cream; cook, stirring constantly, until mixture is smooth and thickened. Place blazer pan in water jacket over low heat. Stir small amount of hot mixture into egg yolks; return to hot mixture. Cook, stirring constantly, until smooth and thickened. Stir in lobster; heat through. Stir in wine, lemon juice, and salt; sprinkle with paprika. Serve in toast cups. Yield: 4-6 servings.

Mrs. Betty J. Knoll
Xi Gamma Upsilon X 3204, Niles, Michigan

LOBSTER BALLS

2 cans drained lobster or
   2 lb. cooked lobster
3 hard-boiled egg yolks, mashed
1 egg
Butter
1 tbsp. cornstarch
1 tbsp. milk
Salt to taste
2 tsp. minced tarragon
1/4 tsp. fresh ground pepper
Flour
1 c. sour cream
2 tsp. lemon juice
1 tbsp. chopped chives

Grind lobster; combine with egg yolks, egg, 2 tablespoons butter, cornstarch, milk, salt, tarragon and pepper. Mix well. Shape into walnut-sized balls; roll in flour. Chill thoroughly. Melt small amount of butter in blazer pan of chafing dish; brown lobster balls in butter. Place blazer pan in water jacket over low heat. Combine sour cream, salt, lemon juice, and chives; mix well. Serve as dip for lobster balls.

Dolly Rudd, Pres., City Coun.
Xi Alpha Chi X2603, Alamagordo, New Mexico

PINEAPPLE SHRIMP EN CROUSTADES

1/3 c. butter
1 1/2 lb. large cooked deveined
   shrimp
3 tbsp. cornstarch
1 tsp. salt
Dash of hot sauce
1 tsp. paprika
1/2 tsp. monosodium glutamate
1 tbsp. Worcestershire sauce
1 1/2 c. whipping cream
1/2 c. sour cream
1/4 c. dry sherry
1   1-lb. 4 1/2-oz. can pineapple
   chunks, drained
Croustades or patty shells

Melt butter in chafing dish; add shrimp. Stir until shrimp are coated. Sprinkle cornstarch into shrimp mixture, stirring until blended.

Add seasonings. Stir in whipping cream gradually. Heat, stirring, until mixture bubbles and thickens. Stir in sour cream and sherry gradually. Add pineapple chunks; heat gently. Serve in croustades. Yield: 6-8 servings.

LUAU SHRIMP

2 lb. Velveeta cheese, cubed
1 c. diced green pepper
4 c. diced onions
1 clove of garlic, minced
1 c. diced celery
1/2 c. butter or margarine
1   8-oz. can mushrooms
1 can chilies and tomatoes
1 No. 2 can tomatoes
2 lb. frozen shrimp
Cooked rice

Melt cheese in top of double boiler over hot water. Saute green pepper, onions, garlic and celery in butter in skillet; stir into cheese. Pour cheese mixture into chafing dish. Stir in mushrooms, chilies and tomatoes, tomatoes and shrimp; heat through. Keep warm over hot water. Serve with rice. Yield: 8-10 servings.

Carolyn Lackland, City Coun. Pres.
Xi Eta Omicron X2252, Arlington, Texas

FOO YUNG FRITTERS

6 eggs
1 c. flour
1 1/2 tsp. baking powder
1/2 tsp. salt
1 tbsp. soy sauce
1/2 tsp. Worcestershire sauce
1 can bean sprouts
1 can mushrooms stems and pieces
1 can shrimp
1 env. onion soup mix
Salad oil

Beat eggs slightly in large bowl; blend in flour, baking powder, salt, soy sauce, and

Worcestershire sauce. Beat thoroughly. Rinse bean sprouts; drain and chop. Drain mushrooms; drain and chop shrimp. Stir bean sprouts, mushrooms, shrimp and soup mix into batter. Pour salad oil into fryer to depth of 1/2 inch; set temperature at 375 degrees. Drop batter by teaspoonfuls into hot oil; fry until golden, turning once. Drain well. Serve in chafing dish with cocktail picks. Serve with additional soy sauce or desired dip.

Kay Craft, Pres., Nu Iota No. 8514
Saint Joseph, Missouri

SCAMPI

1 lb. large shrimp, shelled
Flour
2 tbsp. oil
1 tbsp. sherry
1 tbsp. brandy
Minced garlic to taste
Chopped parsley to taste
Chopped chives to taste
1/2 c. half and half

Butterfly shrimp; flour lightly. Saute in oil in chafing dish until lightly browned. Flame with sherry and brandy. Stir in garlic, parsley and chives. Add half and half; blend well. Keep warm over hot water.

Betty W. Cote, Alpha Preceptor XP133
Derry, New Hampshire

SHRIMP IN JACKETS

1 lb. medium shrimp, shelled
1/2 tsp. garlic salt
3/4 lb. bacon

Sprinkle shrimp with garlic salt; cut bacon slices into thirds. Wrap each shrimp with bacon; arrange on broiler rack. Broil 3 to 4 inches from source of heat for 8 minutes or until bacon is crisp; turn occasionally. Keep warm in chafing dish. Serve with cocktail picks.

Mrs. Eugene Gille, Nu Chi No. 6841
Belvidere, Illinois

CREOLE SHRIMP DIP

4 cans shrimp
2 sm. onions, chopped
4 c. chopped celery
1/4 c. oil
2 No. 2 1/2 cans tomatoes
1 sm. can tomato sauce
1 tsp. salt
1/2 to 1 tsp. pepper
1 tbsp. parsley flakes
1/2 c. sherry

Rinse shrimp; drain well. Saute onions and celery in oil in large saucepan; stir in tomatoes and tomato sauce. Add salt, pepper, and parsley; blend well. Simmer until well thickened; stir in shrimp and sherry. Simmer for 15 minutes. Transfer to chafing dish; keep warm over hot water. Serve with crackers or large corn chips.

Norma Kasten, Pres., Xi Zeta Sigma X3203
Youngstown, Ohio

INDONESIAN SHRIMP CURRY

2 lg. onions, chopped
2 pieces of gingerroot, peeled
2 cloves of garlic, minced
4 apples, finely diced
2 bay leaves
1/4 tsp. cinnamon
Butter
3 tbsp. flour
2 tbsp. (about) curry powder
1 tbsp. sugar
1 c. chicken stock
2 c. Coconut Milk
Salt to taste
2 lb. cooked shrimp, chicken or
    lamb

Saute onions, gingerroot, garlic, apples, bay leaves, and cinnamon in small amount of butter in top of double boiler until lightly browned. Combine flour, curry powder, and sugar; stir into apple mixture. Simmer, stirring, for 5 minutes. Blend in stock; simmer for 10 minutes longer. Place top of double boiler over hot water. Stir Coconut Milk into mixture; simmer for 45 minutes. Remove gingerroot. Stir in salt and shrimp just before serving; heat through. Transfer to chafing dish; keep warm over hot water. Serve with rice and following condiments: mango chutney, chopped peanuts, chopped candied ginger, Bombay duck, and chopped green onions.

Coconut Milk

2 1/2 c. milk
1 pkg. grated coconut

Pour milk over coconut in top of double boiler; simmer over hot water for 1 hour. Cool; refrigerate overnight. Squeeze through cheesecloth.

Dr. Hope S. Ross
International Honorary Member, BSP
Enid, Oklahoma

SHRIMP BALLS

1 1/2 lb. shelled shrimp
1 med. onion, minced
1 green pepper, minced
2 or 3 stalks celery, minced
3 cloves of garlic, minced
1 egg
Flour
Salad oil
1 can tomatoes
1 can tomato paste
1 bay leaf
1 tsp. Worcestershire sauce
Salt and pepper to taste

Grind shrimp; mix with half the onion, green pepper, celery and garlic. Mix with egg; roll into small balls. Roll balls in flour; fry in a small amount of cooking oil in skillet. Remove balls; saute remaining onion, green pepper, celery, and garlic in skillet until tender. Add tomatoes, tomato paste, bay leaf, Worcestershire sauce, salt, and pepper; blend well. Stir in shrimp balls. Simmer until thickened. Transfer to chafing dish. Serve as appetizer or main dish with rice.

Merline McCoy, Prog. Chm., Xi Iota Mu X2806
Port Neches, Texas

SHRIMP CREOLE

1 1/2 c. chopped onions
1 c. finely chopped celery
2 green peppers, finely chopped
2 cloves of garlic, minced
1/2 c. butter, melted
1 15-oz. can tomato sauce
2 tsp. minced parsley
1 tsp. salt
1/8 tsp. cayenne pepper
2 bay leaves, crushed
1 lb. shelled shrimp
3 c. cooked rice

Saute onions, celery, green peppers, and garlic in butter in large skillet for 5 minutes or until vegetables are tender; remove from heat. Stir in tomato sauce, 1 cup water, parsley, salt, cayenne pepper, and bay leaves; blend well. Simmer for 10 minutes; add water, if needed. Stir in shrimp; bring to a boil. Cook, covered, over medium heat for 10 minutes or until shrimp are tender. Serve with rice. Yield: 6 servings.

Mrs. Larry Thompson, Phi No. 542
Grand Junction, Colorado

SWEET AND PUNGENT SHRIMP

2 lb. shrimp
2 9-oz. cans pineapple chunks
1 c. (packed) brown sugar
1/4 c. soy sauce
1 c. vinegar
6 tbsp. cornstarch
2 green peppers
2 onions
1/2 c. toasted almonds (opt.)
4 c. cooked rice

Shell and devein shrimp; cook in water to cover in saucepan for 5 minutes. Drain thoroughly. Drain pineapple; reserve syrup. Combine brown sugar, soy sauce, vinegar, and 2 cups water with reserved syrup in large skillet; bring to a boil. Combine cornstarch with 1/2 cup water; stir into vinegar mixture. Cook, stirring constantly, until smooth and thickened. Cut green peppers into strips.

Slice onions; separate into rings. Stir green peppers, onions and pineapple into sauce; blend well. Simmer for 2 minutes; stir in shrimp. Heat through. Transfer to chafing dish; keep warm over hot water. Sprinkle with almonds; serve over rice. Yield: 6 servings.

Jane A. Perks, Treas., Preceptor Delta XP472
Millville, New Jersey

SHRIMP STROGANOFF

3 tbsp. butter
1/2 c. chopped onion
1 sm. clove of garlic, minced
1/4 c. all-purpose flour
1 tsp. salt
1/2 tsp. dillweed
1 10 1/2-oz. can beef broth
1 2-oz. can sliced mushrooms
2 c. cooked shrimp
1 c. yogurt, at room temperature

Melt butter in chafing dish blazer pan. Add onion and garlic; saute until onion is tender. Stir in flour, salt, and dillweed; remove from heat. Stir in beef broth and mushrooms with liquid gradually; cook over medium heat, stirring constantly, until thickened. Add shrimp; cook over low heat for 5 to 10 minutes. Stir in yogurt; heat to serving temperature. Do not boil. Place blazer pan over water pan. Serve shrimp mixture over rice or noodles. Yield: 4-6 servings.

Photograph for this recipe on page 42.

HOT SHRIMP DIP

1 lg. or 2 sm. garlic cheese rolls
1 can frozen shrimp soup, thawed
A-1 sauce to taste

Melt cheese in blazer pan of chafing dish over low heat; stir in soup and A-1 sauce. Blend thoroughly. Place blazer pan in water jacket; keep warm over hot water.

Tina Risch, Hist., Kappa Tau No. 4814
Marion, Ohio

GRAPEFRUIT-SHRIMP CURRY

1/3 c. butter or margarine
1/2 c. finely chopped onion
6 tbsp. flour
1 1/2 tsp. salt
1 tbsp. curry powder
1 chicken bouillon cube
2 1/2 c. milk
1/2 c. Florida grapefruit juice
2 lb. cleaned cooked shrimp
2 c. Florida grapefruit sections
1/4 c. chopped parsley
4 c. hot cooked rice
Chopped peanuts
Flaked coconut

Melt butter in saucepan. Add onion; cook until tender but not brown. Blend in flour, salt, and curry powder; add bouillon cube. Stir in milk and grapefruit juice gradually; cook, stirring constantly, until mixture thickens and comes to a boil. Add shrimp and 1 cup grapefruit sections; heat to serving temperature over low heat. Turn into chafing dish. Combine parsley and rice; serve with curry. Serve with remaining grapefruit sections, chopped peanuts, and flaked coconut as curry condiments. Yield: 6 servings.

VEGETABLES

ASPARAGUS WITH CHEESE

1 bunch asparagus
1 tsp. salt
1/2 c. grated cheese
1/8 tsp. pepper
1 tbsp. butter

Cut asparagus into small pieces. Place salt and 1 cup water in saucepan. Add asparagus; bring to a boil. Cook for 10 minutes. Drain; place in baking dish. Sprinkle with grated cheese and pepper; dot with butter. Bake at 350 degrees until heated through. Place in chafing dish.

Mrs. Lora Miller Burke
International Honorary Member, BSP
Moberly, Missouri

NEW YEAR'S LUCK

4 c. dried black-eyed peas
2 lg. hot onions, chopped
Salt
3 c. cornmeal
1/2 c. flour
1 tsp. soda
1 1/2 tsp. baking powder
3 tbsp. sugar
2 eggs
Buttermilk
1/2 c. shortening
2 cans water chestnuts
1/2 c. jalapeno pepper juice (opt.)
Chicken broth or bouillon
Bacon slices, cut in half

Place peas in large saucepan; add onions, 2 tablespoons salt, and enough water to cover. Bring to a boil; reduce heat. Cover; simmer for 4 hours. Let stand overnight. Mix cornmeal, flour, 2 teaspoons salt, soda, baking powder, and sugar. Add eggs and enough buttermilk to make thick batter; mix well. Heat shortening in iron skillet until melted. Pour cornmeal batter into skillet; cook over low heat for several minutes. Bake at 400 degrees for about 30 minutes or until done. Reheat peas. Drain water chestnuts; chop.

Add to peas; add jalapeno pepper juice. Mash with potato masher. Crumble corn bread; stir into peas mixture. Add enough chicken broth, if needed, to moisten. Shape into walnut-sized balls; wrap each ball with 1/2 slice bacon. Secure with toothpick; place in shallow baking pan. Broil until bacon is brown. Place in chafing dish; keep hot.

Marene Johnson-Johnson
International Honorary Member, BSP
Eastland, Texas

RINKTUM DITTY WITH BEANS

1 can tomato soup
2 c. shredded sharp Cheddar cheese
1/4 tsp. dry mustard
1/2 tsp. Worcestershire sauce
2 or 3 dashes of hot sauce
1 egg, slightly beaten
2 c. cooked drained Idaho Great
    Northern dry beans
Salt and pepper to taste

Heat soup, cheese, and seasonings over hot water in chafing dish or double boiler until cheese is melted. Add egg quickly, stirring constantly until smooth; stir in hot beans. Add salt and pepper; heat through. Serve over crisp, piping-hot buttered toast. One-

fourth cup minced onion, cooked in butter, may be added before serving, if desired.

MARINATED MUSHROOMS

1/4 lb. butter
1 sm. onion, finely chopped
1 8-oz. jar mushroom crowns,
    drained
1 tsp. dried sweet basil
1 tsp. crushed oregano
1/2 tsp. garlic salt
1/2 tsp. thyme
1/2 tsp. hot sauce
2 tbsp. lime juice
1/2 tsp. salt
1/4 c. dry sherry

Melt butter in frypan. Add onion; saute over low heat until soft, stirring frequently. Add mushrooms; stir until coated with butter. Combine basil, oregano, garlic salt, and thyme; add to frypan. Sprinkle hot sauce, lime juice, salt, and sherry over onion mixture; mix well. Cover; simmer until dry. Place in chafing dish; keep hot. Serve with picks.

Linda J. Snvder, Pres., Epsilon Tau No. 2618
Mansfield, Ohio

MUSHROOMS À LA CRÈME GEORGE

1 can button mushrooms
1 can mushroom stems and pieces
2 tbsp. butter
2 tbsp. dry sherry
1 c. grated Parmesan cheese
1 c. sour cream
Salt and freshly ground pepper
    to taste

Drain mushrooms; reserve liquid. Saute mushrooms in butter for 2 minutes. Add sherry; cook for 1 minute. Add cheese, sour cream, salt, and pepper; cook until thick. Place in chafing dish; keep hot. Dilute with reserved mushroom liquid if mixture becomes too thick. Yield: 4 servings.

Jeanette Sue Lewis, Pres.
Gamma Lambda No. 1144, Houston, Texas

MUSHROOMS À LA GREQUE

1 c. water
1 c. red wine vinegar
1 c. olive oil
2 cloves of garlic
2 bay leaves
1/2 tsp. crumbled thyme
1/2 tsp. onion powder
2 tsp. salt
12 peppercorns
2 lb. medium mushrooms

Combine all ingredients except mushrooms in large saucepan; bring to a boil. Reduce heat; simmer for 5 minutes. Add mushrooms; simmer for 10 minutes. Let stand until cool; chill. Place in chafing dish; reheat. Serve with picks. Yield: 6-8 servings.

Leona Jean Alonso, Past Pres.
Xi Alpha Zeta X539, Pacific Grove, California

RUTABAGA AND POTATO CASSEROLE

4 c. diced potatoes
4 c. diced rutabagas
2 3/4 tsp. salt
4 tbsp. butter or margarine
4 egg yolks

1 tsp. sugar
1/4 tsp. ground white pepper
1 tbsp. finely chopped onion

Cook potatoes and rutabagas in separate saucepans in 1 inch boiling water and 1 teaspoon salt for 20 minutes or until tender. Drain and mash each separately; place rutabagas over low heat to evaporate excess moisture. Combine potatoes, rutabagas, butter, egg yolks, sugar, remaining salt, white pepper, and onion; mix well. Reserve 2 cups rutabaga mixture. Turn remaining rutabaga mixture into greased 1-quart casserole. Place reserved rutabaga mixture in pastry bag or tube; make rosettes over casserole, covering entire surface. Bake in preheated 400-degree oven for 30 minutes or until brown. Place over water pan of chafing dish or over candle warmer to keep hot. Yield: 6 servings.

CHAFING DISH SPINACH SALAD

1 lb. fresh spinach
2 green onions and tops, sliced
Coarsely ground pepper to taste
5 slices bacon, diced
2 tbsp. wine vinegar
1 tbsp. lemon juice
1 tsp. sugar
1/2 tsp. salt
1 hard-cooked egg, coarsely
    chopped

Wash spinach, discarding stems; pat dry on paper towels. Tear in bite-sized pieces; place in bowl. Add onions; sprinkle with pepper. Chill. Fry bacon bits in deep chafing dish or electric skillet over low heat until crisp. Add vinegar, lemon juice, sugar, and salt. Add spinach; toss just until leaves are coated and slightly wilted. Sprinkle with egg.

Diane Cooper, Pres., Xi Nu Delta X3060
Palmdale, California

GREEN BEANS DELUXE

2 lb. fresh green beans
1/2 c. sliced onions

2 tbsp. minced parsley
2 tbsp. butter or margarine
2 tbsp. flour
1 tsp. salt
1/4 tsp. pepper
1/2 tsp. grated lemon peel
1 c. sour cream
1/2 c. grated cheese

Remove ends from beans; cut beans into small pieces. Cook in boiling, salted water until tender; drain. Cook onions and parsley in butter in chafing dish over high flame until onions are tender but not brown. Add flour, salt, pepper and lemon peel; blend well. Add sour cream. Stir in cheese; cook until cheese melts. Add green beans; heat through. Yield: 4 servings.

Dovie T. Papke, Serv. Com. Chm.
Alpha Rho No. 2445, Oak Ridge, Tennessee

RATATOUILLE

2 tbsp. olive oil
1 onion, finely chopped
1 clove of garlic, crushed
1 green pepper, finely chopped
1 zucchini, chopped
1 sm. eggplant, diced
2 med. tomatoes
1/4 tsp. basil
1/4 tsp. oregano
2 tbsp. tomato puree

Heat oil. Add onion and garlic; cook until translucent. Add green pepper, zucchini, and eggplant. Cover; simmer for 15 minutes. Peel, seed, and chop tomatoes; add to onion mixture. Add herbs; cook, uncovered, for 15 minutes longer. Add tomato puree; place in chafing dish. Serve hot over rice or cold over crackers. One cucumber, chopped, may be substituted for zucchini. Yield: 6 servings.

Mrs. Dorothy Riess
International Honorary Member, BSP
Claremont, California

BROCCOLI DIP

1 pkg. frozen chopped broccoli
1 garlic cheese roll, cubed

1 sm. green onion, chopped fine
2 or 3 stalks celery, chopped fine
1 sm. can chopped mushrooms, drained
Dash of hot sauce
Dash of cayenne pepper
Dash of paprika
Dash of Worcestershire sauce
1 can mushroom soup

Cook broccoli according to package directions; drain. Add cheese roll; let melt. Saute onion, celery, and mushrooms in small amount of fat in saucepan until tender; add to broccoli mixture. Add hot sauce, cayenne pepper, paprika, Worcestershire sauce and undiluted soup; heat through. Place in chafing dish; keep hot. Serve with chips or cauliflower.

Romona Wiseman, Pres., Gamma Rho No. 8518
Dallas, Texas

DESSERTS

FLAMING CHERRIES SUPREME

1 16-oz. can dark sweet cherries
2 tbsp. cornstarch
2 tbsp. sugar
1/4 c. lemon-lime carbonated drink
6 sugar cubes
Vanilla

Drain cherries, reserving syrup. Combine cornstarch and sugar in small saucepan, mixing well. Stir in reserved syrup and 1/4 cup water gradually. Cook, stirring constantly, over medium heat until thickened and bubbly. Stir in cherries; heat through. Remove from heat; stir in carbonated beverage. Place in chafing dish. Soak sugar cubes in small amount of vanilla. Place cubes over cherries. Ignite cubes; serve flaming. Yield: 6 servings.

Allena Brunken, Treas., Gamma Mu No. 7789
Hopkinsville, Kentucky

CHERRIES FLAMBÉ

1 No. 2 1/2 can pitted Bing cherries
3/4 c. currant jelly
1/2 c. brandy
Vanilla ice cream

Drain cherries well. Melt jelly in chafing dish over direct heat; stir frequently. Add cherries to jelly; heat through, stirring occasionally. Pour brandy into center of cherry mixture; heat to warm brandy. Ignite; spoon cherries over 8 portions ice cream. Serve immediately.

Karen Maycock, Phi Lambda Chap.
Des Moines, Iowa

BANANAS CONNOISSEUR

4 lg. green-tipped bananas
3 tbsp. lime juice
1/4 c. butter or margarine
1/2 c. sugar
1/2 c. apricot brandy
1 c. sour cream

Slice bananas diagonally into 1-inch pieces; sprinkle with lime juice. Melt butter in large blazer pan over medium flame. Add bananas; heat through. Stir in sugar and all except 1 tablespoon apricot brandy. Heat remaining

apricot brandy in ladle or large serving spoon over flame. Ignite; pour over bananas. Shake pan or stir until flame dies; serve bananas topped with sour cream. Yield: 4 servings.

APRICOT-PEACH-PLUM COMPOTE

1 No. 2 1/2 can apricots
1 No. 2 1/2 can peaches
1 No. 2 1/2 can plums
1/3 c. (packed) brown sugar
1 tsp. grated lemon rind
1/2 c. orange juice

Drain apricots, peaches, and plums thoroughly; place in 1 3/4-quart chafing dish. Combine brown sugar, lemon rind, and orange juice; pour over fruits. Bring to a boil over direct heat; reduce heat. Simmer for 10 minutes, stirring occasionally. Serve hot or cold. Yield: 4-6 servings.

Gwen Sharp, 1st VP, Xi Iota X2580
Winnipeg, Manitoba, Canada

FIGS IN CLARET

8 figs
Blanched almonds, halved
1/2 c. claret
1 tbsp. sugar
1 tsp. lemon juice
Heavy cream

Stuff figs with almonds. Heat claret, sugar and lemon juice in blazer pan of chafing dish over simmering water. Add figs; cook, covered, for 8 minutes. Serve with heavy cream.

Mrs. Ted G. Tudor, Corr. Sec.
Xi Iota Mu X2806, Port Neches, Texas

ORANGE CRÊPES SUZETTE

2 c. warm water
2 c. flour
1 pkg. yeast
4 eggs
1 tsp. soda
1 tsp. salt
1 tbsp. sugar

1/4 c. melted shortening
Salad oil
1/2 c. soft butter
1/2 c. confectioners' sugar
1 tbsp. grated orange rind
3 tbsp. grenadine
1/3 c. orange juice
1 c. orange sections

Place water, flour, and yeast in medium mixing bowl; mix well. Cover. Let stand in warm place for 6 to 12 hours. Add eggs, soda, salt, sugar, and shortening; mix well. Brush hot 7 or 8-inch skillet lightly with salad oil. Pour 2 to 3 tablespoons batter onto skillet; tip skillet so that mixture covers bottom evenly. Cook until brown. Loosen with spatula; flip over. Brown; turn out onto foil or waxed paper. Repeat until all batter is used. Cream butter with confectioners' sugar and orange rind; blend in grenadine. Spread about 1/2 teaspoon over each crepe on last-browned side; roll as for jelly roll. Place remaining butter mixture in large chafing dish; stir in orange juice. Heat until bubbly. Add crepes; heat through, spooning sauce over each crepe. Add orange sections; heat for 2 to 3 minutes longer.

Verle Weiss, Pres., Xi Beta Omega X2713
Denison, Iowa

CRÊPES SUZETTE

3 eggs
1 c. milk
3/4 c. unsifted flour
Sugar
1/4 tsp. salt
1/2 c. margarine
1 tsp. grated orange peel
1/3 c. cointreau

Beat eggs and milk in small mixing bowl; beat in flour, 1 tablespoon sugar and salt. Pour batter, 2 tablespoons at a time, into lightly greased 5 or 6-inch skillet; cook over medium heat until lightly browned and top is bubbly. Turn; brown other side. Fold each crepe in quarters; set aside. Melt margarine in large skillet or chafing dish. Add 2/3 cup sugar and grated orange peel; cook until mixture bubbles. Place folded crepes in sauce; cook for 5 minutes or until sugar starts to caramelize, basting crepes occasionally with sauce. Pour cointreau over top; ignite. Serve immediately. Yield: 16 crepes.

Photograph for this recipe on page 4.

MONT BLANC BRANDIED ORANGES

6 oranges
2 c. water
1 1/2 c. sugar
3/4 c. brandy
6 whole cloves
2 c. small curd cottage cheese
1 tbsp. lemon juice
1 tbsp. grated orange peel

Wash and section oranges. Blend water, 1 cup sugar, 1/2 cup brandy and cloves. Mash cottage cheese through fine sieve; beat in remaining sugar, lemon juice, and orange peel. Place in serving dish; chill. Place orange sections, brandy mixture, remaining brandy, and cheese mixture on tray. Place orange sections and brandy mixture in blazer pan; simmer for 10 minutes. Remove cloves. Pour brandy over oranges; ignite. Serve immediately over cottage cheese.

Carol Lynne Abel, City Coun. Sec.
Xi Beta Iota X2495, North Bend, Oregon

PRUNE-CHUTNEY HORS D'OEUVRES

18 lg. prunes
6 1-oz. wedges process Gruyere cheese
1 9-oz. jar chutney

Remove pits from prunes. Cut each cheese wedge into 3 wedges; insert cheese wedge in center of each prune. Place in chafing dish. Heat chutney in small saucepan; pour over prunes.

Linda S. Smith, Pres., Iota Omega No. 4642
Findlay, Ohio

PEACHES CHANTILLY

4 canned or fresh peach halves
Vanilla ice cream
Whipped cream
4 tbsp. raspberry jelly
4 tbsp. Grand Marnier or
    orange-flavored liqueur

Arrange peach halves and ice cream in 2 sherbet glasses. Top with whipped cream; place in freezer. Melt raspberry jelly in blazer of chafing dish directly over flame. Blend in 3 tablespoons Grand Marnier; heat until bubbly. Heat remaining Grand Marnier in large serving spoon over flame. Ignite; stir into raspberry sauce. Ladle over peaches and ice cream; serve with wafers, if desired.

PEARS POACHED IN WINE

1 c. claret or burgundy
1 c. sugar
2 3-in. sticks cinnamon
6 whole cloves
1/8 tsp. nutmeg
3 med. Anjou or Comice pears

Mix claret and sugar in blazer pan. Add cinnamon, cloves, and nutmeg; bring to a simmer, stirring until sugar is dissolved. Rinse pears; cut into quarters lengthwise. Core; pare. Add to wine mixture; cover. Simmer

for 25 to 30 minutes or until pears are tender, turning occasionally. Place blazer over water pan; keep warm.

Mary Ann Zaorski, Pres., Xi Kappa X1457
Pittsfield, Massachusetts

PEAR FLAMBÉE AU PORT

1 c. canned pear juice
1/2 c. sugar
3 tbsp. cornstarch
1 c. port
Lemon juice to taste
8 canned pear halves
Brandy to taste

Combine juice, sugar and cornstarch in blazer pan of chafing dish over direct low heat; stir constantly until sauce is clear and thickened. Stir in port and lemon juice. Place blazer pan in water jacket; add pears to sauce. Cook over hot water for 10 minutes. Pour brandy over pears; ignite. Serve immediately.

Marylou Burns, Pres., Xi Gamma Zeta X1072
Rockford, Illinois

WINE-FRUIT MEDLEY

1 13 1/2-oz. can pineapple chunks
1 16-oz. can apricot halves
1 16-oz. can peach halves
1 16-oz. can pitted dark sweet
    cherries
1/4 c. (packed) brown sugar
1/4 tsp. ground cinnamon
1/3 c. port
1 tbsp. lemon juice

Drain pineapple and apricots, reserving pineapple syrup and 1/2 cup apricot syrup. Drain remaining fruits well. Blend sugar and cinnamon in blazer pan; add reserved syrups, port, and lemon juice. Heat until bubbly. Add pineapple, apricots, and peaches; heat through. Add cherries; place over water pan. Yield: 6-8 servings.

Lila Jean Stewart, VP, Xi Gamma Epsilon X3099
Longmont, Colorado

BLINTZES

1 7 3/4-oz. can salmon
1 c. cottage cheese
1 egg
2 tbsp. sugar
3/4 tsp. salt
1/4 tsp. cinnamon
12 Pancakes
Butter
1 c. sour cream
1/2 c. cherry or strawberry
    preserves

Drain and flake salmon. Add cottage cheese, egg, sugar, salt, and cinnamon; mix thoroughly. Place about 2 tablespoons salmon mixture on browned side of each Pancake; spread to within 1 inch of edge. Fold bottom edge of Pancake up about an inch over filling. Fold 2 sides in about 3/4 inch over filling; roll Pancake from bottom. May be refrigerated until ready to use, if desired. Place Blintzes in single layer in small amount of melted butter in 10-inch frypan or chafing dish blazer pan; cook over moderate heat for 5 to 6 minutes or until brown. Turn carefully; cook for 5 to 6 minutes longer or until brown. Drain on absorbent paper. Place 2 Blintzes on small plate for each serving; top with sour cream and cherry preserves.

Pancakes

3/4 c. all-purpose flour
1/4 tsp. salt
1 c. milk
2 eggs, beaten
Oil

Combine flour and salt in bowl. Combine milk and eggs. Add to flour mixture gradually; stir until smooth. Pour 2 tablespoons batter for each pancake into lightly oiled 6-inch frypan; tip frypan so that batter completely covers bottom. Cook over moderate heat for 3 to 4 minutes or until brown on bottom and set on top; remove from frypan.

BUFFET

Buffet service is an enjoyable and easy way to serve a small group or a crowd. You plan carefully in advance so that there are no unexpected problems on the day of your party. You cook your favorite, most praised dishes. Finally, you set the foods and your very best china, silver, and crystal out on a flat surface so that your guests can serve themselves. Then you relax and enjoy yourself.

Does it all sound marvelous? Of course it does, and such a delightful buffet can be yours. In the next four pages, you'll discover detailed hints on how to plan and serve a buffet with a creative flair all your own. Some of the hints tell you the secrets of advance planning, others talk about serving a buffet with and without household help. Still others suggest table settings.

And all this valuable information is followed by hundreds of recipes that are just right for buffet meals. Every recipe you'll find has been home-tested for flavor and for the ease with which it can be handled. You can rest assured that every salad, every main dish, every dessert can be easily served and just as easily handled by a diner who has limited space in which to use his knife and fork!

Beginning with accompaniments, you'll find page after page of recipes suitable for virtually every kind of buffet meal, from a formal reception or tea to a casual before-the-game party. Accompaniments are followed by buffet-perfect soups; salads; cereal, cheese, egg, and pasta dishes; meats; poultry; seafood; vegetables; breads; and, finally, desserts. As you browse through this section, you'll find yourself mentally mixing and matching all these recipes to create buffet menus uniquely yours!

When buffet meals are an important part of your at-home entertaining, depend on this section to answer just about every question that will arise and to provide you with a varied menu you'll serve with pride.

buffet
FUNDAMENTALS

PLANNING YOUR MENU

A successful buffet party depends as much on your careful planning as it does on the foods you serve. Begin planning your party by making your guest list with one rule of thumb in mind: All the entertainment your buffet party should need is conversation carried on among mutually interested and interesting groups of people. Plan your guest list accordingly, so that you include both talkers and listeners. Of course you'll want people of diverse ideas and interests, but they should have a few things in common, too.

Decide whether you will phone or mail your invitations. Regardless of which you do, issue your invitations in plenty of time to allow your guests the fun of anticipation. Consider, too, using place cards, especially if you are serving a sit-down buffet (more about that later). Unless your guests know each other well, place cards are almost a necessity — and a thoughtful gesture on your part.

Once you have determined how many guests you will have, turn your attention to the menu. You'll want a menu that is within your budget yet delicious. You'll enjoy featuring foods that mix and match well and can be prepared early, long before your guests arrive. Most of all, you'll want foods that can stand on the buffet table without losing flavor, texture, or attractiveness.

Decide on an entree and build the remainder of your menu around it. For a seated buffet, any entree is appropriate. But if your guests are going to be eating from plates in their laps or on small trays, choose an entree that does not require cutting with a knife. A seafood casserole, a chafing dish entree such as beef stroganoff, or a stew are all excellent main course selections for buffets. And you'll want to serve first courses, salads, soups, and desserts that complement the entree.

After choosing your recipes, read them carefully and list all the ingredients you'll need. Check your cupboards and refrigerator to see which you have on hand, and shop for those you'll need. Unless you are buying perishables like fresh fruit, vegetables or seafood, you'll want to do your shopping at least a day or two in advance of the buffet. Experienced hostesses recommend that you make a schedule showing what tasks you will do on each day before the party. As many foods as possible should be prepared in advance of the party date and frozen, then thawed the day of your buffet.

All these advance preparations will help you achieve the goal of every buffet — to relax and enjoy the occasion just as much as your guests.

SERVING THE BUFFET

As your guests arrive, seat them in the living room, on the patio, or in any room other than the one where food has been laid out. When most are present, serve appetizers and beverages. Serving this first course in the living room keeps your guests away from the buffet and kitchen areas while the finishing touches are put on the meal. It also enables any late-arriving guests to join the others inconspicuously.

Choose appetizers that are easy to eat without a fork or plate — antipasto, bits of seafood or meat on toothpicks, and other "finger foods." A few minutes before the first course ends, excuse yourself and fill the water glasses, remove cold foods from the refrigerator, and prepare hot foods for serving. (Here's a helpful hint: If for some reason you don't have your husband available to assist you, ask your older son or another relative to serve as host

with you. The logistics of serving a buffet are such that almost always two people must share the hostess' functions.) Even if you are lucky enough to have household help in preparing your buffet, you'll want to give the arrangements one last looking over before you call the guests in.

As hostess, you should be near the buffet table, perhaps serving the entree or salad. While you are doing this, the host or your servant should clear the first course from the living room. If the host performs this task, he will join the buffet line when he finishes.

Your guests' first sight of the buffet should be impressive. On this occasion, you can prepare a spectacularly beautiful centerpiece without having to wonder about people trying to look around or over it during conversations. You can bring out your very best serving pieces, and convert other pretty pieces into servers. That silver or pewter bowl can hold sharply flavored vegetable condiments. That huge punch bowl might be just what you

need to serve stew or bouillabaisse from. Yes, a buffet is one social occasion when you can bring out and use all those often-neglected serving pieces.

Arrange the buffet table in careful sequence, following our diagram below. You'll want plates, entree, vegetables (if any) and salads following each other in that order. If your guests

Rolls and relishes may be passed from guest to guest after all have been seated. Buffet breads should always be pre-buttered.

You may want to include accompaniments to your buffet meal. One that invariably sparks up a buffet is sweet jam or jelly, especially the jewel-bright kinds. Try mint jelly with lamb,

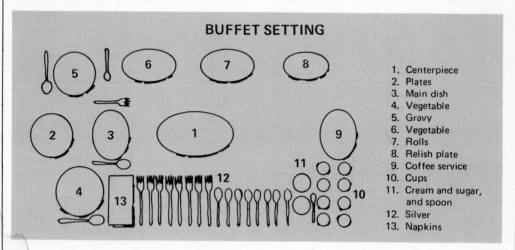

BUFFET SETTING

1. Centerpiece
2. Plates
3. Main dish
4. Vegetable
5. Gravy
6. Vegetable
7. Rolls
8. Relish plate
9. Coffee service
10. Cups
11. Cream and sugar, and spoon
12. Silver
13. Napkins

are eating from their laps or trays, arrange silverware, napkins, and beverage glasses at the end of the serving table. It is preferable, if at all possible, to have people eating at tables where silver, napkins, and glasses are set up in readiness for them.

Although both entree and vegetable can fit on a dinner plate without any problem, there may be difficulty managing the salad. In such cases, serve the salad as a separate course either before or after the entree or, plan a salad that is a self-contained unit. A great buffet salad might be half an avocado filled with crabmeat or with a vegetable salad. Other equally suitable salad recipes can be found in the pages that follow.

orange or pineapple marmelade with ham, cranberry jelly with poultry or pork, and apple jelly with beef.

Whatever foods you choose to serve, hot dishes should be very hot and cold ones should be icy. Casseroles can be placed over candle warmers that will keep them hot. If you have chafing dishes, by all means use them. They are lovely to look at as well as extremely effective for keeping hot foods at their proper temperature. (For some hints on using chafing dishes, see pages 44 to 47.) Cold foods can be kept at their proper temperature by setting the serving dish into a bowl of crushed ice. Mix a little rock salt with the ice, and it will not melt quickly, even at room temperature.

When your guests have finished the main course, you or a guest you ask to assist should offer them coffee and tea. Plates may be removed either by a servant, if you're fortunate enough to have one, or by you. Some hostesses ask their guests to bring their plates to a serving cart or a table cleared just for that purpose.

If you do have a servant, particularly if it is someone hired just for the occa-

from beautiful and elaborate cherries jubilee or crepes suzette to fruit plucked at random from the buffet centerpiece. You may want to prepare the dessert plates in the kitchen and serve them to each guest or you may present dessert as a separate course and allow guests to go through the buffet line once again. (If the latter is your choice, see the illustration below for the suggested table setting.)

BUFFET DESSERT SETTING

1. Centerpiece
2. Coffee service
3. Dessert
4. Serving silver
5. Dessert plates

sion, let her practice clearing the table. The correct procedure for her to follow is to stand at the guest's left, and, with her left hand, remove the dinner plate. Transfer the plate to her right hand. Remove salad plate with left hand, put it on top of the already-removed dinner plate. (All this goes on behind the guest's back.) She moves to another guest and repeats the same procedure, beginning this time with the salad plate. When she has completely cleared two places, she takes the plates to the kitchen and returns to clear another two.

After the plates have been cleared and while coffee and tea are being served, you, the hostess, take charge of dessert. The dessert you serve may range

Be certain that your guests have a dessert that complements the main course and, like it, can be easily handled. Don't forget – they'll be trying to manage coffee at the same time!

Buffets are not always limited to evening affairs. There are breakfasts, brunches, luncheons, afternoon teas, and so on. But every buffet has certain elements in common, and most important among these is the need for advance planning. Careful planning and a step-by-step schedule will enable you to relax and enjoy both the party and your guests' company. And with the family-proven favorite recipes you'll find in the pages that follow, you can always be certain of serving buffet-perfect foods!

SALADS

APPLE-BANANA WALDORF

2 c. cubed unpeeled red apples
1/2 c. broken pecans
1/2 c. chopped celery
1 banana, diced
Lemon juice to taste
1/2 c. mayonnaise
1/4 c. whipped cream

Combine apples, pecans, and celery. Sprinkle banana with lemon juice; add to apple mixture. Combine mayonnaise and whipped cream; pour over top. Toss to coat lightly.

SNOW APPLES

4 firm apples
Sugar
40 red cinnamon candies
Chopped dates
Chopped nuts
Lettuce leaves
2 tbsp. butter
2 eggs, beaten
Juice of 2 lemons
1/2 c. whipped cream

Pare apples; remove cores carefully. Combine 3 cups sugar and 3 cups water in large

saucepan; add cinnamon candies. Boil to heavy syrup consistency. Drop apples into boiling syrup; cook until clear and tender. Tint with red food coloring if desired. Remove apples from syrup; cool. Fill apple centers with dates and nuts; arrange on lettuce leaves on individual salad plates. Chill. Cream 1/2 cup sugar and butter together until fluffy. Add beaten eggs, lemon juice, and 2 tablespoons water. Place in double boiler over hot water. Cook, stirring constantly, until thickened. Cool; fold in whipped cream. Spoon over apples.

Ethel G. Swanbeck
International Honorary Member, BSP
Huron, Ohio

MARINATED FRUIT MEDLEY

1 fresh pineapple
1 c. fresh banana slices
1 c. unpeeled fresh apple cubes
1 c. seeded fresh orange cubes
1 c. fresh cantaloupe pieces
Sugar to taste

Cut pineapple in half lengthwise; scoop out centers of each half. Cut pineapple into chunks; place in bowl. Add banana slices, apple cubes, orange cubes, cantaloupe, and sugar; mix well. Place cantaloupe mixture in pineapple shells; place in serving bowl.

Photograph for this recipe on page 85.

ORANGE SHERBET SALAD

3 3-oz. packages orange gelatin
2 1/2 c. boiling water
3 11-oz. cans mandarin orange sections
1 pt. orange sherbet
3 bananas

Dissolve gelatin in boiling water. Drain orange sections; reserve 1 1/2 cups liquid. Add reserved orange liquid to gelatin; stir in sherbet until dissolved. Refrigerate until partially set. Peel bananas; slice. Add gelatin mixture; stir in oranges. Pour into 6-cup mold; chill until firm. Yield: 6-8 servings.

Dr. Elta Pfister
International Honorary Member, BSP
Burbank, California

GINGERED APPLE SALAD MOLD

1 env. unflavored gelatin
3 1/2 c. ginger ale
3/4 c. mayonnaise
1/4 tsp. salt
3/4 c. sour cream
1 egg white, stiffly beaten
1/4 c. chopped nuts
2 3-oz. packages lemon gelatin
1 c. chutney
2 to 3 Washington apples
Lettuce

Soften unflavored gelatin in 1/2 cup ginger ale; dissolve over hot water. Combine gelatin mixture, mayonnaise, salt, and sour cream; blend well. Chill until partially set. Fold in egg white and nuts; spoon into 8-cup mold. Chill until set. Dissolve lemon gelatin in remaining ginger ale over boiling water. Chill until slightly thickened; stir in chutney. Pare

and core apples; chop finely. Add 2 cups chopped apples to lemon gelatin mixture; pour over congealed layer. Chill until firm. Unmold on lettuce-lined salad platter. To prepare other photograph, divide chutney mixture in half. Pour 1/2 into bottom of mold; chill until set. Pour sour cream layer over congealed layer; chill until set. Pour remaining chutney mixture over sour cream layer; chill until set.

MELBA PEACH SALAD

1 No. 303 can peach halves
1 3-oz. package cream cheese
Mayonnaise
Lettuce leaves
Paprika

Drain peaches; reserve 1/2 cup syrup. Soften cream cheese at room temperature. Mix cream cheese, reserved syrup, and enough mayonnaise to moisten. Arrange lettuce leaves on serving platter; place peaches on lettuce. Fill the peach halves with cream cheese mixture; sprinkle with paprika. Yield: 6 servings.

Photograph for this recipe on page 128.

CRANBERRY SALAD

1 8 1/2-oz. can crushed pineapple
1/4 c. water
1 3-oz. package black cherry
   gelatin
1 can cranberry sauce
1 c. chopped celery
1 c. chopped nuts
1/4 c. lemon juice

Combine pineapple and water; bring to a boil. Remove from heat. Add gelatin; stir until gelatin is dissolved. Add remaining ingredients; mix well. Place in mold; chill until firm. Yield: 8 servings.

Jessie Allen Taylor, Pres.
Delta Omega No. 6560, Carthage, Tennessee

CHECKERBOARD SOUFFLE SALAD

1   1-lb. can whole cranberry sauce
3 c. boiling water
2   3-oz. packages lemon gelatin
1 tbsp. lemon juice
1/4 tsp. salt
1/2 c. real mayonnaise
1 peeled apple or orange, diced
1/4 c. chopped walnuts

Heat cranberry sauce until melted; strain, reserving berries. Mix cranberry liquid with boiling water; add gelatin, stirring until dissolved. Mix in lemon juice and salt. Chill until thick enough to mound slightly when dropped from spoon. Reserve 1 1/2 cups thickened gelatin mixture; pour remaining mixture into chilled 13 x 9 1/2 x 2-inch pan. Chill until set. Add mayonnaise to reserved gelatin; beat with rotary beater until light and fluffy. Fold in cranberries, diced apple and walnuts. Spoon evenly over congealed gelatin in pan; chill until firm. Cut into 12 squares; unmold. Arrange squares, inverting half, checkerboard fashion on salad greens. Chill until ready to serve. Yield: 12 servings.

GREENGAGE PLUM SALAD

1 env. unflavored gelatin
1 No. 303 can sliced pineapple
1 No. 303 can greengage plums
1 sm. package lemon gelatin
Dash of salt
1/2 c. sherry
1   3-oz. package cream cheese
1 c. whipping cream
Salad dressing to taste
Powdered sugar to taste

Sprinkle gelatin over 1/4 cup cold water; let stand for 5 minutes. Drain pineapple and plums; reserve syrups. Add enough water to reserved syrups to make 2 cups liquid; bring to a boil. Stir in lemon gelatin, softened gelatin and salt until dissolved; chill until thickened. Blend pineapple, plums, and sherry; add to gelatin. Cut cream cheese into small cubes. Add to gelatin mixture; mix well. Place in large mold or individual molds; chill until firm. Whip cream until stiff peaks form; fold in salad dressing and powdered sugar. Serve with salad.

Mrs. Clara Nielsen
International Honorary Member, BSP
Midland, Texas

SOUR CREAM SALAD

1 c. orange sections
1 c. pineapple chunks
3 tbsp. powdered sugar
1 c. coconut
1/2 c. chopped pecans
1 c. miniature marshmallows
1 c. sour cream

Drain orange sections and pineapple. Add sugar, coconut, and pecans; mix. Fold in marshmallows and sour cream. Place in bowl; chill. Other nuts may be substituted for pecans. Yield: 8 servings.

Hazel Palmer
International Honorary Member, BSP
Sedalia, Missouri

FESTIVE CHICKEN AND FRUIT SALAD

1   5-lb. roasting chicken, cooked
3/4 c. diced celery
1 c. halved seedless grapes
1 c. mandarin orange sections
1/2 c. mayonnaise
1/4 c. slivered almonds
1/2 c. sour cream
2 tbsp. minced onion
2 tbsp. chopped parsley
1/2 tsp. herb salad dressing mix
1/2 tsp. salt
1/2 tsp. pepper
6 lettuce cups

Cut chicken into bite-sized pieces. Add remaining ingredients except lettuce; toss well. Serve in lettuce cups; garnish with additional grapes and orange sections.

Patti Sellers, Pres., Delta Kappa No. 6073
Albany, Georgia

HOT CHICKEN SALAD

1   8-oz. can water chestnuts
2 c. diced cooked chicken
2 c. diced celery
1 c. mayonnaise
2 tbsp. lemon juice
2 tsp. minced onion
1/2 tsp. salt
1/2 c. toasted slivered almonds
Crushed potato chips
1/2 c. sharp grated cheese

Drain water chestnuts; dice. Combine all ingredients except potato chips and cheese. Sprinkle potato chips into casserole to cover bottom; add chicken mixture. Cover with potato chips; add cheese. Bake at 450 degrees for 15 minutes. Yield: 6 servings.

Wilma Clark, Xi Alpha Alpha X1398
Chappell, Nebraska

CORNED BEEF AND SLAW SALAD

2 env. unflavored gelatin
2 tbsp. sugar
3/4 tsp. salt
4 tbsp. lemon juice
1/4 c. vinegar
2 tbsp. chopped green peppers
2 c. finely shredded cabbage
3/4 c. mayonnaise
1/4 c. minced onion
1/2 c. chopped sweet pickle
1/2 c. diced celery
1   12-oz. can corned beef, minced

Mix 1 envelope gelatin, sugar and 1/2 teaspoon salt in small saucepan; add 1/2 cup water. Place over low heat until gelatin is dissolved, stirring constantly. Remove from heat; stir in 3/4 cup water, 2 tablespoons lemon juice, and vinegar. Chill until consistency of unbeaten egg white; fold in green peppers and cabbage. Turn into 8-inch square pan; chill until firm. Sprinkle remaining gelatin into 1/2 cup cold water to soften. Place over low heat; stir until gelatin is dissolved. Remove from heat. Stir in remaining lemon juice and salt; add mayonnaise gradually. Stir in remaining ingredients; place on congealed layer. Chill until firm. Unmold; cut into squares. Serve with additional mayonnaise. Yield: 8-12 servings.

Mrs. Maureen Brisebois, Xi Epsilon X2431
Montreal, Quebec, Canada

MEXICAN FIESTA SALAD

1 head lettuce
1/2 c. fresh spinach
1 ripe avocado, pared
1 c. corn chips
1/2 c. shredded Cheddar cheese
1/4 c. sliced green onion
1   12-oz. can corned beef, chilled
1 c. prepared green goddess dressing
1/3 c. sour cream
1 1/2 tbsp. fresh lemon juice
Hot sauce to taste

Tear lettuce and spinach into pieces into salad bowl; cut half the avocado into slices. Combine greens, avocado slices, corn chips, cheese, and onion. Cut corned beef into cubes; add to salad. Mash remaining avocado with fork; blend in remaining ingredients. Spoon dressing over salad; toss well and serve.

Frances V. Scofield, Preceptor Rho XP500
Akron, Ohio

HAM MOUSSE

1/2 c. finely ground cooked ham
1 c. tomato juice
1 c. beef consomme
1/2 tsp. paprika
1 env. unflavored gelatin
4 tbsp. cold water
2 c. whipping cream, whipped
Salt to taste
Watercress
Mayonnaise
Lemon juice
Heavy cream
Finely chopped chives to taste

Mix ham, tomato juice, consomme, and paprika; bring to a boil. Remove from heat. Soften gelatin in water. Add to ham mixture; stir until dissolved. Refrigerate, stirring occasionally, until slightly thickened. Fold in whipped cream and salt; place in large mold or individual molds. Refrigerate until firm. Unmold; garnish with watercress. Mix mayonnaise with several drops of lemon

juice, small amount of heavy cream, and chives; serve with mousse.

Mrs. Richard M. Nixon
International Honorary Member, BSP
Washington, D. C.

CRAB-RICE SALAD

2   6-oz. packages frozen crab
3 c. cold cooked rice
1 tsp. curry powder
1/2 c. chopped parsley
3 tbsp. French dressing
1 c. quartered ripe olives
1/2 c. diced celery
1/3 c. mayonnaise
1 lg. ripe pineapple

Thaw crab; drain. Place rice, curry powder, and parsley in large bowl; toss lightly. Drizzle with French dressing; toss well. Fold in olives, celery, crab, and mayonnaise, being careful not to break up crab chunks; refrigerate until chilled. Cut pineapple lengthwise through green top; remove pulp with grapefruit knife, leaving 1/2-inch thick shell. Refrigerate shells. Chop 1 cup pineapple pulp; fold into crab mixture. Place in pineapple shells; arrange on platter.

Rhoda M. Borden, Preceptor Delta
Dartmouth, Nova Scotia, Canada

HOT CRAB MEAT SALAD

1/2 c. butter
2/3 c. sifted flour
2 2/3 c. milk
2 c. flaked crab meat
1 lg. stalk celery, diced
1/3 green pepper, minced
1 lg. pimento, minced
1/3 c. blanched quartered almonds
4 hard-cooked eggs, chopped
2 tsp. salt
Buttered fine bread crumbs
Lettuce cups
Mayonnaise
Chopped sweet pickles

Melt butter; stir in flour. Add milk slowly; cook, stirring constantly, until thick. Add crab meat, celery, green pepper, pimento, almonds, eggs, and salt; mix well. Place in buttered 12 x 7 1/2 x 2-inch baking dish; cover with bread crumbs. Bake at 350 degrees for 35 minutes. Serve hot in lettuce cups; top with mayonnaise mixed with pickles. Yield: 8 servings.

Katherine Stromberg, Past City Coun. Pres.
Xi Iota X839, Ogden, Utah

SEAFOOD GRAPEFRUIT CUP

2 grapefruit
1 can lobster meat, drained
1 can crab meat, drained
1 can shrimp, drained
Salt and pepper to taste
Garlic salt to taste
Mayonnaise

Cut grapefruit in half; remove pulp. Drain. Mix remaining ingredients in bowl, adding enough mayonnaise to moisten. Add grapefruit; mix well. Fill grapefruit cups; chill well.

Jo-Anne M. Collins, Corr. Sec.
Theta No. 3800, Pointe Claire, Quebec, Canada

CURRIED SEAFOOD SALAD

1 c. solid-pack or chunk-style tuna
3/4 lb. cooked cleaned shrimp
1/2 c. mayonnaise
2 tbsp. lemon juice
1 tsp. curry powder
1/2 c. chopped celery
1/4 c. chopped ripe or stuffed
 olives
3 c. cold cooked rice
2 to 3 tbsp. French dressing
1/2 c. snipped parsley

Drain and flake tuna. Combine tuna and shrimp; chill well. Combine mayonnaise, lemon juice and curry powder. Add curry mixture to seafood; stir in celery and olives, tossing well. Mix rice and French dressing together, blending well. Spoon rice mixture onto serving platter; top with seafood salad. Garnish with parsley. Serve chilled.

Virginia Rossiter, Xi Kappa Zeta X3022
Canyon, Texas

TUNA-OLIVE MOUSSE

4 env. unflavored gelatin
1 c. boiling chicken broth
4 7-oz. cans tuna, drained
4 5-oz. cans shrimp, drained
4 hard-cooked eggs, chopped
1 c. sliced pimento-stuffed olives
1 c. heavy cream, whipped
1 c. mayonnaise
2 tsp. dillweed
2 tsp. lemon juice
1 tsp. lemon peel
1/4 c. dry sherry
Watercress

Soften gelatin in 1 cup cold water; dissolve in boiling broth. Combine 2 cans tuna, 2 cans shrimp and gelatin mixture in electric blender container. Blend until smooth. Chop remaining shrimp; break remaining tuna into chunks. Add to pureed mixture. Stir in eggs, sliced olives, whipped cream, mayonnaise, dillweed, lemon juice, lemon peel and sherry. Turn into 3-quart mold; chill until set. Unmold; garnish with additional sliced olives and watercress.

ROCK LOBSTER JELLIED IN SHELL

3 9-oz. packages frozen South
    African rock lobster-tails
4 env. unflavored gelatin
1/2 c. cold water
2 3-oz. packages cream cheese
3 c. tomato juice
1 c. mayonnaise
1/4 c. lemon juice
2 c. chicken broth
Strips of pimento

Drop lobster-tails into boiling, salted water; cook for 2 to 3 minutes after water reboils. Drain immediately; drench with cold water. Cut away underside membrane. Remove lobster from shells; dice. Reserve shells. Soak gelatin in cold water for 5 minutes. Place over low heat; stir until gelatin is dissolved. Soften cream cheese; beat in tomato juice gradually. Beat in mayonnaise and lemon juice; beat in chicken broth gradually. Stir in gelatin and lobster; chill until slightly thickened. Stir to blend; spoon into reserved lobster shells. Chill until firm; garnish with pimento strips. Any remaining gelatin mixture may be chilled in small decorative mold and used to decorate platter. Yield: 12 servings.

Photograph for this recipe on page 82.

ROCK LOBSTER-STUFFED TOMATOES

4 9-oz. packages frozen South
    African rock lobster-tails
12 lg. ripe tomatoes
Salt and pepper to taste
Shredded lettuce
3 c. cooked pastina
1 c. chopped celery
1/2 c. chopped stuffed olives
1/4 c. chopped onion
1 c. mayonnaise

Drop lobster-tails into boiling, salted water; cook for 2 to 3 minutes after water reboils. Drain immediately; drench with cold water. Cut away underside membrane. Remove lob-

ster from shells; dice. Core tomatoes; turn upside down. Cut tomato into 8 sections without cutting all way through. Open out tomato; sprinkle with salt and pepper. Place tomatoes on bed of lettuce. Combine remaining ingredients with lobster; blend well. Stuff in tomatoes; chill until ready to serve. Yield: 12 servings.

Photograph for this recipe on page 82.

SALMON MOUSSE

2 sm. packages lemon gelatin
1 3/4 c. boiling water
2 tbsp. vinegar
1 tsp. salt
2 c. flaked salmon
1 c. diced cucumbers
1/2 c. diced celery
3 tbsp. pickle relish
1/2 c. mayonnaise
1/2 can water chestnuts, chopped
1 pimento, chopped
1/2 c. whipped cream

Dissolve gelatin in water. Stir in vinegar and salt; chill until slightly thickened. Fold in remaining ingredients in order listed; place in mold. Chill until firm. Garnish with chopped nuts and grapefruit sections.

Sauce

1 c. mayonnaise
1 tsp. lemon juice
1/2 c. chili sauce

Mix all ingredients; serve with salad.

Mrs. Arrigo M. Young
International Honorary Member, BSP
Carmel, California

SHRIMP À LA ROEBLING

2 to 3 lb. cooked lg. shrimp
2/3 c. mayonnaise
2 tbsp. cream
2 tbsp. tarragon
2 tbsp. chopped parsley

2 tbsp. chopped chives
1/2 tsp. celery seed
1/2 tsp. sweet basil
1/2 tsp. salt
1/4 tsp. cracked pepper
Garlic powder to taste
Avocado halves

Shell and devein shrimp. Mix remaining ingredients except avocado halves in bowl. Add shrimp; refrigerate overnight. Drain shrimp; place in avocado halves. Shrimp may be served on Boston lettuce and garnished with sliced avocados and tomatoes, if desired.

Mrs. Mary G. Roebling
International Honorary Member, BSP
Trenton, New Jersey

SHRIMP-POTATO SALAD

3 lb. cleaned shrimp
Bay leaves to taste
5 lb. boiled potatoes, peeled
1 c. chopped celery
1 1/2 c. chopped green onions with tops
1 1/2 c. salad olives
12 hard-boiled eggs, chopped
1 c. piccalilli
1 pt. mayonnaise
Salt and pepper to taste

Cook shrimp with bay leaves in boiling salted water to cover until tender; drain and chop. Cut potatoes into cubes. Combine shrimp, potatoes, celery, onions, olives, eggs, piccalilli, mayonnaise, and seasonings. Mix well. Cover; let stand in refrigerator overnight.

Bettye Mires, Pres., Xi Kappa Delta X3011
Dallas, Texas

DELICIOUS ASPARAGUS SALAD

2 lb. asparagus
1   14-oz. can chicken broth
6 tbsp. olive oil
4 tbsp. white wine vinegar
2 tbsp. finely chopped green onion

2 tbsp. finely chopped pimento
1 tsp. Dijon mustard
1/4 tsp. salt
1/8 tsp. pepper
Shredded iceberg lettuce
2 hard-cooked eggs, quartered
Cherry tomatoes, halved
Pitted ripe olives
1   2-oz. can anchovy fillets (opt.)

Break off white fibrous ends of asparagus; discard. Wash asparagus well. Heat chicken broth to boiling point in large frying pan. Add asparagus; simmer for 7 to 9 minutes or until tender. Remove asparagus to deep bowl with tongs. Reserve broth for future use, if desired. Blend olive oil, vinegar, green onion, pimento, mustard, salt, and pepper. Pour over asparagus; cover. Chill for 4 to 6 hours. Arrange bed of lettuce on large platter; place asparagus on lettuce in several piles. Garnish with eggs, tomatoes, olives, and anchovy fillets; drizzle remaining dressing over all. Yield: 4-6 servings.

Mrs. Arlene Engelhart, Pres.
Xi Pi Delta X3713, Woodside, California

SCHNIPPLED BEAN SALAD

1 qt. green or yellow string beans
1 sm. onion
Salt and pepper
1 tsp. sugar
1 tsp. vinegar
3/4 c. (about) sour cream

Cut stems off beans; wash. Cut beans on slant in very thin slices, each bean being cut into 3 or 4 slices. Cook in boiling, salted water until crisp-tender. Drain; cool. Peel and slice onion; sprinkle generously with salt. Stir; let stand for at least 15 minutes, stirring occasionally. Mix sugar, vinegar, 1/2 teaspoon salt, dash of pepper, and sour cream. Squeeze excess moisture from onion; add to dressing. Add beans; mix until beans are coated. May be refrigerated for 2 days.

Mrs. Edna Cress Staebler
Honorary International Member, BSP
Waterloo, Ontario, Canada

FRESH VEGETABLE SALAD

Fresh asparagus
Italian salad dressing
Fresh chick-peas
Chopped hard-boiled eggs
Pimento-stuffed green olives
Ripe olives
Sliced cucumbers
Fresh mushrooms
Cauliflowerets
Salad tomatoes
Lettuce

Wash asparagus; break off stalk as far down as snaps easily. Remove scales with knife; wash again to remove sand. Place in saucepan; add 1-inch boiling, salted water. Bring to boiling point; cook for 5 minutes. Reduce heat; cover. Cook for 15 minutes or until asparagus is crisp-tender; drain. Cover with Italian salad dressing; chill overnight. Cook chick-peas in boiling, salted water until crisp-tender; drain. Chill. Drain asparagus; reserve salad dressing. Arrange asparagus, eggs, green olives, ripe olives, cucumbers, mushrooms, cauliflowerets, tomatoes, and chick-peas on lettuce-lined platter. Garnish center with luncheon meat; serve with reserved dressing.

Photograph for this recipe on page 126.

CAESAR SALAD

3/4 c. Parmesan cheese
3 cloves of garlic, peeled
1 c. salad oil
8 slices bread
1 tbsp. Worcestershire sauce
1/4 tsp. dry mustard
3/4 tsp. salt
1 lg. head romaine lettuce
1 sm. bunch watercress
1 1-minute coddled egg
Juice of 2 sm. lemons

Combine 1/2 cup cheese, 2 garlic cloves, and 1/2 cup oil in blender container; blend for 1 minute. Remove crusts from bread; cut into cubes. Toss bread cubes with cheese mix-ture. Place on baking sheet. Bake at 300 degrees until crisp; cool. Combine remaining garlic and oil, Worcestershire sauce and seasonings in blender container; blend for 1 minute. Tear salad greens into bite-sized pieces into large salad bowl. Pour oil mixture over greens, tossing to coat well. Blend in egg. Add lemon juice; toss well. Add bread cubes, tossing. Sprinkle with remaining cheese; toss well. Yield: 6-8 servings.

Mrs. Mary Lee Burnett, Xi Delta Eta X3162
Webster Groves, Missouri

CONGEALED VEGETABLE SALAD

2 env. unflavored gelatin
1 tsp. salt
1/2 to 3/4 c. sugar
1/4 c. lemon juice
1/4 c. vinegar
1 c. shredded cabbage
1 sm. onion, minced
1/2 green pepper, minced
1/2 c. carrots, chopped
1 c. chopped celery
1/2 c. chopped olives

Soften gelatin in 1/4 cup cold water; dissolve in 1 1/4 cups boiling water. Add salt, sugar, lemon juice, and vinegar. Add vegetables and olives. Pour into wet mold; chill until set. Yield: 8-10 servings.

Lorena Swisher, Preceptor Alpha Theta XP797
Warrensburg, Missouri

DELICIOUS CUCUMBER SALAD

1 env. unflavored gelatin
1/4 c. cold water
1/4 c. sugar
2 tbsp. vinegar
1 tsp. salt
1/2 c. hot water
1 c. grated cucumber
Grated onion to taste
1 c. sour cream

Soften gelatin in cold water. Add sugar, vinegar, salt, and hot water; cook, stirring, until gelatin is dissolved. Do not boil. Chill until thickened. Add cucumber, onion, and sour cream; mix well. Spoon into individual molds; chill until firm. Yield: 6 servings.

Esther Kellner
International Honorary Member, BSP
Richmond, Indiana

CHILLED CUCUMBER SLICES

1 lg. cucumber
1/4 tsp. salt
Dash of pepper
1 sm. clove of garlic
1/8 tsp. dillweed
1/4 tsp. sugar
1 tbsp. lemon juice
1/2 c. yogurt
1 tsp. minced parsley
Salad greens

Score cucumber lengthwise with fork; cut into thin slices. Sprinkle with salt and pepper. Cover; refrigerate for 1 hour. Mash garlic in bowl; blend in dillweed and sugar. Add lemon juice; stir in yogurt. Drain cucumbers; fold in yogurt mixture. Sprinkle with parsley; serve on salad greens. Yield: 4 servings.

Photograph for this recipe on page 123.

GARDEN SALAD WITH HERB DRESSING

2 6-oz. jars marinated
   artichoke hearts
Olive oil
1/3 c. tarragon vinegar
1 tsp. salt
1/2 tsp. pepper
1/2 tsp. garlic salt
1/4 tsp. oregano
1/4 tsp. basil
1/8 tsp. paprika
1 head iceburg lettuce
1 head romaine
1/2 lb. fresh spinach
1/2 lb. fresh mushrooms, thinly
   sliced

2 cucumbers
2 green peppers
2 lg. red onions
2 pt. cherry tomatoes
Anchovy fillets
1 8-oz. can ripe olives, drained

Drain artichoke hearts; reserve oil. Add enough olive oil to reserved oil to make 1 cup liquid. Combine oil, vinegar and seasonings in small jar with lid; shake well. Chill until serving time. Tear lettuce, romaine and spinach into salad bowl. Cut mushrooms, cucumbers, and green peppers into thin slices. Slice onions thinly; separate into rings. Add sliced ingredients and artichoke hearts to salad greens. Add tomatoes, anchovy fillets and ripe olives. Pour dressing over salad; toss lightly and serve.

Judith E. Johnson, Treas.
Alpha Kappa No. 1452, Beloit, Wisconsin

CAULIFLOWER SALAD

3/4 c. wine vinegar
1/2 c. olive oil
2 tbsp. sugar
1 tsp. salt
1/2 tsp. oregano
1/4 tsp. pepper
1/2 sm. cauliflower
2 carrots
2 stalks celery
1 sm. green pepper
1 4-oz. jar pimentos, drained
1 3-oz. jar green olives, drained

Mix wine vinegar, olive oil, sugar, salt, oregano, pepper, and 1/4 cup water in large saucepan. Separate cauliflower into flowerets. Cut carrots into 2-inch strips; cut celery into 1-inch strips. Cut green pepper into strips; chop pimentos. Add cauliflowerets, carrots, celery, green pepper, pimentos, and olives to vinegar mixture; simmer for 5 minutes. Chill for 24 hours; drain well before serving.

Maureen A. Krull, Beta Pi No. 7020
Canfield, Ohio

GREEK SALAD SUPREME

1 clove of garlic
1 head lettuce
1/2 bunch endive
3 or 4 tomatoes, quartered
6 green onions with tops,
  chopped
1 green pepper, diced
1 cucumber, sliced
3 stalks celery, diced
2 carrots, shredded
6 radishes, sliced
2 tbsp. chopped parsley
1 tsp. salt
Pepper to taste
3/4 c. olive oil
1/4 tsp. oregano
1/4 c. wine vinegar
1/2 c. feta cheese
8 radish rosettes
8 Greek black olives
5 to 6 anchovy fillets

Rub wooden salad bowl with garlic. Break lettuce and endive into bowl in bite-sized pieces. Add tomatoes, onions, green pepper, cucumber and celery. Add carrots, reserving 1/4 cup for garnish. Place sliced radishes and parsley in bowl; sprinkle salad with salt and pepper. Combine olive oil, oregano and vinegar in small jar with lid; shake well. Pour desired amount of dressing over salad; toss lightly. Crumble cheese; add to salad, tossing again. Garnish with reserved carrots, radish rosettes, olives and anchovy fillets.

Pat Kandis, Publ. Chm.
Xi Gamma Omega X1471, Victoria, Texas

ORIENTAL SALAD

1 pkg. fresh spinach
1 can bean sprouts, drained
1 6-oz. can water chestnuts,
  sliced
3 hard-boiled eggs, diced
1/2 lb. bacon, diced
1/2 c. salad oil
1/2 c. sugar
1/2 c. catsup
1/4 c. vinegar
1 tsp. salt
1 tsp. Worcestershire sauce
1 med. onion, diced

Tear spinach into bite-sized pieces into salad bowl. Add bean sprouts, water chestnuts and eggs. Chill until serving time. Fry bacon in skillet until crisp; drain well and set aside. Combine oil, sugar, catsup, vinegar, salt, Worcestershire sauce and onion in small jar with lid; shake well. Add bacon to salad; pour dressing over salad, tossing well.

Mrs. Judy Shannon, Beta Pi No. 1209
Hillsdale, Michigan

HOT POTATO SALAD WITH BACON

4 lb. pared potatoes, sliced
1/2 c. chopped onion
2/3 c. bacon drippings
1/2 c. vinegar
2 tbsp. chopped parsley
2 tsp. sugar
1 tsp. paprika
1/2 tsp. salt
1/4 tsp. pepper
12 slices fried bacon, crumbled

Cook potatoes in saucepan in 2 inches salted water until tender; drain. Saute onion in bacon drippings until tender; stir in vinegar, parsley, sugar, paprika, salt and pepper. Combine potatoes, bacon, and onion mixture. Toss gently. Serve warm with pork roast and sauerkraut.

Photograph for this recipe on page 135.

GERMAN POTATO SALAD

2 lb. sliced potatoes
1/4 tsp. caraway seed
1 med. onion, diced
3 strips bacon, diced
1/2 c. cider vinegar
1/2 c. hot water
2 tbsp. sugar
1/4 tsp. freshly ground pepper

Cook potatoes in salted water to cover, adding caraway seed, until done; drain. Add onion. Fry bacon in skillet; pour off about 2 tablespoons fat. Add remaining fat and bacon to potatoes. Combine vinegar, hot water, sugar, and pepper; add to potato mixture gently. Serve warm; garnish with chives, parsley or hard-cooked egg slices.

Vida E. Diener, Xi Epsilon Rho X2282
St. Marys, Ohio

BAVARIAN POTATO SALAD

3 1/2 lb. medium potatoes
1 c. chopped onion
1/2 lb. bacon, diced
2 tbsp. flour
1/4 c. sugar
2 tbsp. butter
1 1/2 tsp. salt
1/4 tsp. pepper
1/2 c. cider vinegar
1 c. sour cream
2 tbsp. parsley flakes

Cook potatoes, covered, in boiling salted water to cover for 35 to 40 minutes or until fork tender. Peel warm potatoes; slice. Add onion. Cook bacon in large skillet until crisp; remove from heat. Remove bacon with slotted spoon; set aside. Pour off fat, reserving 1/4 cup in skillet. Stir flour into fat; add sugar, butter, salt, pepper, vinegar and 1 cup water. Bring to a boil, stirring. Remove from heat; cool slightly. Stir in sour cream, potato mixture and half the bacon and parsley. Sprinkle with remaining bacon and parsley. Serve warm or cold.

Gloria Budd, Treas., Iota Eta No. 3998
Troy, Ohio

SALADE NICOISE

3/4 c. olive oil
1/4 c. wine vinegar
1/4 tsp. salt
1/4 tsp. pepper
2 tbsp. chopped parsley
2 tbsp. chives
4 lg. boiling potatoes

1 1/2 lb. green beans
2 lg. tomatoes
2 to 3 hard-cooked eggs
10 anchovy fillets
1/2 c. pitted lg. ripe olives
Capers
Butter lettuce
1 can solid-pack white tuna

Shake oil, vinegar, salt, pepper, parsley and chives together; chill. Cook potatoes in boiling salted water until barely tender; cool under cold water. Peel and slice. Pour just enough dressing over potatoes to coat slices. Cover; chill for at least 2 hours. Cut beans into 1 1/2-inch lengths; cook until crisp tender. Cool with cold water. Drain beans; coat lightly with dressing. Cover; chill for 2 hours or longer. Mound potatoes down center of shallow bowl. Arrange beans along both sides. Peel tomatoes; cut into wedges. Quarter eggs; arrange eggs and tomatoes beside green beans. Crisscross anchovy fillets over potatoes. Garnish with olives and capers. Cover with foil; chill until serving time. Add border of butter lettuce; pour remaining dressing over salad. Drain and flake tuna; arrange on separate dish. Serve salad with tuna.

Betty A. Womack, VP, Xi Omicron Omega X3619
Portola, California

SWEET-SOUR SAUERKRAUT SALAD

1 lg. jar sauerkraut
1 green bell pepper, chopped fine
1 onion, chopped fine
1 sm. jar pimento, chopped fine
1/2 c. salad oil
1/2 c. vinegar
2 1/2 c. sugar

Drain sauerkraut; squeeze out excess moisture. Add remaining ingredients; mix well. Refrigerate for 1 day for better flavor. Yield: 4-6 servings.

Kathy Ewell, Alpha Nu XP926
Pullman, Washington

SPECIAL SLAW

1 med. cabbage
1 lg. onion
1 red pepper
1 green pepper
1/2 c. honey
2/3 c. salad oil
1 c. vinegar
2 tbsp. salt
2 tbsp. sugar

Shred cabbage; cut onion and red and green peppers into short strips. Place alternate layers of cabbage, onion, and peppers in bowl. Mix remaining ingredients; cook over low heat for several minutes. Pour over slaw. Cover; refrigerate for 1 to 2 days. Will keep for long time in refrigerator. Yield: 6-8 servings.

Aileene C. Hatton
International Honorary Member, BSP
Chillicothe, Ohio

SWEET-SOUR VEGETABLE MOLD

2 pkg. sour cream sauce mix
2 3-oz. packages lemon gelatin
2 tbsp. lemon juice
1 tsp. dried dillweed
2 sm. pared carrots, sliced
1 med. green pepper, seeded
1 med. pared cucumber, halved

Prepare sour cream sauce mix according to package directions. Dissolve gelatin in 2 cups boiling water; add 1/2 cup cold water, sour cream sauce, lemon juice, and dillweed. Beat until blended. Chill until partially set. Place vegetables in blender container; cover with cold water. Blend for several seconds, until vegetables are coarsely chopped; drain well. Stir vegetables into gelatin mixture; turn into 5 1/2-cup mold. Chill until firm. Unmold on lettuce; fill center with additional assorted vegetables. Yield: 8 servings.

Barbara S. Ferrell, Ext. Off.
Xi Beta Gamma X2849, Roanoke, Virginia

HAM-STUFFED CHERRY TOMATOES

1/2 c. minced cooked ham
1/4 c. Roquefort cheese,
   crumbled
1/4 c. sour cream
1/4 tsp. lemon juice
Dash of pepper
36 cherry tomatoes
Parsley

Combine ham, cheese, sour cream, lemon juice, and pepper; blend well. Refrigerate. Cut tops off tomatoes; scoop out pulp. Spoon about 1/2 teaspoon ham mixture into each tomato, mounding slightly. Garnish each tomato with small sprig of parsley. Refrigerate until serving time.

Nancy Fine, Pres., Xi Mu Zeta X2923
Garden Grove, California

ITALIAN TOMATO SALAD

1 sm. onion
8 sm. ripe tomatoes
2 tbsp. salad oil
1/2 tsp. powdered thyme
1/2 tsp. salt

Slice onion; separate into rings. Cut tomatoes into segments; mix with onion rings in salad bowl. Chill well. Combine salad oil, thyme, and salt; pour over tomato mixture. Chill for about 15 minutes. Yield: 4 servings.

Lillian Bueno McCue
International Honorary Member, BSP
Colorado Springs, Colorado

BLUE CHEESE DRESSING

1/2 c. salad oil
1/4 c. finely crumbled blue
   cheese
3 tbsp. wine vinegar
1/2 tsp. salt
1/2 tsp. dry mustard
1/2 tsp. paprika

Combine all ingredients in mixing bowl; beat with mixer until blended. Use as marinade for cooked vegetables such as cauliflower, artichoke hearts, snap and wax beans or fresh tomatoes. Chill well before serving. Yield: About 3/4 cup.

Photograph for this recipe on page 46.

ACCOMPANIMENTS

SPICED PINEAPPLE

2 15-oz. cans pineapple chunks
3/4 c. vinegar
1 1/4 c. sugar
Dash of salt
8 whole cloves
1 4-in. stick cinnamon

Drain pineapple, reserving 3/4 cup juice. Add vinegar, sugar, salt, cloves, and cinnamon to reserved syrup. Pour into saucepan; heat for 10 minutes. Add pineapple chunks; bring to a boil. Remove from heat; cool. Chill until serving time. Drain pineapple; place on serving dish. Serve with wooden picks.

Shenda Oliphant, City Coun. Pres.
Preceptor Gamma XP238, Billings, Montana

ANTIPASTO MISTO

1 c. white vinegar
3 c. water
2 to 4 cloves of garlic, peeled
1 tbsp. pickling spice
1 tbsp. salt
Carrot sticks
Celery sticks
Small onions, sliced
Cauliflowerets
1 sm. hot pepper
Green unpitted olives
Black unpitted olives
Italian olives

Combine vinegar, water, garlic, pickling spice and salt, stirring until salt is dissolved. Place vegetables and olives in large glass jar with lid; pour vinegar mixture over vegetables. Seal. Let stand in refrigerator for at least 2 weeks. Will keep for 6 weeks.

Betty D. Norton, W and M, Beta Eta No. 6236
Grantsville, Utah

VICHYSSOISE

1/4 c. butter
1 1/2 c. thinly sliced leeks
3 c. thinly sliced potatoes
1 c. hot water
4 chicken bouillon cubes
3 c. milk
1 tsp. salt
1/8 tsp. white pepper
1/8 tsp. paprika
1 c. cream
2 tbsp. finely chopped chives

Melt butter in large heavy saucepan; add leeks. Cook, stirring, until transparent. Add potato slices, water and bouillon cubes; cover. Cook over moderate heat until tender. Press through fine sieve or puree in blender. Return to saucepan; add milk, stirring rapidly to blend. Stir in salt, white pepper and paprika. Add cream; heat only to serving temperature. Serve hot; garnish with chopped chives. May chill quickly and serve cold. Yield: 6 servings.

FRUIT PUNCH

2 pkg. red gelatin
Sugar to taste
1 lg. can frozen lemon juice
1 lg. can pineapple juice
1 bottle ginger ale
Sliced bananas (opt.)
Cherries (opt.)

Dissolve gelatin in 1 quart boiling water; cool. Add sugar, juices, and ginger ale; chill. Place ice in punch bowl; pour in punch. Add bananas and cherries.

Mrs. John P. Lester
International Honorary Member, BSP
Mena, Arkansas

BAKED CURRIED FRUIT

1 can peach halves
1 can sliced pineapple
1 can pear halves
1 sm. bottle cherries with stems
1/3 c. butter
3/4 c. (packed) light brown sugar
4 tsp. curry powder

Preheat oven to 325 degrees. Drain fruits; dry well on paper towel. Arrange in 1 1/2-quart casserole. Melt butter; add brown sugar and curry powder. Spoon over fruits. Bake for 1 hour. May be reheated. Yield: 8-10 servings.

Frances R. Frye, Preceptor Alpha
Lexington, South Carolina

PINEAPPLE SUPREME

1 can crushed pineapple
1 lg. can chunk pineapple
1/2 lb. American cheese, grated
1/4 c. flour
1/4 c. sugar

Drain pineapple; reserve juice. Arrange layers of pineapple and cheese in baking dish. Combine flour and sugar; sprinkle over

layers. Pour reserved juice over layers. Bake at 350 degrees for 45 minutes. Serve with ham if desired.

Iva Sharp, Exemplar Preceptor Iota XP274
Independence, Missouri

ANTIPASTO DELUXE

Leaf lettuce
1/2 lb. each sliced salami, ham,
    prosciutto and capocollo
1/2 lb. each American, Swiss and
    provolone cheese
1 can tuna, drained
1 can sardines, drained
1 can anchovies, drained
1 jar stuffed green olives, drained
1 can black pitted olives, drained
1 can pimentos or roasted peppers,
    drained
Celery sticks
Carrot curls or sticks
Midget dill pickles
Mixed sweet pickles
Sliced or cherry tomatoes
12 deviled egg halves
1 green pepper, cut into strips
1 bunch scallions
1 jar pickled mushrooms, drained
1 jar artichoke hearts, drained
1 jar pickled eggplant strips,
    drained
Radish roses

Line large tray with lettuce. Roll sliced meats. Slice, cube or cut cheeses into sticks. Place all foods on tray in attractive arrangement; lettuce cups may be used to hold some of the foods.

Gloria D. Dubuc, Ext. Off.
Xi Eta Mu No. 3532, Milan, Ohio

ANTIPASTO CAPRI

1   1-qt. jar mixed vegetables
    in wine vinegar
2 jars marinated artichoke hearts
    in oil
1   4-oz. can mushrooms, drained

1 can pitted olives, drained
3 8-oz. cans tomato sauce
5 tbsp. white vinegar
1 can tuna, drained

Drain mixed vegetables; cut into slices. Combine all ingredients in large mixing bowl; cover. Let stand in refrigerator for 3 days before serving. Serve with crackers.

Gayle Brewer, Iota Lambda No. 3379
Auburn, California

CHEESE, EGGS, & CEREAL

ALMOND-CHEESE LOGS

1 3-oz. package cream cheese
1/2 lb. natural Cheddar cheese
1 c. unblanched almonds
1 pimento
1 tbsp. lemon juice
1 1/2 tsp. salt
1 tsp. Worcestershire sauce
1 tsp. grated onion
Dash of cayenne pepper
Crackers
Paprika
Finely chopped almonds

Process cream cheese, Cheddar cheese, unblanched almonds, and pimento through food chopper, using fine blade. Add lemon juice, salt, Worcestershire sauce, onion, and cayenne pepper. Mix well. Shape into two 7-inch long rolls. Wrap in waxed paper; chill. Cut into thin slices to serve; place on crackers. Sprinkle with paprika and chopped almonds.

Mary Kay Owens, 2nd VP, Mu Psi No. 4028
Midland, Texas

BLUE CHEESE BALLS

2 3-oz. packages cream cheese, softened
2 oz. blue cheese, crumbled
2 tbsp. minced celery

1 tbsp. minced onion
Dash of cayenne pepper
Dash of hot sauce
1 tbsp. mayonnaise
3/4 c. chopped walnuts

Blend cheeses together well; mix in celery, onion, cayenne pepper, hot sauce, and mayonnaise. Shape into small balls; roll each ball in walnuts, coating well. Chill until serving time.

Jo Levine, Xi Alpha Rho X3229
Chattanooga, Tennessee

CHEESE WAFERS

1 1/2 c. flour
1/2 tsp. salt
1 lb. sharp Cheddar cheese, grated
1/4 lb. butter
Dash of cayenne pepper
Dash of hot sauce

Combine all ingredients; mix well with hands. Shape into 2-inch wide roll; wrap in foil. Chill for several hours or overnight. Slice; place slices on greased cookie sheet. Bake at 350 degrees for 12 minutes or until lightly browned. Will keep for several weeks in covered container.

Dorotha Moore
International Honorary Member, BSP
Moro, Oregon

NACHOS

1 pkg. tortillas
1 c. oil
1 lb. Cheddar cheese, grated
1/2 tsp. garlic powder
4 or 5 hot peppers, chopped

Cut each tortilla into 4 pie-shaped pieces. Fry in oil in skillet until crisp; drain on absorbent paper. Combine cheese, garlic powder, and hot peppers. Spoon small amount of cheese mixture on fried triangles; place on baking sheet. Broil until cheese is melted. Serve hot.

Mary Joyce Dillon, Delta Eta Chap.
Dayton, Ohio

BAKED CHEESE DISH

Bread strips
1/4 c. chopped celery
1/4 c. finely chopped onion
1 c. cubed Imperial cheese
1 c. cubed Velveeta cheese
4 eggs, beaten
1 c. milk
1/2 c. light cream
Salt and pepper to taste

Line bottom and side of greased baking dish with bread strips. Combine remaining ingredients; spoon into bread-lined dish. Bake at 325 degrees for 50 minutes to 1 hour. Yield: 6-8 servings.

Mrs. John Diefenbaker
International Honorary Member, BSP
Ottawa, Ontario, Canada

CREAM CHEESE BALLS

2 lg. packages cream cheese
1 tbsp. onion juice
3/4 tsp. garlic juice
1 tbsp. Worcestershire sauce
1/4 tsp. salt
3 oz. dried beef, shredded
Chopped parsley to taste
Chopped chives to taste (opt.)
Paprika to taste (opt.)

Let cream cheese soften to room temperature; add onion juice, garlic juice, Worcestershire sauce, and salt. Mix thoroughly. Chill until firm. Shape into 1-inch balls. Combine dried beef, parsley, chives, and paprika. Roll balls in mixture until thoroughly coated. Insert wooden pick in each ball; arrange on serving tray. Chill until serving time.

Mildred Ross, VP, Xi Beta Alpha X1876
Niles, Michigan

DATE-CHEESE TIDBITS

1/2 lb. sharp Cheddar cheese
1/2 c. margarine
2 c. sifted flour

Dash of red pepper
2 1-lb. packages pitted dates
Pecan halves

Let cheese and margarine soften to room temperature. Place cheese in mixer bowl; beat with electric mixer until thoroughly mixed. Add margarine; beat until blended. Add flour and red pepper; beat well. Roll dough out on floured board to 1/8-inch thickness. Cut with biscuit cutter. Stuff dates with pecan halves. Fold dough around each date. Place on baking sheet. Bake at 350 degrees for 20 minutes.

Mrs. Alice N. Heard, Ext. Off.
Alpha Omicron No. 8330, Oxford, Alabama

EASY CHEESE PUFF

4 tbsp. butter
8 slices bread
1/2 lb. sharp cheese
4 eggs
1/2 tsp. salt
1/4 tsp. mustard
2 1/2 c. milk

Spread butter on bread slices; cut into 1-inch squares. Cut cheese into fine pieces. Beat eggs; add salt, mustard, and milk. Arrange layers of bread and cheese in greased casserole. Pour milk mixture over layers; let stand for several minutes. Bake at 350 degrees for about 50 minutes. Yield: 4-6 servings.

Dr. Helen K. Mackintosh
International Honorary Member, BSP
Alexandria, Virginia

HOT TOTS

1 c. butter or margarine
1/2 lb. sharp Cheddar cheese, grated
1 1/2 tsp. hot sauce
1/2 tsp. cayenne pepper
1/4 tsp. salt
2 c. sifted flour
3 tbsp. cold water
Pecan quarters

Soften butter and cheese to room temperature; cream together well. Stir in hot sauce, cayenne pepper, and salt. Blend in flour and water gradually, mixing well. Roll dough out on lightly floured board; cut into 1 1/2-inch circles. Wrap each circle around pecan quarter, forming crescent. Place on ungreased baking sheet. Bake at 350 degrees for 18 to 20 minutes.

Ollie Kuykendall
Preceptor Alpha Sigma XP760, San Angelo, Texas

MIDDLE AGE SPREAD

1 c. mayonnaise
1/2 c. sour cream
1/4 c. vinegar
1/2 tsp. lemon juice
1/2 c. parsley flakes
1/4 c. chopped onion
1 tbsp. anchovy paste
1 clove of garlic, crushed
1/4 lb. bleu cheese, crumbled
Sherry to taste (opt.)

Combine mayonnaise and sour cream, blending well. Stir in vinegar, lemon juice, parsley flakes, onion, anchovy paste, garlic, cheese, and sherry. Mix well; chill. Serve as dip with cauliflowerets and broccoli pieces.

Doris Littrell, Xi Epsilon Theta Chap.
Columbia, Missouri

NIPPY CHEESE BALL

4 oz. Danish blue cheese
4 oz. Old English cheese
4 oz. sharp Cheddar cheese
1 3-oz. package cream cheese
1/8 tsp. dry mustard
1/8 tsp. onion powder
1/2 tbsp. Worcestershire sauce
1/2 to 3/4 c. finely chopped
   walnuts

Let cheeses soften to room temperature. Combine all ingredients except walnuts in mixer bowl. Beat well with electric mixer until blended. Place on waxed paper; shape

into ball. Roll ball in walnuts, coating well. Mixture will be soft. Chill until firm. Place in center of large plate; surround with desired crackers. Cut wedge from cheese to serve.

Mrs. Philip W. Jean
International Honorary Member, BSP
Vancouver, British Columbia, Canada

PIZZA SNACKS

1 bunch green onions, chopped
1 lb. mild Cheddar cheese, grated
1 sm. can chopped black olives,
   drained
1 6-oz. can tomato paste
1 8-oz. can tomato sauce
1/3 c. oil
Oregano to taste
Salt and pepper to taste
Garlic salt to taste
Sliced French bread

Combine onions, cheese, and olives. Add tomato paste, tomato sauce, oil, and oregano. Season with salt, pepper, and garlic salt. Mix well; chill for 1 to 2 days. Spread pizza mixture on sliced French bread; place on baking sheet. Broil until bubbly; serve hot. Yield: 25-30 servings.

Jackie Elardo, Theta Phi No. 3224
Los Gatos, California

SWEET GHERKIN-CHEESE DIP

1 lg. package cream cheese,
   softened
1/2 c. finely chopped sweet
   gherkins
1 tsp. salt
1 tsp. dry mustard
10 drops of hot sauce
1 c. sour cream

Combine cream cheese, gherkins, salt, mustard, and hot sauce. Blend in sour cream. Serve with chips. Yield: 2 1/3 cups.

Martha Spencer, Coun. Pres.
Xi Alpha Nu X608, Los Angeles, California

PECAN-CHEESE BALL

6 oz. Roquefort cheese
6 oz. sharp soft Cheddar cheese
10 oz. cream cheese
1 tsp. Worcestershire sauce
2 tbsp. grated onion
2 tbsp. sherry
1 c. chopped pecans
1/2 c. finely chopped parsley

Soften cheeses; add remaining ingredients, reserving 1/2 cup pecans and 1/4 cup parsley. Shape into ball; chill until firm. Combine reserved pecans and parsley; roll ball in mixture until coated. Serve with crackers.

Betty D. Thornton
International Honorary Member, BSP
Jacksonville, Florida

DEVILED HAM-CHEESE BALL

2 8-oz. packages cream cheese
1/2 lb. sharp cheese, shredded
2 tsp. grated onion
1 tsp. lemon juice
1 tsp. mustard
3 tsp. Worcestershire sauce
1 tsp. paprika
1/2 tsp. seasoning salt
2 1/4 tbsp. chopped dried parsley
1 tbsp. chopped pimento
2 lg. cans deviled ham
Chopped nuts

Soften cheeses; beat all ingredients together except nuts. Cover; chill for 2 hours. Shape into 2 large balls; roll in nuts.

Mary Laine Hampton, Pres.
Delta Gamma No. 4815, Wenatchee, Washington

PATTY SHELLS BENEDICT

6 baked patty shells
1 c. shredded cooked ham
6 eggs
1 recipe hollandaise sauce

Fill patty shells loosely with ham. Place on baking sheet. Bake at 350 degrees for 10 minutes. Poach eggs in skillet in enough salted water to cover. Remove eggs with slotted spoon; place on paper towel to drain. Trim eggs with 2-inch cookie cutter. Place 1 egg over ham in each patty shell; cover with hollandaise sauce. Garnish with parsley.

Nan Gardner Weber
International Honorary Member, BSP
Farmington, Missouri

SPINACH-CHEESE PIE

4 frozen patty shells
1 10-oz. package frozen chopped
   spinach
6 eggs, beaten
1 3-oz. package cream cheese,
   softened
1/4 c. shredded sharp process
   American cheese
2 tbsp. sliced green onion
1 tbsp. snipped parsley
1/2 tsp. salt
Dash of pepper
2 tbsp. grated Parmesan cheese

Thaw patty shells in refrigerator for about 2 hours. Roll shells out on lightly floured surface to fit 10-inch pie plate, sealing edges together. Let rest for 5 minutes. Place pastry in pie plate; flute edges. Cook spinach according to package directions; drain well. Combine eggs, cream cheese, and shredded cheese; beat until blended. Stir in spinach, green onion, parsley, salt, and pepper. Turn into prepared shell; top with Parmesan cheese. Bake at 425 degrees for 15 minutes; remove from oven. Let stand for 10 minutes. Yield: 8 servings.

Susan Swift, Alpha Nu No. 936
Cincinnati, Ohio

SWISS CHEESE AND ONION TART

2 slices bacon, diced
3 c. thinly sliced onions
3 eggs
3/4 tsp. salt

1 c. grated Swiss cheese
1 c. light cream
1 unbaked 10-in. pie shell
1 tbsp. butter

Fry bacon in skillet until crisp; drain on paper toweling. Saute onions in bacon drippings until transparent; cool thoroughly. Add eggs to onion mixture, one at a time, beating well after each addition. Add salt, cheese, cream, and bacon; mix well. Spoon filling into pie shell; dot with butter. Bake at 350 degrees for 35 minutes. Yield: 4-6 servings.

Dora Purchard
International Honorary Member, BSP
San Diego, California

BETTY'S RICE

1/4 lb. butter
1 c. rice
1 minced onion
6 peppercorns
5 cardamom seed
Dash of cinnamon
Salt to taste
1/2 bay leaf, broken
Pinch of saffron
1/2 c. seedless raisins
12 blanched almonds
3 c. chicken broth

Melt half the butter in skillet; add rice. Cook, stirring, until browned. Add onion and remaining butter. Cook over low heat for 5 minutes; stir in peppercorns, cardamom seed, cinnamon, salt, bay leaf, and saffron. Add raisins and almonds. Do not stir. Add broth, 1 cup at a time, cooking, covered, over low heat until each cup broth has been absorbed.

Agnes Moorehead
International Honorary Member, BSP
New York, New York

MUSHROOM RICE

3 tbsp. butter
1 c. rice

3 c. boiling water
2 tbsp. soy sauce
1/2 c. sauteed chopped mushrooms
2 tbsp. dried parsley
2 tbsp. chopped pimento
Salt to taste

Melt butter in large frying pan over medium heat. Add rice; stir until rice is lightly browned. Add remaining ingredients; stir well. Cover; cook for 30 to 40 minutes, stirring occasionally, until rice is tender. Spoon into serving dish; sprinkle with additional parsley if desired. Yield: 4-6 servings.

Joyce Lynette Smith, Kappa Omicron No. 3523
Victoria, Texas

ORIENTAL RICE

1/4 tsp. curry powder
3 tbsp. butter, melted
4 c. hot cooked rice
1/3 c. finely chopped parsley
1 tsp. salt
1/4 c. finely chopped peanuts

Blend curry powder into butter in blazer pan of chafing dish. Add rice with remaining ingredients. Keep hot over water pan. Yield: 6 servings.

CARAWAY SEED-NOODLE RING WITH CREAMED TUNA

1/2 lb. noodles
1 tbsp. caraway seed
4 tbsp. butter or margarine
3 tbsp. flour
1 1/2 c. milk
2 6-oz. cans tuna
3/4 tsp. salt
1/4 tsp. ground thyme
1/8 tsp. pepper

Cook noodles according to package directions; drain and rinse. Add caraway seed and 1 tablespoon butter; toss lightly. Turn into greased 1 1/2-quart ring mold. Place in pan of hot water to keep warm. Melt remaining butter in saucepan; blend in flour. Stir in milk gradually. Cook until of medium thickness, stirring constantly. Drain tuna; flake. Add to white sauce. Add seasonings; mix well. Heat, stirring as little as possible. Turn noodle ring out on hot platter. Fill center with creamed tuna. Garnish with parsley flakes. Yield: 6 servings.

CHINESE-FRIED RICE

3 chicken bouillon cubes
2 1/2 c. boiling water
6 strips bacon
1/4 c. chopped onion
1/4 c. chopped green pepper
1 c. rice
1/2 lb. shrimp, chopped
Butter
2 eggs, slightly beaten
Salt and pepper to taste
1 to 2 tbsp. soy sauce
2 green onions, sliced

Dissolve bouillon in boiling water; set aside. Fry bacon in skillet until crisp; crumble and set aside. Saute chopped onion and green pepper in bacon drippings until crisp-tender. Add rice; stir until lightly browned. Add bouillon; simmer for 20 to 30 minutes or until rice is tender. Saute shrimp in butter for 1 minute. Add eggs; cook quickly, stirring. Season with salt and pepper. Stir egg mixture into rice mixture; season with soy sauce. Top with crumbled bacon and sliced green onions. May be prepared and served in electric skillet. Yield: 6-8 servings.

Kathy Knowles, Pres.
Missouri Nu No. 427, Macon, Missouri

RICE BALLS

1 pkg. herb-seasoned stuffing mix
2 c. grated Cheddar cheese
1 egg

2 tbsp. horseradish
3 tsp. Worcestershire sauce
1/4 tsp. cayenne pepper
1/4 tsp. pepper
1 tsp. salt
3 jalapeno peppers, minced
2 c. cooked rice
Oil

Place stuffing mix in blender container; blend to fine crumb consistency. Set aside. Combine grated cheese, egg, horseradish, Worcestershire sauce, cayenne pepper, pepper, salt and jalapeno peppers in large bowl. Mix well; add hot rice. Chill for 2 hours. Roll into 1 1/2-inch balls; roll each ball in stuffing crumbs. Fry in hot oil until brown.

Bootsie Clark, City Coun. Pres.
Xi Mu Chi X3728, El Campo, Texas

BEEF

BEEF AND NOODLE CASSEROLE

1 lb. ground steak
1/3 c. chopped onion
1 tsp. oregano
1/2 tsp. salt
1 med. clove of garlic, minced
2 c. medium noodles, cooked
1 can tomato soup
1 c. grated cheese

Brown steak and onion in large skillet; stir in oregano, salt, and garlic. Add noodles, soup and 1/3 cup water; mix well. Turn into greased casserole; sprinkle with cheese. Bake at 350 degrees for 30 minutes or until bubbly. Yield: 6-8 servings.

The Hon. F. Elsie Inman
International Honorary Member, BSP
Ottawa, Canada

ROLLED SHOULDER MEDLEY

1 4-lb. rolled boneless beef
  shoulder roast
1/4 c. flour
2 tbsp. salad oil

2 tsp. salt
1/8 tsp. pepper
1/4 tsp. thyme leaves
1/2 tsp. oregano leaves
1 bay leaf
2 beef bouillon cubes
1 c. water
1 c. red wine
6 med. pared carrots, slivered
1 lb. small white onions, peeled
2 10-oz. packages frozen Brussels
  sprouts

Roll roast in flour until coated on all sides. Heat oil in Dutch oven over medium heat. Brown roast for about 15 to 20 minutes, turning as necessary. Add seasonings, bouillon cubes, water and wine. Cover tightly; simmer over low heat, turning occasionally for about 3 hours and 15 minutes or until roast is tender. Add carrots and onions to roast mixture. Cook for 10 minutes. Add Brussels sprouts; simmer for 15 minutes longer. Place roast in center of large heated serving platter; surround with vegetables. Boil gravy until reduced to desired consistency; remove bay leaf. Spoon off fat from surface of gravy. Spoon some of the gravy over roast and vegetables; serve remaining gravy in bowl.

BEEF AND FRUIT KABOBS

3/4 lb. round steak
Instant meat tenderizer
1 11-oz. can mandarin oranges
1 13 1/2-oz. can pineapple chunks
1/2 c. (packed) brown sugar
1/4 c. honey
1 tbsp. butter or margarine, melted

Cut steak into 1-inch cubes; sprinkle with tenderizer according to label directions. Drain oranges, reserving 1/4 cup syrup; drain pineapple. Alternate steak and fruits on 4 small skewers. Combine reserved syrup with brown sugar, honey, and butter; blend well. Broil kabobs over hot coals on hibachi for 10 minutes or until steak is of desired doneness. Turn to brown on all sides, basting frequently with sauce. Yield: 2 servings.

Nancy M. Russell, City Coun. Pres.
Omicron No. 1060, Wheeling, West Virginia

MARY HELEN'S BEEF BRISKET

1 4-lb. beef brisket
1 onion, sliced
1 lemon, sliced
2 c. catsup
2 tbsp. Worcestershire sauce
1/4 tsp. hot sauce
2 tsp. dry mustard
1 tsp. salt
2 tbsp. liquid smoke
1/4 c. (packed) brown sugar

Trim fat from brisket; arrange onion and lemon slices over brisket. Seal well in foil; place in shallow baking pan. Bake at 250 degrees for 6 hours. Combine remaining ingredients with 2 cups water in saucepan; mix well. Simmer, stirring, for 5 minutes. Remove brisket from foil; discard onion and lemon. Cool brisket; slice thinly. Arrange brisket in shallow baking pan; pour sauce over brisket to cover partially. Bake at 350 degrees for 1 hour. Serve with remaining sauce, if desired. Yield: 8 servings.

Marilee Clark, Pres., Gamma Iota No. 2224
Chillicothe, Missouri

STIFADO

4 lb. beef chuck or round steak
2/3 c. vegetable oil
1 6-oz. can tomato paste
1 1/2 c. red wine
8 peppercorns
2 bay leaves
1 1/2 tbsp. ground allspice
2 cloves of garlic, halved
5 whole cloves
Salt and pepper to taste
3 lb. small white onions, peeled
3 c. rice
6 c. chicken consomme
1 1/2 c. chopped parsley
1/3 c. butter

Cut beef in 1-inch squares; saute in oil until well browned. Add tomato paste, wine, peppercorns, bay leaves, allspice, garlic, cloves, salt, and pepper. Bring to a boil; simmer, covered, for 1 hour. Add wine, if needed. Add onions; cook for 30 minutes or until beef is tender and sauce is thickened. Discard garlic and cloves, if desired. Prepare rice according to package directions, using consomme. Stir in parsley, butter, salt, and pepper. Serve with Stifado. Yield: 12 servings.

Fran Miller, Pres., Preceptor Pi XP512
Great Bend, Kansas

BEEF MOUSSAKA

Butter
1 c. finely chopped onions
1 1/2 lb. ground chuck
1 clove of garlic, minced
1/2 tsp. oregano
1/2 tsp. cinnamon
Salt and pepper to taste
2 8-oz. cans tomato sauce
2 med. eggplant
2 tbsp. flour
2 c. milk
2 eggs
1/2 c. grated Parmesan cheese
1/2 c. grated Cheddar cheese
2 tbsp. dry bread crumbs

Melt 2 tablespoons butter in 3 1/2-quart Dutch oven; saute onions, chuck, and garlic in butter for 10 minutes or until browned. Stir in oregano, cinnamon, salt, pepper, and tomato sauce; bring to a boil. Reduce heat; simmer for 30 minutes. Cut eggplant in half lengthwise; cut crosswise into 1/2-inch slices. Sprinkle with salt; brush lightly with 1/2 cup melted butter. Broil 4 inches from source of heat for 4 minutes on each side or until golden. Melt 2 tablespoons butter in medium saucepan; stir in flour, salt and pepper. Remove from heat; add milk gradually. Return to heat; cook, stirring constantly, until mixture is smooth and thickened. Remove from heat. Beat eggs with whisk. Beat small amount of hot mixture into eggs; return to hot mixture. Return to heat; cook, stirring constantly, until sauce is smooth and thickened. Preheat oven to 350 degrees. Arrange half the eggplant in shallow 2-quart casserole; overlap slices. Sprinkle with 2 tablespoons cheeses. Stir bread crumbs into meat sauce; spoon over eggplant. Sprinkle with 2 tablespoons cheeses. Arrange remaining eggplant over top. Pour cream sauce over all. Sprinkle with remaining cheeses. Bake for 35 minutes or until set and top is golden brown. Yield: 12 servings.

Linda Bennett, Pres., Delta Xi No. 5839
Knoxville, Tennessee

BEEF IN SAVORY SAUCE

1 1/2 lb. thinly sliced round steak
2 tbsp. flour
1 tsp. paprika
1/2 tsp. salt
Dash of pepper
1 med. onion, sliced
1 4-oz. can sliced mushrooms, drained
2 tbsp. shortening
1 10 3/4-oz. can beef gravy
1/2 c. sour cream
Hot buttered noodles

Cut steak into thin strips. Combine flour, paprika, salt, and pepper; coat steak. Brown steak, onion, and mushrooms in skillet in shortening; add beef gravy. Cover; cook over low heat for about 1 hour and 15 minutes. Uncover; cook for 15 minutes longer, stirring. Blend in sour cream; serve with noodles. Yield: 4-6 servings.

BEEF AND PEPPER CASSEROLE

1   2 1/2-lb. flank steak
1/4 c. vegetable oil
1 clove of garlic, crushed
1 tsp. powdered ginger
2 green peppers, cut into strips
3/4 c. chopped onions
2   8-oz. cans tomato sauce
4 tbsp. soy sauce
2 tsp. sugar
Pepper to taste
1 can bean sprouts

Tenderize steak as desired; cut into strips. Combine oil, garlic, and ginger in large skillet over medium heat; blend well. Add steak; cook, stirring constantly, for 5 minutes. Remove steak. Add green peppers and onions; cook, stirring, for 2 minutes. Stir in tomato sauce, soy sauce, sugar, and pepper; cook for 3 minutes longer. Rinse and drain bean sprouts. Add steak and bean sprouts to onion mixture; cook for 2 minutes longer. Serve with rice. Yield: 6 servings.

Daphne W. Merrill
International Honorary Member, BSP
Auburn, Maine

BEEF WITH SNOW PEAS

1   1-lb. flank steak
4 tbsp. soy sauce
1 tbsp. cornstarch
1 tbsp. dry sherry
1 tsp. sugar
1/4 tsp. monosodium glutamate
3 tbsp. cooking oil
1 slice gingerroot
1/4 to 1/2 lb. snow peas

Cut steak across grain into 1/4 x 2-inch strips. Combine soy sauce, cornstarch, sherry, sugar, and monosodium glutamate; mix well. Pour sauce over steak. Marinate steak, covered, in refrigerator for at least 30 minutes. Pour oil into skillet over medium heat; stir in steak and gingerroot. Saute lightly; stir in snow peas. Cook, stirring gently, just until peas are crisp-tender and

mixture is heated through. Powdered ginger to taste may be substituted for gingerroot. Yield: 6 servings.

Virginia Gilley, Pres.
Preceptor Delta XP371, Falls Church, Virginia

BEEF STROGANOFF

2 lb. beef fillet, sliced 1/4 in.
   thick
2 tbsp. flour
2 med. onions, chopped
6 tbsp. butter
1/2 lb. sliced fresh mushrooms
2 tbsp. prepared mustard
2 tbsp. catsup
2 tbsp. Worcestershire sauce
2 c. sour cream
Salt and pepper to taste
1/2 c. sherry

Pound beef slices; cut across grain into 1/2 x 1 1/2-inch strips. Dredge with flour; keep at room temperature. Saute onions in 2 tablespoons butter in large skillet until transparent; add 2 tablespoons butter. Stir in mushrooms. Cook for 3 minutes longer; remove onions and mushrooms from skillet. Add remaining butter; stir in beef. Cook, stirring, until red color is gone; remove from skillet. Blend mustard, catsup, and Worcestershire sauce into pan juices; mix well. Have sour cream at room temperature; blend into mustard mixture thoroughly. Heat through over low heat. Stir in mushrooms, onions, beef, and sherry; simmer until just heated through. Serve with rice. Yield: 6 servings.

Margaret Ruth Thomas
International Honorary Member, BSP
New City, New York

GREEK BEEF STEW

3 lb. lean beef, cubed
Salt and pepper to taste
1/2 c. butter
2 lb. small onions, peeled
1/2 c. red wine
1   6-oz. can tomato paste

2 tbsp. red wine vinegar
1 tbsp. (packed) brown sugar
1 minced clove of garlic
3/8 tsp. ground cumin
1 whole bay leaf
1 cinnamon stick
4 to 5 whole cloves
1/4 c. dried currants or raisins

Season beef well with salt and pepper. Melt butter in heavy kettle; add beef, stirring just to coat with butter. Add onions. Combine wine, tomato paste, vinegar, brown sugar, garlic, cumin, bay leaf, cinnamon, cloves, and currants in bowl; mix well. Pour sauce over beef and onions; do not stir. Simmer, tightly covered, for 3 hours or until beef is tender. Blend sauce carefully when serving. Yield: 6-8 servings.

Mary Davis, Pres., Preceptor Rho XP 453
Arvada, Colorado

LASAGNA

1 8-oz. package lasagna
1 tbsp. olive oil
1 1/2 lb. ground beef
1/2 c. chopped onion
1 clove of garlic, minced
1 6-oz. can tomato paste
1 8-oz. can tomato sauce
1 can mushrooms
1 tsp. basil
1 tsp. parsley
1/4 tsp. oregano
1/4 tsp. thyme
1/4 tsp. chili powder
1/4 tsp. pepper
1 tsp. salt
2 c. small curd cottage cheese
1/4 c. diced salami
1 egg
2 c. shredded mozzarella cheese

Cook lasagna according to package directions; drain. Place olive oil in large skillet; add beef, onion, and garlic. Saute until crumbly and lightly browned; drain off excess grease. Stir in tomato paste, tomato sauce, and mushrooms; mix well. Add basil, parsley, oregano, thyme, chili powder, pepper, salt, and 1 cup water; blend well. Simmer, stirring occasionally, for 1 hour. Combine cottage cheese, salami, and egg. Alternate layers of lasagna, beef mixture, cottage cheese mixture, and mozzarella in 13 x 9 x 2-inch baking dish. Bake at 350 degrees for 45 minutes. Let stand for 15 minutes before serving. May be made ahead and frozen. Yield: 8 servings.

Floy Deen Leetch, Zeta Theta No. 4454
Lee's Summit, Missouri

MEATBALL CURRY

2 lb. lean ground beef or lamb
1 finely minced onion
1 tbsp. minced green pepper or
    green chili pepper
Curry powder
1/8 tsp. salt
1 med. coarsely chopped onion
3 tbsp. vegetable oil
3 tbsp. sour cream or yogurt
3 c. meat broth or hot water
3 lg. tomatoes, chopped

Combine beef, minced onion, green pepper, 1/2 teaspoon curry powder, and salt; blend thoroughly. Form into walnut-sized balls. Cook chopped onion in oil in large skillet over medium heat until soft; move onion to side of pan. Stir in 2 tablespoons curry powder until well blended with oil. Remove from heat; blend curry powder mixture with onions. Return to heat; brown, stirring constantly, for 2 minutes. Stir in sour cream and broth; blend well. Bring to a boil; blend in tomatoes. Cook, stirring, for 2 minutes longer; add meatballs, one at a time. Bring to a boil; reduce heat. Cook, stirring occasionally, for 20 minutes longer; reduce heat. Simmer, covered, for 20 minutes longer or until gravy is thickened. Serve with saffron rice and peas. Yield: 6-8 servings.

Mrs. G. J. Watumull
International Honorary Member, BSP
Honolulu, Hawaii

Core apples; peel and halve. Melt butter in skillet; add curry powder. Cook, stirring, over moderate heat for about 30 seconds. Add water, brown sugar and lemon juice; bring to a boil. Add apple halves; spoon liquid over apples. Simmer until apples are just tender, turning occasionally. Remove apples. Dissolve cornstarch in cold water; add to sauce. Cook, stirring, until thickened. Replace apples in sauce briefly to reheat; coat with sauce. Reserve sauce. Stud apples with whole cloves; garnish beef ring with apples.

Curried Rice

2 tbsp. butter
1 tbsp. chopped green onion
1 tbsp. curry powder
1 tsp. salt
1 beef bouillon cube
2 c. water
1 c. rice
Minced green onion tops

Melt butter in saucepan; add onion. Saute until onion is tender. Stir in curry powder, salt, bouillon cube and water; bring to a boil. Add rice; cover. Cook over low heat for about 15 to 20 minutes or until rice is tender and liquid is absorbed. Pile rice into center of beef ring; garnish with green onion tops. Spoon reserved sauce over apples and beef ring. Serve.

ORIENTAL BEEF RING

2 eggs
1/2 c. milk
2 c. fresh bread crumbs
1/4 c. minced onion
1 tbsp. prepared mustard
2 tsp. salt
2 lb. ground beef
1 5-oz. can sliced water
   chestnuts, drained

Beat eggs slightly; stir in milk and bread crumbs until blended. Add remaining ingredients; mix thoroughly. Shape beef mixture into 8-inch ring with 4-inch hole in center in shallow baking dish. Bake at 350 degrees for about 45 minutes. Lift carefully to serving dish. Keep warm.

Curried Apples

3 med. Washington apples
2 tbsp. butter
2 tsp. curry powder
1/2 c. water
2 tbsp. brown sugar
1 tbsp. lemon juice
1 tbsp. cornstarch
1 tbsp. cold water
Whole cloves

CASTLE VALLEY CASSEROLE

1 12-oz. package spaghetti
1 lb. ground beef
1 sm. onion, chopped
Butter
3 tbsp. flour
3 c. milk
Salt and pepper to taste
1 can tomato soup
1 can cream of mushroom soup

Prepare spaghetti according to package directions; drain. Saute ground beef and onion in small amount of butter in large skillet over medium heat until lightly browned; remove from skillet. Add 3 tablespoons butter to pan drippings; stir in flour. Add milk gradually; cook, stirring, until sauce is smooth and slightly thickened. Stir in salt, pepper, and soups; blend thoroughly. Arrange alternate layers of spaghetti, beef mixture, and sauce in large casserole, ending with sauce. Bake at 300 degrees for 20 minutes. Yield: 8-10 servings.

Mrs. Margaret D. Lee
International Honorary Member, BSP
Salt Lake City, Utah

HORSERADISH MEATBALLS

2 egg yolks or 1 egg
1/2 c. fine bread crumbs
2 tbsp. prepared horseradish
1 can water chestnuts, finely
   ground
1 lb. ground chuck
1/3 c. orange marmalade
1 clove of garlic, minced
1/4 c. soy sauce
2 tbsp. lemon juice

Beat egg yolks with 1/2 cup water; stir in crumbs, horseradish and water chestnuts. Add ground chuck; mix thoroughly. Shape into 1-inch meatballs; place in shallow baking pan. Bake at 350 degrees for 15 minutes or until browned. Combine marmalade, garlic, soy sauce, and lemon juice with 1/3 cup water in small saucepan; blend well. Bring to a boil, stirring constantly. Remove from heat; serve hot with meatballs.

Mrs. Lovern Stockwell, Serv. Chm.
Xi Alpha Alpha No. 3884, Bangor, Maine

HOT CORNED BEEF TEMPTERS

2 12-oz. cans corned beef
1 med. onion, minced
1 tbsp. minced parsley
1/2 c. melted butter
1 c. all-purpose flour
1 tsp. dry mustard
1 tsp. salt
1 c. milk
1 1-lb. can sauerkraut, drained

2 eggs
Fine dry bread crumbs

Let corned beef stand until at room temperature; flake and mix with onion. Saute corned beef mixture and parsley in butter for 5 minutes; stir in flour, mustard, and salt. Add milk gradually; cook, stirring constantly, until thickened. Chop sauerkraut finely; add to corned beef mixture. Mix thoroughly; cool. Shape into 1/2-inch balls; chill. Beat eggs with 1/4 cup water. Dip balls into egg mixture; roll in bread crumbs. Fry in 375-degree deep fat for about 2 minutes or until golden brown. Spread balls on paper-lined cookie sheet to drain. Pile balls in serving bowl; serve with cocktail picks.

Barbara L. Jacob, City Coun., Chap. VP
Iota Theta No. 4193, Belleville, Illinois

SINA'S MEAT SPAGHETTI SAUCE

4 lb. ground beef
2 c. chopped onions
8 cloves of garlic, minced
2 6-oz. cans broiled sliced
   mushrooms
1 c. chopped parsley
4 No. 2 1/2 cans tomatoes
1 16-oz. can tomatoes
2 tbsp. oregano
4 tsp. salt
2 tsp. monosodium glutamate
1 tsp. thyme
1/2 tsp. pepper
4 crumbled bay leaves
1 tbsp. sugar

Combine beef, onions, and garlic in large kettle; cook, stirring, until beef is lightly browned. Add mushrooms with liquid. Stir in remaining ingredients except sugar; mix well. Blend in 4 cups water; mix well. Bring to a boil; reduce heat. Simmer, stirring occasionally, for 2 hours or until of desired consistency. Stir in sugar. Yield: 48 servings.

Mrs. John Cantrell, Pres.
Omicron Chi No. 4422, McKinney, Texas

BEEF-PEACH PIE

  1   1-lb. 13-oz. can cling peach
      halves
1 1/2 lb. ground lean beef
1 1/2 c. soft bread crumbs
1/2 c. finely chopped onion
1 1/4 tsp. salt
2 eggs, slightly beaten
  1   8-oz. can tomato sauce with
      mushrooms

Drain peaches, reserving 1/4 cup syrup. Combine beef, crumbs, onion, salt, eggs, reserved syrup and 1/2 cup tomato sauce. Turn into 8-inch round baking dish or 9-inch pie plate. Do not pack. Make depressions in beef mixture around edge of dish with back of spoon. Place peach halves, cup sides up, in depressions; cover. Bake at 350 degrees for about 1 hour. Remove cover. Spoon remaining tomato sauce into peach cups and over surface of beef mixture. Bake, uncovered, for 15 to 20 minutes longer. Cut into pie-shaped wedges to serve. Yield: 6-7 servings.

JUMBO CORNBURGER

3 eggs
1 1/2 lb. ground beef
  1   8-oz. can tomato sauce
1 1/2 tsp. salt
Pepper to taste
1 tsp. Worcestershire sauce
  1   12-oz. can whole kernel corn
1/2 c. medium-coarse cracker crumbs
1/4 c. diced green pepper
1/4 c. chopped onion
2 tbsp. chopped pimento
1/4 tsp. ground sage
1 med. tomato
1/2 c. shredded sharp American
     cheese

Beat 2 eggs slightly. Combine ground beef, eggs, tomato sauce, 3/4 teaspoon salt, pepper, and Worcestershire sauce; mix well. Beat remaining egg slightly; stir in corn, crumbs, green pepper, onion, pimento, remaining salt, and sage. Spread half the beef mixture in 8-inch round baking dish; spoon corn mixture over beef mixture. Top with remaining beef mixture. Bake at 375 degrees for 55 minutes. Peel tomato and cut into wedges; arrange tomato over top. Sprinkle with cheese; return to oven. Bake for 5 minutes longer or until cheese is melted. Yield: 6 servings.

Julia Perkey, Pres.
Epsilon Omicron No. 3909, Rich Hill, Missouri

ARROZ CON POLLO

1 tbsp. salt
1 tsp. oregano
1/4 tsp. pepper
2 tsp. olive oil
1 tsp. vinegar
1 clove of garlic
1   3-lb. broiler fryer,
    disjointed
3 tbsp. shortening
1/4 lb. cooked ham, diced
1 strip bacon, chopped
1 onion, chopped
1 green pepper, chopped
6 green olives, chopped
1 tomato, chopped
1 tsp. capers
3 tbsp. tomato sauce
2 c. rice
1 can green peas
1 qt. boiling water
1   4-oz. can pimentos, cut in
    strips

Combine salt, oregano, pepper, olive oil, vinegar, and garlic in small bowl; mash together with wooden spoon. Brush chicken pieces with olive oil mixture. Melt shortening in Dutch oven or large skillet. Add chicken pieces; brown lightly on all sides. Add ham, bacon, onion, green pepper, olives, tomato, and capers. Mix lightly; cover. Cook over medium heat for 10 minutes. Add tomato sauce and rice. Cook, covered, for 5 minutes. Drain peas, reserving liquid. Add reserved liquid and boiling water to chicken mixture; mix well. Cook over medium heat for 15 minutes, stirring lightly. Cover; simmer for

20 minutes. Add peas; top with pimento strips. Simmer for 10 minutes longer, covered.

Jan Blaisdell, Omicron Theta No. 7002
Galesburg, Illinois

PARTY-STYLE PAELLA

1   3 1/2-lb. chicken, disjointed
Olive oil
Salt
2 c. rice
1 cloves of garlic, minced
1 bay leaf, crumbled
1/2 tsp. saffron
1/2 tsp. pepper
1 c. canned tomatoes
3 1/2 c. boiling water
1 c. chopped olives
1 green pepper, slivered
1 pimento, sliced
Dash of cayenne pepper
1/2 lb. hot sausage or pepperoni
1 can baby clams, drained
1 lb. cooked fresh shrimp,
    shelled
2 cans lobster
1 c. small peas

Fry chicken in hot oil in skillet until browned. Remove meat from bones, leaving wings and drumsticks in sections. Cut meat into bite-sized pieces. Place chicken in large greased casserole; sprinkle with 1 teaspoon salt. Combine rice and garlic in pan drippings in skillet. Saute, stirring, until rice is lightly browned. Combine 2 1/2 teaspoons salt, bay leaf, saffron, pepper, tomatoes, water, olives, green pepper, pimento, and cayenne pepper in saucepan; bring to a boil. Pour boiling mixture over chicken; cover. Bake at 425 degrees for 25 minutes. Cut sausage into thin slices; brown well in skillet. Add sausage, clams, shrimp, lobster, and peas to chicken mixture. Mix lightly. Reduce oven temperature to 375 degrees; cover casserole. Bake for 15 minutes longer or until heated through. Yield: 10-12 servings.

Sylvia Baillargeon, Eta Beta No. 5881
Ottawa, Ontario, Canada

CHOP SUEY

1 lb. veal
1 lb. pork
1/2 c. shortening
1 c. chopped onions
3 c. chopped celery
2 tsp. salt
1 tbsp. pepper
2 No. 2 cans bean sprouts
2 4-oz. cans mushroom pieces
5 tbsp. cornstarch
2 tsp. sugar
4 tsp. soy sauce

Cut veal and pork into bite-sized pieces. Melt shortening in hot skillet; add veal and pork. Saute until meats are browned. Add onions; cook for 5 minutes. Place meat mixture in large kettle; add celery, salt, pepper, and 1 cup hot water. Drain bean sprouts, reserving juice. Add 1 cup reserved juice to meat mixture. Cover; cool for 5 minutes. Add bean sprouts and undrained mushrooms to meat mixture. Add enough water to remaining reserved juice to make 1 cup liquid. Combine liquid, cornstarch, sugar, and soy sauce; stir into meat mixture. Cook over low heat, covered, for 25 minutes, stirring occasionally, until thickened. Serve with chow mein noodles or rice. Yield: 10 servings.

Maryann Ketchesin, Serv. Chm.
Xi Beta Omega X1163, Elyria, Ohio

CHICKEN-CRAB MEAT ROSEMARY

2 tbsp. chopped onion
1/2 c. butter
1 tbsp. flour
1 tsp. salt
1 tsp. paprika
1 tsp. crushed rosemary
2 c. chicken broth
2 c. sour cream
3 c. diced cooked chicken
1 c. crab meat, flaked
1 1/2 c. cubed avocado
2 tbsp. lemon juice
1 c. toasted bread crumbs

Saute onion in butter in skillet until golden; stir in flour, salt, paprika, and rosemary. Cook, stirring, until bubbly. Add broth gradually; bring to a boil over low heat, stirring constantly. Remove from heat; stir in sour cream gradually. Add chicken and crab meat. Sprinkle avocado with lemon juice; add to sour cream mixture. Blend gently. Turn into 2-quart baking dish; cover with bread crumbs. Bake at 350 degrees for 30 minutes. Yield: 8 servings.

Mrs. Hal. C. Horton, Sr., Spon.
Xi Epsilon Pi X1900, Greenville, Texas

POULTRY

CHICKEN-ASPARAGUS BAKE

1 lb. fresh or frozen asparagus
5 tbsp. butter
5 tbsp. flour
1 1/2 c. chicken broth
1 6-oz. can sliced mushrooms, drained
Dash of pepper
2 lg. chicken breasts, cooked
1/4 c. dry bread crumbs
2 tbsp. snipped parsley
2 tbsp. slivered toasted almonds
2 tbsp. melted butter

Cook asparagus in boiling water until tender. Place butter in large skillet; melt. Blend flour into butter. Add broth; blend thoroughly. Cook over low heat, stirring constantly, until thickened. Stir in mushrooms and pepper. Slice chicken; place in 10 x 6-inch baking dish. Drizzle with half the mushroom mixture. Arrange asparagus over sauce. Top with remaining sauce. Combine crumbs, parsley, almonds, and melted butter, tossing well. Sprinkle over top. Bake at 375 degrees for 20 minutes or until heated through and lightly browned. Yield: 6 servings.

Sharon Van Haven, Pres.
Xi Alpha Nu X3855, Saint Cloud, Minnesota

BUTTERMILK-PECAN CHICKEN

1/2 c. margarine
1 c. buttermilk
1 egg, slightly beaten
1 c. flour
1 c. ground pecans
1 tbsp. paprika
1 tbsp. salt
1/8 tsp. pepper
1/4 c. sesame seed
2 frying chickens, disjointed
1/4 c. pecan halves

Melt margarine in 13 x 9-inch baking dish. Combine buttermilk and egg in shallow dish. Combine flour, ground pecans, paprika, salt, pepper, and sesame seed in shallow pan, mixing well. Dip chicken in buttermilk mixture; coat with flour mixture. Place, skin side down, in melted margarine in baking dish; turn, coating with margarine. Turn skin side up. Place pecan halves on each chicken piece. Bake at 350 degrees for 1 hour and 15 minutes or until tender and browned. Yield: 8-10 servings.

Joyce Homan, Pres.
Xi Zeta Theta X2030, Abilene, Texas

CHICKEN ALOHA

1 1/2 c. sliced celery
1 green pepper, cut in strips
3 tbsp. butter
2 tsp. instant chicken bouillon
3 c. cooked diced chicken
1 22-oz. can pineapple pie filling
1/4 c. soy sauce

Saute celery and green pepper in butter in skillet until just crisp-tender. Dissolve bouillon in 1/3 cup water. Add chicken, pie filling, soy sauce, and bouillon mixture to celery mixture; mix thoroughly. Heat through, stirring frequently. Serve over chow mein noodles, garnished with parsley and kumquats, if desired. Yield: 6 servings.

LaVera M. Stalnecker
Sigma Zeta Chapter, Riverside, California

CHICKEN-ALMOND SWIRLS

1 8-oz. can refrigerator crescent rolls
1 5-oz. can chicken spread
1 tbsp. chopped toasted almonds
1 tbsp. mayonnaise
1/2 tsp. lemon juice
Seasoned salt

Separate dough into 4 rectangles; press along perforations to seal. Combine chicken, almonds, mayonnaise, lemon juice, and salt, mixing well; spread on rectangles. Roll up each rectangle, jelly roll fashion, starting with long side. Slice each roll into 8 slices. Place, cut side down, on greased cookie sheet. Bake at 375 degrees for 12 minutes or until lightly browned. Serve warm. Yield: 32 appetizers.

Ruth Galyean, Corr. Sec.
Preceptor Beta XP428
West Asheville, North Carolina

CHICKEN SPAGHETTI CASSEROLE

1 1/4 c. spaghetti
1/2 lb. grated sharp cheese
1 3/4 c. diced cooked chicken
1/4 c. diced pimento
1/4 c. diced green pepper
1/4 c. diced onion
1 can cream of chicken soup
1/2 c. chicken broth
1/2 tsp. salt

Cook spaghetti according to package directions; drain. Reserve 1/2 cup cheese for topping. Combine remaining cheese, chicken, pimento, green pepper, onion, soup, broth, and salt, mixing well. Toss with spaghetti. Turn into greased baking dish. Top with reserved cheese. Bake at 350 degrees for 1 hour. Yield: 8-10 servings.

Virginia Docking
International Honorary Member, BSP
Topeka, Kansas

CHICKEN AND OLIVES IN CREAM

1/4 c. butter or margarine
3 boned chicken breasts, skinned
   and split
Salt and white pepper to taste
1/4 c. chicken broth
1/4 c. dry vermouth
1 c. heavy cream
1/3 c. sliced pimento-stuffed olives
2 tbsp. chopped parsley
Hot cooked rice or noodles

Heat butter in large skillet with heat-proof handle until melted and foaming decreases. Add chicken pieces, turning to coat on all sides. Cook until lightly browned. Sprinkle with salt and pepper; cover skillet with greased waxed paper. Bake at 400 degrees for 6 to 8 minutes or until chicken is firm to touch. Remove chicken; place on serving platter. Keep warm. Add broth and vermouth to butter in skillet; boil until syrupy. Stir in cream and olives; simmer, stirring, until thickened. Season with salt and pepper.

Pour sauce over chicken. Sprinkle with parsley; garnish with additional sliced olives if desired. Serve with rice or noodles.

CHICKEN BREASTS DELUXE

6 chicken breasts
2 c. sour cream
1/2 c. lemon juice
4 tsp. Worcestershire sauce
4 tsp. celery salt
2 tsp. paprika
4 cloves of garlic, chopped
4 tsp. salt
1/2 tsp. pepper
1 3/4 c. bread crumbs
1/2 c. margarine
1/2 c. shortening

Divide chicken breasts in half. Combine sour cream, lemon juice, Worcestershire sauce, celery salt, paprika, garlic, salt, and pepper in large bowl, mixing well. Marinate chicken in sour cream mixture in refrigerator, covered, overnight. Preheat oven to 350 degrees. Remove chicken from sour cream mixture.

Roll in crumbs, coating evenly. Arrange in single layer in large shallow baking pan. Melt margarine and shortening in small saucepan. Spoon half the margarine mixture over chicken. Bake for 45 minutes. Spoon remaining margarine mixture over chicken. Bake for 10 minutes or until tender and browned. Yield: 12 servings.

Joyce Angela Garthune, Pres., Xi Beta X290
Winchester, Virginia

HANNIBAL'S BARBECUED CHICKEN

3   3-lb. fryers, cut in half
Salt to taste
1 c. fresh lemon juice
1/4 c. vinegar
1/2 c. melted butter
Pinch of thyme
1/4 c. Worcestershire sauce

Place chickens on grill over low coals; cook for about 30 minutes, turning occasionally. Mix remaining ingredients. Cook chickens for 30 to 45 minutes longer or until done, brushing with sauce and turning frequently.

Photograph for this recipe on page 85.

CHICKEN STROGANOFF

1 c. flour
1 tbsp. salt
1 tbsp. paprika
2 tsp. poultry seasoning
1/2 tsp. pepper
2   3-lb. chickens, disjointed
1/4 c. butter
1 lb. fresh mushrooms, halved
   and sliced
1/2 c. chicken broth
2 c. sour cream
Chopped parsley

Combine flour and seasonings, mixing well. Coat chicken with flour mixture. Reserve remaining flour mixture. Melt butter in skillet. Brown chicken, adding butter, if necessary. Remove from skillet. Saute mushrooms in pan drippings for 8 minutes or until tender. Remove from skillet; drain. Pour pan drippings into baking dish. Arrange chicken, skin side up, in dish. Bake at 350 degrees for 30 minutes or until tender and browned. Place chicken on serving platter; keep warm. Drain off all but 3 tablespoons drippings. Blend in 3 tablespoons reserved seasoned flour. Add broth gradually, stirring until blended. Cook over low heat, stirring constantly, until thickened and bubbly. Cook for 2 minutes longer. Add mushrooms; cook for 1 minute, stirring constantly. Stir in sour cream. Pour over chicken. Sprinkle with parsley. Yield: 8 servings.

Susan Berryman, VP, Xi Eta Psi X2078
San Jose, California

TOMATO ASPIC

1 pkg. lemon gelatin
1 pkg. orange gelatin
2   8-oz. cans tomato sauce
3 tbsp. vinegar
1 tsp. celery salt
1 tsp. onion juice
1/2 tsp. sugar

Dissolve gelatins in 2 cups hot water; stir in remaining ingredients. Pour into lightly oiled fluted mold; chill until firm. Unmold onto plate; garnish with lettuce. Serve as accompaniment with poultry.

CHICKEN BREASTS SUPREME

6 chicken breasts
Margarine
2 boxes frozen broccoli spears,
   thawed
3 cans cream of mushroom soup
1 c. mayonnaise
Grated sharp Cheddar cheese

Brown chicken in small amount of margarine in skillet. Place broccoli spears in 13 x 9-inch baking pan; place chicken over broccoli. Combine soup and mayonnaise; pour over chicken. Top with cheese. Bake at 350 degrees for 1 hour or until tender and browned. Yield: 6 servings.

Karren L. Smith, Prog. Chm., Beta No. 573
Reno, Nevada

FIVE-CAN CASSEROLE

1 can cream of chicken soup
1 can mushroom soup
1 sm. can evaporated milk
1 can Chinese noodles
1 can boned chicken
Potato chips, crushed

Combine soups and milk in bowl, mixing well. Pour layer of soup mixture into greased casserole. Add layer of noodles; top noodles with layer of chicken. Repeat layers until all ingredients are used. Sprinkle potato chips over top. Bake at 350 degrees for 1 hour.

Myrtle E. Miller
International Honorary Member, BSP
Saint Joseph, Missouri

CHICKEN SAUCE ORIENTAL

1/4 tsp. ginger
1 clove of garlic, crushed
1 tsp. salt
3/4 tsp. monosodium glutamate
4 tsp. sugar
4 tsp. soy sauce
1/2 tsp. vinegar
1/2 tsp. brandy
1 tsp. oil
1/2 tsp. oyster sauce
2 lb. sectioned chicken wings,
   tips removed
1/2 c. flour
1/4 tsp. pepper

Combine ginger, garlic, 1/2 teaspoon salt, 1/4 teaspoon monosodium glutamate, sugar, soy sauce, vinegar, brandy, oil, and oyster sauce; mix well. Marinate chicken in ginger mixture for 4 hours. Drain chicken. Combine flour, remaining salt and monosodium glutamate, and pepper in shallow dish; blend well. Coat chicken with flour mixture. Fry in hot deep fat at 375 degrees until lightly browned.

Penny Y. Dunn, Pres., Theta No. 7712
Ponce, Puerto Rico

CHICKEN WITH SNOW PEAS

3 fryer chicken breasts
1   1 lb. 4 1/2-oz. can pineapple
   chunks
1 chicken bouillon cube
1/4 c. butter
1   5-oz. can water chestnuts,
   drained
1 c. diagonally sliced celery
1 1/2 tsp. salt
1 tsp. monosodium glutamate
2 tbsp. chopped chives
1 tsp. dried leaf tarragon
1 pkg. frozen snow peas, thawed
2 tbsp. cornstarch
1   4-oz. can diced pimentos

Bone and skin chicken breasts; cut into thin strips. Drain pineapple; reserve 1/2 cup syrup. Combine reserved syrup, 3/4 cup water and bouillon cube. Place butter in electric skillet; turn to high setting. Add chicken; cook, stirring constantly, for 3 minutes. Slice water chestnuts into thin slices. Add celery, water chestnuts, salt, monosodium glutamate, chives, and tarragon to chicken; mix thoroughly. Cook for 2 minutes, stirring constantly. Add pineapple, syrup mixture, and snow peas, blending well.

Bring to a boil. Reduce to medium heat. Cook, covered, for 4 minutes. Combine cornstarch and 1/4 cup cold water, blending well. Add to chicken mixture; cook, stirring constantly, until thickened and bubbly. Stir in pimentos. Serve over rice. Yield: 4-6 servings.

Barbara S. Kelly, Pres.
Beta Beta No. 1830, Denver, Colorado

CORNISH CURRY

1 1-lb. 1-oz. can whole apricots
2 fresh or frozen Rock Cornish hens
1/4 c. soft butter
1 6-oz. package curry rice
1/4 c. melted butter
1/2 c. sliced onion
1/2 c. sliced celery
2 tbsp. flour
1 tsp. curry powder
1 c. water
2 chicken bouillon cubes

1/4 c. medium pitted ripe olives
Parsley

Drain apricots; reserve 1/2 cup syrup. Thaw frozen hens; remove giblets. Split hens; place in 13 x 9-inch baking pan, skin side up. Brush with butter. Bake in preheated 350-degree oven for 1 hour to 1 hour and 15 minutes or until fork-tender, basting occasionally with remaining butter. Bake rice in 1 1/2-quart covered casserole according to package directions while hens are baking. Place melted butter in saucepan; saute onion and celery in butter until almost tender. Stir in flour and curry powder; remove from heat. Stir in water and reserved syrup gradually. Add bouillon cubes; cook, stirring constantly, until mixture thickens and cubes melt. Cook for 2 minutes longer. Add apricots and olives; heat to serving temperature. Arrange rice, hens, apricots and olives on heated platter; spoon some sauce over all. Garnish with parsley; serve with remaining sauce. Yield: 4 servings.

CHICKEN BREASTS WITH PILAF

4 whole broiler-fryer chicken
  breasts
Salt and pepper to taste
1/2 c. butter or margarine
1/2 tsp. dried leaf tarragon
1/4 tsp. dried thyme
2 tbsp. flour
1 1/2 c. chicken broth

Halve chicken breasts; sprinkle with salt and pepper. Heat butter in large skillet; stir in herbs. Add chicken breasts; cook for about 25 to 30 minutes, until brown on both sides and tender. Remove chicken breasts; keep warm. Blend flour into drippings in skillet; add broth gradually. Cook, stirring constantly, until mixture thickens and comes to a boil.

Pilaf

4 tbsp. butter or margarine
1/2 c. slivered almonds
1 6-oz. can sliced mushrooms
1 1/2 c. diced celery
3 chicken bouillon cubes
1/2 tsp. salt
1 1/2 c. rice
Frosted Grapes

Melt butter in heavy skillet; add almonds. Saute until lightly browned. Drain mushrooms, reserving juice. Add enough water to reserved juice to make 3 cups liquid. Add mushroom liquid, celery, bouillon cubes, and salt to skillet; bring to a boil. Add rice gradually; cover. Reduce heat; simmer for 15 to 25 minutes or until rice is tender and liquid is absorbed. Fluff with fork; add mushrooms. Mound rice mixture on heated serving platter; surround with chicken pieces. Spoon sauce over top. Garnish with Frosted Grapes.

Frosted Grapes

White seedless grape clusters
Unbeaten egg white
Sugar

Dip grape clusters into egg white; shake to remove excess. Roll in sugar. Chill.

CHICKEN YUM-YUM

1   8-oz. bottle Russian salad
      dressing
1 env. dry onion soup mix
1   10-oz. jar pineapple and
      apricot preserves
1/4 tsp. curry powder
2 broiler-fryer chickens,
      disjointed

Combine Russian dressing, soup mix, preserves, and curry powder in small bowl; mix well. Place chickens in single layer, skin side up, in large shallow baking dish. Pour dressing mixture over chickens. Bake at 325 degrees, basting occasionally with pan drippings, for 1 hour and 30 minutes or until tender. Yield: 6-8 servings.

Gay Quoidbach Barrett
International Honorary Member, BSP
Longview, Washington

CHICKEN BAKE FOR TWELVE

8 oz. medium noodles
1/2 c. butter
3 1/2 c. milk
1/4 c. flour
1/2 tsp. salt
1/8 tsp. white pepper
2   10 3/4-oz. cans chicken gravy
4 c. diced cooked chicken
2 tbsp. chopped pimento
1/2 c. fine dry bread crumbs
1 1/2 tbsp. melted butter
1/2 c. American cheese, grated

Cook noodles according to package directions; drain. Add 2 tablespoons butter and 1/2 cup milk; mix well. Melt remaining butter in kettle. Blend in flour, salt, and white pepper. Add remaining milk all at once. Cook, stirring constantly, until mixture is thickened and bubbly. Stir in chicken gravy, chicken, pimento, and noodles, mixing well. Spread in 13 x 9 x 2-inch baking dish. Bake,

covered, at 350 degrees for 25 minutes. Combine bread crumbs and melted butter; blend in cheese. Sprinkle around edges of baking dish; bake for 10 minutes longer. Yield: 12 servings.

Maxine M. Johnson, XI Nu X1943
Charleston, South Carolina

CHICKEN WING APPETIZERS

16 chicken wings
3/4 c. dry bread crumbs
1/4 c. grated Parmesan cheese
1 1/2 tbsp. dried parsley
1/2 tsp. garlic salt
1/3 c. melted butter

Preheat oven to 350 degrees. Disjoint wings, discarding tips. Combine crumbs, cheese, parsley, and salt; mix well. Dip wings in butter; roll in crumb mixture. Place in lightly greased shallow pan. Bake for 18 minutes. Increase oven temperature to 450 degrees. Bake for 15 minutes or until lightly browned. Yield: 32 servings.

Anne M. Peitzmeier, Past Pres.
Beta Alpha No. 574, Boone, Iowa

YAKITORI

1/2 c. soy sauce
1/4 c. mirin, honey, or sweet sherry
2 or 3 tbsp. sugar
2 tsp. cornstarch
3 green onions
3 green peppers, seeded
3 boned chicken breasts, cubed

Mix first 3 ingredients; bring to a boil over low heat. Simmer for 5 minutes. Mix cornstarch with small amount of water; stir into sugar mixture. Cook until thickened; remove from heat. Cut onions and green peppers into bite-sized pieces. Arrange chicken, onion, and green pepper pieces alternately on bamboo skewers; marinate in sauce for at least 1 hour. Place in broiler pan. Broil for about 7 minutes on each side or until done.

Carolyn B. Genshock, Corr. and Rec. Sec.
Omicron Rho No. 4521, Costa Mesa, California

ITALIAN MEATBALL SPAGHETTI

3/4 c. chopped fresh onions
1 tsp. garlic salt
2 lb. fresh tomatoes, chopped
2 6-oz. cans tomato paste
1 tbsp. sugar
1 1/2 tsp. salt
1/2 tsp. pepper
1 bay leaf
1 1/2 tsp. crushed oregano
Meatballs
1 lb. spaghetti, cooked

Cook onions with garlic salt in small amount of hot fat in skillet until tender, but not brown. Combine 1 cup water, tomatoes tomato paste, sugar, salt, pepper, bay leaf, and oregano; add to onions. Simmer for 45 minutes; remove bay leaf. Drop Meatballs into simmering sauce; cook for 15 minutes. Serve sauce and Meatballs over spaghetti.

Meatballs

1 lb. ground beef
1 c. dry bread crumbs
1/2 c. grated Parmesan cheese
1 tbsp. chopped fresh parsley
1 tsp. garlic salt
1/2 c. milk
2 eggs, beaten
1/2 tsp. salt
Dash of pepper

Combine all ingredients; shape into balls. Brown in small amount of hot fat in skillet.

CHICKEN LIVER PÂTÉ TURNOVERS

3 green onions, chopped
1 tbsp. butter
1/2 lb. chicken livers
1/3 c. chicken broth

3 tbsp. white wine
3/4 tsp. salt
1/8 tsp. pepper
Dash of cayenne pepper
Dash of nutmeg
Dash of allspice
1/4 c. melted butter
1/4 c. heavy cream
1 c. finely chopped toasted
    walnuts
1 recipe 2-crust pie pastry

Saute onions in butter until soft but not browned. Add chicken livers; brown lightly. Add broth, wine, salt, pepper, cayenne pepper, and spices, mixing well. Simmer for 10 minutes or until pink color disappears from livers. Turn liver mixture into blender; blend until smooth. Add melted butter and cream; blend well. Pour into mixing bowl; cool. Stir in walnuts. Roll pastry in thin layer on floured surface. Cut into 2 1/2-inch squares. Place scant teaspoon liver mixture onto each square; moisten edges, folding to make triangle. Seal edges securely. Prick top generously. Place on cookie sheet. Bake at 425 degrees for 10 minutes or until browned. Yield: 6 dozen.

Marcheta Fritz, Pres.
Xi Gamma Alpha X2782, Pontiac, Michigan

COQ AU VIN

2   2 1/4-lb. frying chickens
Salt to taste
White pepper to taste
1/4 c. margarine
1 c. burgundy
2 c. brown sauce
10 sm. canned white onions
8 fresh sm. mushroom caps
8 med. boiled potatoes
3 bread slices

Quarter chickens; remove backbones. Season lightly with salt and white pepper. Saute chicken in margarine in large skillet until lightly browned. Remove chicken; pour off excess fat. Pour burgundy into skillet; bring to a boil. Cook until burgundy is reduced to 1/2 cup. Stir in brown sauce; add chicken. Simmer until chicken is tender. Saute onions and mushrooms in additional margarine in skillet until mushrooms are tender; drain. Add onions, mushrooms, and potatoes to chicken mixture. Cut bread slices into 1-inch squares. Place on cookie sheet. Bake at 400 degrees until lightly browned. Sprinkle over chicken. Heat through over low heat. Yield: 4 servings.

Mrs. Kathy Fleps, W and M Chm.
Theta Gamma No. 3386, Cleveland, Ohio

BREAST OF CHICKEN PAPRIKA IN CHAMPAGNE

3 chicken breasts
3 tbsp. paprika
Salt and pepper to taste
2 tbsp. chopped shallots
3/4 c. butter
1 pt. champagne
1 pkg. long grain and wild rice mix
1 1/2 c. chopped celery
1 1/2 c. sliced mushrooms
1   2-oz. jar sliced pimentos
1/2 c. chopped parsley
1 pkg. herb-seasoned stuffing mix
1 c. chicken broth or bouillon

Split breasts in half and remove skin. Sprinkle with paprika and salt and pepper. Arrange in casserole. Add shallots, 1/4 cup butter, and champagne. Bake, covered, at 350 degrees for 45 minutes. Remove chicken; place on platter, keeping warm. Prepare rice according to package directions. Saute celery and mushrooms in remaining butter in skillet for 2 minutes. Add pimentos and parsley, mixing well. Stir in rice and stuffing mix. Add broth, mixing well. Place rice mixture in casserole; top with chicken. Reduce oven temperature to 325 degrees. Bake, covered, until heated through. Remove cover. Bake for 10 minutes or until browned.

Ann Roach, Pres., Preceptor Beta XP185
White Rock, New Mexico

RED SNAPPER WITH CORN BREAD STUFFING

1 3 to 4-lb. red snapper, dressed
2 c. cornmeal
Butter
3 med. onions, chopped
Salt and pepper to taste
2 eggs, beaten
3 slices salt pork

Place snapper in shallow baking pan. Combine cornmeal, 1/2 cup melted butter, onions, salt, pepper, and eggs in bowl; mix well. Stuff into snapper; place salt pork over snapper. Cover. Bake at 375 degrees for 1 hour. Uncover; bake until brown. Snapper may be wrapped in foil before baking, if desired.

CREAM OF CHICKEN MARENGO

1/4 lb. mushrooms
1/4 c. dry white wine
2 cloves of garlic
1/4 c. flour
1/4 tsp. pepper
1/2 tsp. rosemary
2 med. tomatoes, quartered
1 lg. onion, quartered
1/4 c. parsley sprigs
1 1/2 tsp. salt
1/4 tsp. dry tarragon

1/2 c. butter
4 lb. chicken pieces

Remove stems from mushrooms; reserve caps. Place mushroom stems, wine, garlic, flour, pepper, rosemary, tomatoes, onion, parsley, salt, and tarragon in blender container. Blend, covered, at high speed for 40 seconds, stopping to stir down, if necessary. Melt butter in skillet. Saute chicken in butter until browned. Pour sauce and mushroom caps over chicken. Simmer, covered, for 50 minutes or until tender, stirring occasionally. Serve with rice. Yield: 6-8 servings.

Faye Taylor, Alpha Omicron No. 3024
Suffolk, Virginia

PICK-UP CHICKEN STICKS

3 lb. chicken wings
1 c. butter or margarine
1 1/2 c. sifted flour
1/3 c. sesame seed
1 tbsp. salt
1/2 tsp. ground ginger

Cut off tips of wings and discard. Cut each wing in half through joint; wash and drain. Melt butter in large, shallow baking pan. Mix flour, sesame seed, salt, and ginger in pie plate. Roll chicken pieces in butter; roll in flour mixture to coat generously. Arrange in single layer, not touching, in butter in baking pan. Bake in 350-degree oven for 1 hour or until tender. Broil for 3 to 5 minutes to brown.

Frances Reck, Pres.
Omicron Epsilon No. 7089, Cincinnati, Ohio

CHICKEN LIVERS AND AVOCADO IN SOUR CREAM

1/4 c. chopped onion
1/4 c. chopped green pepper
1 clove of garlic
1/2 lb. chicken livers
2 tbsp. butter
1 sm. avocado, diced
3/4 c. sour cream

1/2 tsp. Worcestershire sauce
2 slices cooked bacon, crumbled
1/2 tsp. paprika
Salt and pepper to taste

Saute onion, green pepper, garlic, and livers in butter for 10 minutes or until livers lose pink color and are tender. Remove garlic. Add avocado; heat through. Stir in sour cream. Add Worcestershire sauce, bacon, paprika, and salt and pepper, blending well. Serve on hot buttered toast rounds.

Joyce Fry, Preceptor Gamma XP238
Billings, Montana

CHICKEN INDIENNE

1/4 c. butter
1   3-lb. chicken, disjointed
1 onion, coarsely chopped
1 green pepper, coarsely chopped
2 tbsp. lemon juice
2 c. chicken stock
1 1/3 c. prepared mincemeat
1 tsp. salt
Dash of pepper
1 c. rice
1 tbsp. curry powder

Melt butter in large skillet. Brown chicken in butter; remove from skillet. Saute onion and green pepper in pan drippings until transparent. Add lemon juice, chicken stock, mincemeat, salt, pepper, rice, and curry powder; mix thoroughly. Turn mixture into buttered 2 1/2-quart casserole. Arrange chicken pieces over rice mixture. Bake, covered, in 350-degree oven for 1 hour or until tender. Yield: 6 servings.

Mrs. Welthy Fisher
International Honorary Member, BSP
Southbury, Connecticut

INDIA CHICKEN CURRY

1   3-lb. fryer, disjointed
4 tbsp. butter
1 med. onion, chopped
1 clove of garlic, minced
1 tbsp. curry powder
2 tsp. ground ginger
1 tsp. ground cumin
1 tsp. ground coriander
1   1-lb. can tomatoes
1 c. peeled chopped apple
2 c. chicken broth
1 tsp. salt
Cooked rice

Wash and dry chicken; remove skin. Cook chicken in butter in skillet until golden brown; remove from skillet. Combine onion, garlic, spices, tomatoes, and apple in blender container; blend until smooth. Mix with chicken broth and salt in skillet; simmer for about 5 minutes. Add chicken; cover. Simmer for about 40 minutes or until tender. Serve with rice and condiments of salted peanuts, flaked coconut, chopped green onion, and crumbled bacon. Three pounds chicken breasts may be used instead of fryer. Yield: 6 servings.

Emily Douglas, Xi Iota No. 986
Bentonville, Arkansas

TAK GUI

2 lb. chicken drumsticks
1/2 c. sugar
3/4 c. soy sauce
2 tsp. ginger
1 clove of garlic, minced
1/4 tsp. pepper
1/2 tsp. paprika
1/2 tsp. chili powder

Remove skins from drumsticks. Sprinkle drumsticks with sugar; let stand for 30 minutes. Combine remaining ingredients; pour over chicken, turning to coat well. Let stand for 1 hour. Drain drumsticks; reserve marinade. Place in baking dish. Bake at 350 degrees for 45 minutes to 1 hour, basting with reserved marinade occasionally. Serve with rice. Spareribs may be substituted for drumsticks.

Lynn L. Beko, Pres.
Delta Delta Kappa No. 7924
Seal Beach, California

MANDARIN CHICKEN

2 tbsp. flour
2 tbsp. oil
1/2 c. barbecue sauce
1/2 c. orange juice
1/4 c. (packed) brown sugar
1/4 tsp. salt
4 c. chopped cooked chicken
1 13 1/2-oz. can pineapple chunks,
    drained
1/2 can water chestnuts, sliced
1/2 c. slivered almonds (opt.)
1 tsp. chopped candied ginger
Cooked rice

Mix flour and oil. Add barbecue sauce, orange juice, sugar, and salt; cook until mixture boils and thickens, stirring constantly. Add remaining ingredients except rice; cover. Simmer for 10 minutes. Serve over rice.

Annette Copeland, Ext. Off., Xi Nu Psi Chap.
Dallas, Texas

ROAST TURKEY WITH TROPICAL RICE STUFFING

1 13 1/2-oz. can pineapple
    tidbits
1 10 1/2-oz. can chicken consomme
1 c. rice
1 5-oz. can water chestnuts
1/4 c. butter, melted
1/2 c. chopped green onion
1/2 c. thinly sliced celery
1 tbsp. soy sauce
1 10-lb. turkey
Salt and pepper to taste

Drain syrup from pineapple; combine with consomme. Add enough water to make 2 cups liquid. Pour into saucepan. Stir in rice; heat to boiling point. Cover; cook for 15 minutes or until liquid is absorbed and rice is tender. Mix in pineapple lightly. Drain and slice water chestnuts; stir into rice mixture. Add butter, onion, celery and soy sauce; toss well. Pat turkey cavity dry with paper toweling, leaving outside moist. Sprinkle cavity

with salt and pepper. Stuff rice mixture into neck and body cavity of turkey. Fasten neck skin to body with skewer. Push legs under band of skin at tail. Place turkey, breast side up, in shallow roasting pan. Cover with loose tent of aluminum foil if desired. Bake at 325 degrees for 4 hours and 30 minutes. Let stand for 15 to 20 minutes for easier carving. Place on serving platter; garnish with pineapple slices, grape clusters and holly.

CORNISH HENS ON WILD RICE MINGLE

1/4 c. butter
1/2 c. chopped celery
1 4-oz. can sliced mushrooms,
    drained
2 pkg. long grain and wild
    rice mix
2 1 3/8-oz. envelopes onion
    soup mix
4 Rock Cornish hens
Salt

Preheat oven to 400 degrees. Melt 2 tablespoons butter in skillet. Saute celery and mushrooms in butter until tender. Add rice; saute until lightly browned. Spread rice mixture in roasting pan. Combine onion soup mix and 3 1/2 cups boiling water; pour over rice mixture. Rub cavities of hens with salt. Place hens on rice mixture. Rub hens with remaining butter. Bake for 50 minutes or until browned and tender, basting with pan liquids occasionally. Yield: 4-8 servings.

Alice Lawlor, Xi Epsilon Nu X1604
Pleasanton, California

DUCKLING FLAMBÉ

3 c. toasted bread cubes
2 c. finely diced celery
1 tbsp. grated orange peel
2/3 c. diced orange sections
3/4 tsp. salt
1/2 tsp. poultry seasoning
Dash of pepper
1 egg, beaten
1/4 c. melted butter or margarine
1 5-lb. duckling

Mix bread cubes, celery, orange peel, orange sections, salt, poultry seasoning, and pepper. Combine egg and butter; add to bread mixture, tossing lightly. Place in cavity of duckling; place in baking pan. Bake at 325 degrees for 2 hours to 2 hours and 30 minutes. Place duck on serving platter.

Sauce

1/2 c. white wine
2 lumps sugar
2 tsp. vinegar
1 c. brown gravy
Juice of 1 orange
Juice of 1 lemon
Salt
Rind of 1 orange, cut in thin strips
2 tbsp. rum or brandy

Pour off excess fat from roasting pan. Add wine, sugar, and vinegar to pan; cook, stirring, for several minutes. Stir in brown gravy, fruit juices and salt to taste. Add orange peel and rum; ignite. Let flame burn out. Pour sauce over duck; serve hot. Ignite again at table, if desired, using 2 more tablespoons of rum.

Sarah Dabdoub, W and M Chm.
Preceptor Beta XP282, New Orleans, Louisiana

PORK

STUFFED PORK ROAST

1 pkg. herb-seasoned stuffing mix
1 3 1/2 to 4-lb. boneless
pork loin

Prepare stuffing mix according to package directions. Cut the loin lengthwise to within 1 inch of other side. Place stuffing in center of loin lengthwise. Fold loin over; tie securely with string. Place in roasting pan; add 2 cups water. Cover. Bake at 325 degrees for 2 hours. Uncover; bake until brown, basting occasionally. Serve with baked apples.

Photograph for this recipe on page 88.

APPETIZER HAM BALL

2 4 1/2-oz. cans deviled ham
3 tbsp. chopped stuffed green
olives
1 tbsp. prepared mustard
Hot sauce to taste
1 3-oz. package cream cheese,
softened
2 tbsp. milk

Combine deviled ham, olives, mustard, and hot sauce in mixing bowl. Blend thoroughly. Shape into a ball. Place on serving dish; chill. Combine cream cheese and milk, mixing well; frost ball with mixture. Chill; remove from refrigerator 15 minutes before serving. Garnish with parsley. Serve with crackers. Yield: 8 servings.

Mrs. Carol A. Fenn, Prog. Chm.
Xi Mu Epsilon X2873, San Diego, California

FRENCH-STYLE MEAT PIE

2 med. potatoes
1/2 sm. onion
1 tbsp. celery leaves
1/4 lb. ground round beef
1 lb. fresh ground ham or pork
1/2 tsp. cinnamon
1/2 tsp. poultry seasoning
1/2 tsp. sweet basil
1/4 c. water
Salt and pepper to taste
Pastry for 4 pie crusts

Process potatoes, onion and celery leaves through food grinder; add ground meats, cinnamon, poultry seasoning, basil, and water. Simmer in saucepan over low heat until meat is partially cooked. Add salt and pepper. Prepare pie crusts using 1 tablespoon less shortening. Line 2 pie pans with bottom crusts; fill with meat mixture. Place top crusts over pies; prick with fork. Bake at 425 degrees for 15 minutes; reduce oven temperature to 350 degrees. Bake for 20 minutes longer.

Carol Overcast, Pres.
Xi Alpha Omicron X 1814, Yakima, Washington

PORK POLYNESIAN

1 No. 2 1/2 can pineapple
   chunks
1/3 c. vinegar
1/3 c. (packed) brown sugar
4 tsp. soy sauce
1/3 c. flour
1 1/2 tsp. salt
1/2 tsp. garlic salt
1/8 tsp. pepper
2 lb. boneless pork shoulder, cut
   into 1-in. cubes
2 tbsp. butter or margarine
1 med. green pepper, cut into
   thin strips
1 med. tomato, cut into thin
   wedges

Drain pineapple; reserve syrup. Combine reserved syrup, 1/2 cup water, vinegar, brown sugar, and soy sauce. Combine flour, salt, garlic salt, and pepper; dredge pork in flour mixture. Brown pork on all sides in butter in large skillet; add 1 cup syrup mixture. Simmer, covered, for 1 hour or until pork is tender. Add remaining syrup mixture; heat through. Add pineapple, green pepper, and tomato; mix carefully. Simmer for 3 minutes or until vegetables are just heated through. Serve with rice. Yield: 6 servings.

Freda Draper-Gerhardt
International Honorary Member, BSP
Dana Point, California

SAFFRON CREAMED HAM WITH SEASONED RICE

3 cans cream of chicken soup
1/4 tsp. powdered saffron
Beer
1 8-oz. can sliced mushrooms,
   drained
4 c. cooked ham, cubed
1/2 c. chopped pimento
1/2 c. sliced ripe olives
3 tbsp. butter
1 lg. green pepper, chopped
2 sm. onions, chopped
1 tbsp. salt
2 1/4 c. rice
1/2 c. melted butter
1/2 tsp. ground cloves

Combine soup, saffron, and 1 cup beer in large bowl; blend well. Add mushrooms, ham, pimento, and olives, stirring to blend. Place butter in large skillet; melt. Saute green pepper and onions in butter until soft. Add ham mixture, stirring thoroughly. Bring to a boil; remove from heat, keeping hot. Combine 1 quart water, 1 quart beer, and salt in large kettle. Bring to a boil. Add rice gradually to boiling mixture. Cook until tender; drain. Stir melted butter and cloves into rice. Serve ham mixture over rice. Yield: 12 servings.

Julie Imo, Pres., Kappa Beta No. 7019
Saint Louis, Missouri

LOUISIANA YAMS AND HAM BALLS

1 1/2 lb. ground ham
1 c. soft bread crumbs
1 egg, slightly beaten
1 med. onion, finely chopped
1/8 tsp. pepper
1/4 c. butter or margarine
1 1/2 tbsp. prepared mustard
3/4 c. (firmly packed) brown sugar
3/4 c. vinegar
1 1/2 c. water
3   1-lb. cans Louisiana yams,
     drained
1 1/2 tbsp. cornstarch

Combine ham, crumbs, egg, onion and pepper; mix well. Shape into 18 balls. Melt butter in large chafing dish. Add ham balls; cook over low heat until browned on all sides. Discard pan drippings. Combine mustard, brown sugar, vinegar and 1 1/4 cups water. Add to ham balls. Add yams; cook, covered, over low heat for 15 minutes. Remove yams and ham balls from chafing dish. Blend cornstarch with remaining water; add to sauce. Bring to a boil, stirring constantly. Return yams and ham balls to sauce in chafing dish; keep warm over water.

HAM ROLLS

1/4 c. mayonnaise
1 tsp. salad seasoning
8 slices boiled ham
1 can asparagus tips

Combine mayonnaise and salad seasoning in mixing bowl; blend well. Spread ham slices with mayonnaise mixture. Place 3 asparagus spears in center of each ham slice. Roll up; secure with wooden pick. Place rolls on broiler pan. Broil for 5 minutes 5 inches from source of heat; turn. Broil for 3 minutes longer or until heated through. Cut into bite-sized pieces to serve. Yield: 20-24 servings.

Dorothy Daenzer, Rec. Sec.
Xi Delta Mu No. 1617, Fort Worth, Texas

HUNGARIAN GOULASH

1 1/2 lb. onions
1 1/2 lb. lean pork shoulder
1 1/2 lb. beef stew meat
1 tbsp. paprika
Salt to taste
1 6-oz. can tomato paste
1/2 lg. green pepper, sliced
1 c. stock or water
1 tsp. caraway seed
1 1-lb. can sauerkraut
1/2 pt. sour cream

Peel onions; cut into quarters. Brown onions in 2 tablespoons fat in skillet. Cut pork and beef into bite-sized pieces; add to onions. Stir in paprika and salt. Cook for about 30 minutes, adding water as necessary. Add tomato paste, green pepper, stock, and caraway seed. Cover; simmer for at least 1 hour or until meat is tender. Stir in sauerkraut; heat through. Spoon sour cream over top. Serve. Yield: 6-8 servings.

Ingeburg Helm, Pres.
Xi Epsilon Theta X1568, Placerville, California

BITE-SIZED PORK TURNOVERS

1 lb. mushrooms, sliced
2 onions, thinly sliced
Salt and pepper to taste
1 tbsp. cooking oil
1 lb. pork, coarsely ground
Cayenne pepper to taste
Fennel seed to taste (opt.)
1 1-lb. can tomatoes
2 lb. bread dough

Saute mushrooms and onions with salt and pepper in oil in skillet for 7 minutes or until tender and lightly browned; remove to large bowl. Saute pork with additional salt and pepper, cayenne pepper, and fennel seed for 10 minutes or until tender; add to onion mixture. Saute tomatoes, breaking with fork, for 8 minutes or until thickened. Add tomatoes to pork mixture; blend well. Cool. Roll out dough; cut into 3-inch squares. Place 1 teaspoonful pork mixture on side of each square. Fold squares over; seal edges. Place turnovers on greased baking sheet. Bake at 400 degrees for 25 minutes or until golden. Brush tops with additional oil before baking if desired.

Anne J. Cataldo, Prog. Chm.
Xi Alpha Chap., Barrington, Rhode Island

HAM TURNOVERS

1/2 c. margarine, softened
4 oz. cream cheese, softened
1 c. flour
3/4 c. ground cooked ham
2 tbsp. catsup
1 1/2 tsp. mustard
1/2 tsp. Worcestershire sauce
1 tsp. minced onion
Dash of hot sauce

Combine margarine and cream cheese in bowl; blend thoroughly. Add flour, mixing well until mixture clings together. Shape into a ball. Roll out on floured surface. Cut into 2-inch circles. Combine ham, catsup, mustard, Worcestershire sauce, onion, and hot sauce. Mix thoroughly. Spoon ham mixture onto 1/2 of each circle. Fold pastry over, sealing edge with fork. Place on cookie sheet. Bake at 400 degrees for 8 minutes or until browned. Serve hot. Yield: 50 turnovers.

Karen Harkness, VP, Iota Eta Chap.
Columbia, Missouri

PRIZE TOURTIÈRE

1 1/2 lb. ground pork
1 med. onion, minced
1 1/2 tsp. salt
1/2 tsp. thyme
1/2 tsp. sage
1/2 tsp. dry mustard
1/8 tsp. cloves
2 lg. potatoes, mashed
1 recipe 2-crust pie pastry

Combine pork, onion, salt, thyme, sage, mustard, and cloves with 1/2 cup water in saucepan; mix well. Bring to a boil; reduce heat. Simmer for 30 minutes; remove from heat. Stir in potatoes; chill well. Roll out half the pastry; line 9-inch pie pan. Spoon pork mixture into shell. Roll out remaining pastry; arrange over filling. Turn edge under; seal and flute. Cut steam vents in top crust. Bake at 425 degrees for 30 minutes or until golden.

Rae Rowan, Soc. Chm., Xi Zeta X2894
Dartmouth, Nova Scotia, Canada

SAUSAGE-APPLE RING WITH CHEESE-SCRAMBLED EGGS

2 lb. bulk sausage
1 1/2 c. cracker crumbs
2 eggs, slightly beaten
1/2 c. milk
1/4 c. minced onion
1 c. finely chopped apple
Cheese-scrambled eggs
Paprika

Combine sausage, crumbs, eggs, milk, onion, and apple in bowl; mix thoroughly with fork. Press lightly into greased 6-cup ring mold. Turn out into shallow baking pan. Bake at 350 degrees for about 1 hour. Drain excess fat from pan. Place on serving platter. Fill center of sausage ring with eggs. Sprinkle eggs with paprika. Garnish platter with apricot halves and parsley, if desired. Yield: 8 servings.

Jeanne M. Roy, W and M Chm., Eta Mu No. 6490
Overland Park, Kansas

SAUSAGE-CHEESE BALLS

1 lb. hot sausage
1/2 lb. sharp Cheddar cheese, shredded
1 1/2 c. prepared biscuit mix
1/2 c. milk

Combine sausage and cheese, mixing well. Combine biscuit mix and milk, blending thoroughly. Add to sausage mixture; mix well. Chill for 30 minutes. Shape into small balls. Place on rack in broiler pan. Bake at 350 degrees for 15 minutes. Serve hot with wooden picks. Yield: 36 servings.

Betty Jo Wright, VP, Beta Nu No. 3342
Kingsport, Tennessee

ROAST PORK WITH SAUERKRAUT AND APPLE

1   3 1/2-lb. pork loin roast
Onion salt to taste
Marjoram to taste
Pepper to taste
1 qt. drained sauerkraut
2 red apples, thinly sliced
1/2 c. apple brandy
1 tbsp. light brown sugar
2 tbsp. butter

Sprinkle pork with onion salt, marjoram and pepper; secure on spit. Insert meat thermometer. Adjust spit about 8 inches from prepared coals, placing foil pan under pork to catch drippings. Bake for 15 to 20 minutes per pound or until meat thermometer registers 185 degrees. Place on heated serving platter; keep warm. Combine sauerkraut, apple slices, brandy, brown sugar and butter in skillet. Simmer, covered, for 5 minutes or until apples are tender. Spoon into serving dish. Garnish with additional apple slices and parsley. Serve with pork.

ZIPPY HOT APPETIZERS

1 10-oz. package brown and serve
   sausage links
1/2 c. (packed) light brown sugar
1/2 tsp. salt
1 tbsp. cornstarch
1 10-oz. can pineapple chunks
1/4 c. white vinegar
1/2 c. green pepper squares
1/2 c. maraschino cherries, drained

Cut sausage links into thirds, crosswise.
Brown lightly in skillet. Combine brown
sugar, salt, and cornstarch in chafing dish,
mixing well. Drain pineapple, reserving 1/2
cup juice. Combine reserved juice, vinegar,
and 1/2 cup water, blending well. Stir juice
mixture into cornstarch mixture. Bring to a
boil, stirring constantly; cook for 5 minutes
or until thickened. Add green pepper, cherries, pineapple, and sausage; mix. Serve hot
with wooden picks. Yield: 10-15 servings.

Marilyn E. Amato, Pres.
Alpha Alpha No. 1426, Spokane, Washington

BAKED SPARERIBS ALOHA

3 lb. country-style spareribs
Salt and pepper to taste
1/2 c. finely chopped green pepper
2 8-oz. cans tomato sauce
1 tbsp. Worcestershire sauce
1/3 c. vinegar
1 No. 2 can pineapple tidbits
1/4 c. (packed) brown sugar
1/2 tsp. dry mustard
1 can mushrooms

Cut spareribs into serving pieces; sprinkle
with salt and pepper. Place in shallow pan.
Bake at 450 degrees for 30 minutes. Pour off
excess fat; reduce oven temperature to 350
degrees. Mix remaining ingredients; pour
over ribs. Bake, basting frequently, for 1
hour and 30 minutes longer. Yield: 4
servings.

Mrs. Carol Boone, Hist.
Theta Mu No. 7862, Geneva, New York

FRUITED SPARERIBS

3 lb. spareribs
Salt and pepper to taste
2 jars jr. baby food peaches
   or apricots
1/2 c. catsup
1/2 c. vinegar
1/2 c. (packed) brown sugar
2 whole cloves
1 tsp. salt

Season spareribs with salt and pepper; place
on rack in broiler pan. Bake at 450 degrees
for 30 minutes. Cut spareribs into serving
pieces. Combine remaining ingredients; pour
over ribs. Bake at 350 degrees for 1 hour
longer, basting frequently with pan
drippings.

Rosemary G. Ordile, Sec.
Beta Beta No. 3811, Brigantine, New Jersey

SPICY BARBECUED SPARERIBS

3 lb. spareribs
Salt and pepper
2 tbsp. butter
1 med. onion, finely chopped
1/2 c. chopped celery
1 c. catsup
2 tbsp. vinegar
2 tbsp. lemon juice
2 tbsp. Worcestershire sauce
2 tbsp. (packed) brown sugar

Sprinkle spareribs with salt and pepper;
place in roasting pan with small amount of
water. Bake at 325 degrees for 3 hours; remove from oven. Drain off excess fat. Cut
spareribs into serving pieces; return to roasting pan. Melt butter in saucepan; brown
onion in butter. Combine remaining ingredients with 1 teaspoon salt and 1/2 teaspoon
pepper; mix well with onion. Simmer for 20
minutes; pour over spareribs. Return to
oven; heat through. Yield: 6 servings.

Mrs. J. Selby Walker
International Honorary Member, BSP
Calgary, Alberta, Canada

EASY BARBECUED SPARERIBS

1 tsp. pepper
8 tsp. brown sugar
2 tsp. paprika
1 c. chopped onions
8 tsp. Worcestershire sauce
8 tsp. vinegar
2 tsp. prepared mustard
2 tsp. celery salt
1 c. catsup
1 tbsp. cornstarch
1 1/2 tsp. hot sauce
4 lb. spareribs

Mix all ingredients except spareribs with 1 1/2 cups water; blend well. Cut spareribs into serving pieces; arrange in shallow baking pan. Pour sauce over spareribs. Bake, basting occasionally, at 300 degrees for 2 hours or until spareribs are tender.

Helen Beny Gibson
International Honorary Member, BSP
Medicine Hat, Alberta, Canada

SWEET AND SOUR PORK

2 lb. pork shoulder
1 egg, beaten
1/2 c. flour
2 c. cooking oil
1/3 c. (packed) brown sugar
1 c. vinegar
1/4 c. molasses
2 med. tomatoes, peeled and
   diced
2 tbsp. cornstarch
1/4 c. pineapple syrup
2 med. green peppers, cut into
   wide strips
2 c. drained pineapple chunks
1 tsp. salt
1/8 tsp. pepper

Cut pork into bite-sized cubes. Combine egg, flour and 1 cup water; mix well. Dip pork into batter; brown in oil in deep skillet for 8 minutes. Drain; keep warm. Combine brown sugar, vinegar, molasses, and 3/4 cup water in saucepan; mix well. Bring to a boil; reduce heat. Add tomatoes; simmer for 10 minutes. Blend cornstarch with pineapple syrup; add to tomato mixture gradually. Simmer, stirring constantly, until thickened. Add pork, green peppers, pineapple, salt, and pepper; heat through. Serve with rice. Yield: 4-6 servings.

Mrs. Joanne L. Peal, Gamma Zeta No. 6442
Westfield, New Jersey

BRAUNSCHWEIGER SPREAD

1 lb. braunschweiger
1 c. sour cream
1 pkg. dry onion soup mix
1 tbsp. Worcestershire sauce
Milk
1 8-oz. package cream cheese,
   softened
Dried parsley
Paprika to taste

Combine braunschweiger, sour cream, soup, Worcestershire sauce, and 2 tablespoons milk; mix well. Shape into mound; place on serving dish. Blend cream cheese and 3 tablespoons milk together; spread over braunschweiger mixture. Sprinkle with parsley and paprika. Serve with rye bread or crackers.

Linda Nealis, VP, Xi Mu X352
Marion, Indiana

POOR MAN'S PÂTE

1/2 lb. liverwurst
1/4 tsp. onion salt
1/2 tsp. celery salt
1 tsp. Dijon mustard
1 tsp. lemon juice
1/4 c. heavy cream
Dash of cayenne pepper

Mix liverwurst with pastry blender or fork until smooth. Add remaining ingredients, mixing well. Serve as dip or sandwich spread. Will keep for several days in refrigerator in covered jar.

Mrs. Victor Shaw
International Honorary Member, BSP
Fairmont, West Virginia

PICKLED BEEF TONGUE

1   4-lb. beef tongue
Salt
1 onion, sliced
6 cloves of garlic
1 bay leaf
1 c. wine vinegar
2 c. oil
Dash of cayenne pepper
1 tsp. pepper
1/2 c. chopped parsley
1   4-oz. can green chilies, chopped

Wash and trim tongue. Place tongue in water to cover in kettle; add 2 teaspoons salt, onion, 2 to 3 cloves of garlic, and bay leaf. Simmer for 3 to 4 hours or until tongue is tender; drain. Cool slightly; remove skin. Cut into thin slices. Combine vinegar, oil, remaining crushed garlic, 1 teaspoon salt, cayenne pepper, pepper, parsley, and chilies. Arrange layers of tongue slices and chilies mixture in casserole; refrigerate overnight. Yield: 10-12 servings.

Volina L. Leavell, Pres., Chi No. 3437
Yerington, Nevada

FRANKFURTER PARTY PLEASERS

1   1-lb. loaf frozen ready
    to bake bread
2   7-oz. packages cocktail
    frankfurters

Let bread stand at room temperature until thawed and soft. Roll bread dough out into 10 x 16-inch rectangle on lightly floured surface. Cut dough into 2-inch squares. Place 1 frankfurter on each square. Fold edges over; seal well. Place rolls on baking sheet in warm place; let rise until doubled in bulk. Bake at 400 degrees for 10 to 12 minutes. Serve hot with small bowls of catsup and mustard. Yield: 40 servings.

Linda Flatray, Xi Pi Xi X3818
Los Banos, California

SEAFOOD

APPETIZER ABALONE BALLS

2 c. minced abalone
1 tsp. minced onion
Salt and pepper to taste
Chopped parsley to taste
1 c. medium white sauce
1 egg, beaten
Cracker crumbs

Combine abalone, onion, salt, pepper, and parsley; mix well. Blend thoroughly with white sauce; chill well. Roll mixture into small balls. Dip balls into egg; roll in cracker crumbs. Fry in deep hot fat for 10 minutes or until golden; drain well.

Mrs. Jean Vincent, City Coun. Del.
Xi Kappa Psi X2690, Novato, California

SEAFOOD CREAM WITH AVOCADO HALVES

1 lb. fresh mushrooms, sliced
1 c. sliced onions
1 c. butter or margarine
2/3 c. flour
2 1/2 tsp. salt
1 tsp. monosodium glutamate
1/2 tsp. dry mustard
1/2 tsp. pepper
1/4 tsp. thyme leaves
5 c. milk
2 c. light cream
2 eggs, slightly beaten
2 c. grated Swiss cheese
8   7-oz. cans solid white tuna
1 c. sauterne
2 tsp. grated lemon peel
Lemon juice
6   5-oz. cans lobster, drained
2/3 c. chopped toasted blanched
    almonds
12 ripe avocados
Watercress

Saute mushrooms and onions in butter in saucepan until lightly browned; remove with slotted spoon. Stir flour and seasonings into saucepan. Stir in milk and cream gradually; cook stirring, until sauce boils for 1 minute. Stir small amount of hot sauce into eggs; stir back into hot sauce. Stir in cheese; cook, stirring, over low heat until melted. Drain tuna; separate into large pieces. Add sauterne, lemon peel, 2 tablespoons lemon juice, tuna, lobster, almonds, and mushroom mixture to sauce; heat to serving temperature. Cut avocados in half lengthwise, twisting gently to separate halves. Whack sharp knife directly into seeds; twist to lift out. Peel avocado halves; brush with lemon juice. Arrange on serving platter with watercress; garnish with lime slices. Place seafood mixture in serving bowl; serve over avocado halves. Garnish with buttered, toasted fine bread crumbs and sliced truffles. Yield: 24 servings.

Photograph for this recipe on page 3.

CAPTAIN BEN'S CLAM LOAF

1 qt. clams
1 1-lb. loaf unsliced bread
1/2 c. melted butter
1 clove of garlic, minced
1/4 c. chopped onion
1/2 c. chopped celery
1 tbsp. flour
1/8 tsp. pepper
1/4 tsp. thyme
Dash of Worcestershire sauce
1 tbsp. chili sauce
2 eggs, beaten
2 tbsp. chopped parsley

Drain clams; reserve 1/2 cup clam juice. Cut off top of bread; hollow out loaf, leaving 1-inch shell. Crumble enough bread to measure 1 quart. Brush inside of shell with some of the butter. Place shell and bread crumbs on baking sheet. Bake at 350 degrees for 10 minutes. Cook garlic, onion, and celery in remaining butter until tender; blend in flour. Stir in pepper, thyme, Worcestershire sauce, and chili sauce. Add clams and reserved juice; cook until thickened, stirring constantly. Stir

small amount of clam mixture into eggs, stir back into clam mixture. Stir in bread crumbs and parsley; spoon into shell. Wrap in foil; place on baking sheet. Bake at 350 degrees for 1 hour; garnish with lemon slices and parsley sprigs.

E. Jean Yontz, Pres., Epsilon Rho No. 7491
Maryville, Tennessee

DEVILED CLAMS

1 med. onion, chopped
1/2 c. chopped celery
4 tbsp. margarine
1 lg. can minced clams
Dash of salt
Dash of hot sauce
1/2 tsp. mustard
1 c. seasoned bread crumbs
Parsley flakes

Saute onion and celery in margarine in skillet until tender. Add clams; heat through. Remove from heat; add remaining ingredients except parsley. Fill greased ramekins or baking shells with clam mixture; garnish with parsley flakes. Bake at 350 degrees for 20 minutes. Yield: 6 servings.

Amelia K. Waldron, Preceptor Beta XP265
Torrington, Connecticut

BROILED AVOCADOS WITH CRAB

Peeled avocado halves
Cooked crab or shrimp
Minced green onions
Chopped celery
White sauce
Grated Cheddar cheese

Place avocado halves on baking sheet. Mix desired amounts of crab, onions, and celery; pile on avocado halves. Mix white sauce and cheese; heat until cheese is melted, stirring constantly. Spoon over crab mixture. Broil until lightly browned.

Mrs. Billie Porter, Xi Omicron Kappa X3496
Camarillo, California

ALASKA CRAB FONDUE

9 thin slices bread
2   7 1/2-oz. cans King crab
1/2 c. mayonnaise
1 1/2 c. chopped celery
1 tbsp. chopped onion
1/2 tsp. seasoned salt
3 c. milk
4 eggs, slightly beaten
1 c. mushroom soup
1/2 c. grated Cheddar cheese

Dice 4 slices bread; arrange in shallow baking dish. Combine crab, mayonnaise, celery, onion, and seasoned salt; mix well. Spread over bread. Trim crusts from remaining bread; arrange over crab mixture . Combine milk with eggs; pour over all. Refrigerate for several hours or overnight. Bake at 325 degrees for 15 minutes. Spread soup over top; sprinkle with cheese. Bake for 1 hour longer.

Linnea C. Friede
International Honorary Member, BSP
Cleveland Heights, Ohio

ALASKAN KING CRAB CASSEROLE

2 c. crab meat
1/2 c. chopped celery
1/2 c. butter
1 1/2 tbsp. flour
1 c. milk
1 egg yolk, beaten
2 tbsp. lemon juice
Salt and pepper to taste
2 tbsp. chopped pimento
1 c. cooked peas
1 tbsp. melted butter
1/2 c. fine dry bread crumbs

Pick over crab meat; remove pieces of shell. Saute celery in butter in skillet until tender. Blend in flour; add milk gradually. Cook, stirring constantly, until smooth and thickened. Stir small amount of hot sauce into egg yolk; return to hot sauce, stirring until smooth and blended. Add lemon juice, salt and pepper; mix well. Fold in pimento, peas, and crab meat; pour into well-greased casserole.

Combine melted butter and bread crumbs; sprinkle over crab mixture. Bake at 350 degrees for 30 minutes or until heated through and top is golden. Yield: 8 servings.

Lorene Harrison
International Honorary Member, BSP
Anchorage, Alaska

ARTICHOKE-CRAB MEAT CASSEROLE

1 No. 2 can artichoke hearts,
    drained
1 lb. crab meat
1/2 lb. fresh mushrooms
3/8 c. butter
2 1/2 tbsp. flour
1/2 tsp. salt
1 c. cream
1 tsp. Worcestershire sauce
1/4 c. medium dry sherry
Paprika to taste
Cayenne pepper to taste
Pepper to taste
1/4 c. grated Parmesan cheese

Place artichokes in baking dish; place crab meat over artichokes. Saute mushrooms in 2 tablespoons butter in skillet until tender. Spread crab meat with mushrooms. Melt remaining butter in saucepan; stir in flour and salt, blending well. Add cream, blending thoroughly. Place over medium heat; cook, stirring constantly, until bubbly and thickened. Stir in Worcestershire sauce, sherry, paprika, cayenne pepper, and pepper thoroughly. Pour sauce over mushrooms. Sprinkle cheese on top. Bake at 375 degrees for 20 minutes. Yield: 8 servings.

Mrs. Ronald Reagan
International Honorary Member, BSP
Sacramento, California

COCKTAIL QUICHE

1/2 c. mayonnaise
2 tbsp. flour
2 eggs, beaten
1/2 c. milk
1 2/3 c. flaked crab, drained

1/3 c. sliced green onions
1 unbaked 9-in. pie shell
Paprika

Combine mayonnaise, flour, eggs, and milk. Stir in crab and green onions. Spoon filling into pie shell. Sprinkle with paprika. Bake at 350 degrees for 40 to 45 minutes. Yield: 8 servings.

Lucile E. Woods, Sec.
Preceptor Upsilon XP473, Spokane, Washington

CRAB IMPERIAL

1 lb. crab meat
1 tsp. seafood seasoning
1 1/2 tsp. salad dressing or
    mayonnaise
1 tsp. prepared mustard
1 tsp. Worcestershire sauce
1 tsp. salt
1 tsp. pepper
1 tsp. cayenne pepper
1 egg, beaten
1/2 tsp. curry powder
2 bread slices
Milk
Minced parsley to taste
Paprika

Combine crab meat, seasoning, salad dressing, mustard, Worcestershire sauce, salt, pepper, cayenne pepper, egg, and curry powder; blend well. Soak bread slices in enough milk to moisten well. Add bread and parsley; mix well. Turn into greased baking dish. Sprinkle with paprika. Bake at 425 degrees for 25 minutes.

Linda E. Myers, Lambda Nu No. 7642
Lake Worth, Florida

CRAB CAKES

1 lb. crab meat
2 eggs
2 tbsp. mayonnaise
1 tbsp. horseradish mustard
3/4 tsp. salt
3/8 tsp. pepper

1 tbsp. chopped parsley
Cracker crumbs

Combine all ingredients except cracker crumbs; mix well. Shape into cakes; roll in cracker crumbs. Arrange on well-greased baking sheet. Bake at 375 degrees until golden.

Nellie Taylor Ross
International Honorary Member, BSP
Washington, D. C.

CRAB DIP BOMBAY

1 can flaked crab meat
1 c. sour cream
1 tsp. curry powder
1/4 c. grated coconut
Salt and pepper to taste
1/4 c. chili sauce

Combine crab meat, sour cream, curry powder, coconut, salt, pepper, and chili sauce in bowl. Mix thoroughly. Refrigerate, covered, overnight. Serve with potato chips or crackers.

Bernadine Harris, Pres.
Xi Epsilon Nu X3828, Cape Girardeau, Missouri

CRAB MEAT REMICK

1 recipe 2-crust pie pastry
1/2 c. mayonnaise
1 tbsp. chili sauce
1/2 tsp. paprika
Dash of hot sauce
Dash of celery salt
1 c. flaked crab meat

Roll pastry out on floured surface. Cut circles to fit 12 tart pans. Line each tart pan with pastry, fluting edge. Combine mayonnaise, chili sauce, paprika, hot sauce, and celery salt in small bowl, blending well. Add crab meat to sauce; mix thoroughly. Fill tart shells with crab meat mixture. Place tart pans on cookie sheet. Bake at 375 degrees for 18 minutes or until pastry is lightly browned. Yield: 12 tarts.

Helen Mae Morgan, Coord. Chm.
Xi Alpha Chap., Agana, Guam

CRAB QUICHE SUPREME

3 eggs, beaten
1 c. milk
3/4 tsp. salt
Dash of nutmeg
Dash of cayenne pepper
1/3 c. white wine
1 c. flaked crab meat
1 unbaked 9-in. pie shell
1 tbsp. minced green onion
1/2 c. grated Swiss cheese

Combine eggs, milk, salt, nutmeg, cayenne pepper, and wine in bowl; mix well. Arrange crab meat in pie shell. Sprinkle onion over crab meat. Pour egg mixture over top; sprinkle with cheese. Place on bottom shelf in oven. Bake at 400 degrees for 45 minutes or until set. Allow to stand for 10 minutes before serving. Yield: 6-8 servings.

Margaret T. Wolf, Alpha Mu No. 527
Vandalia, Illinois

CREAMED CRAB IN POTATO BASKETS

1 7 1/2-oz. can crab meat
4 med. cooked potatoes, peeled
1 egg
5 tbsp. butter
1 1/2 tsp. salt
1/8 tsp. pepper
Corn flake crumbs
2 tbsp. flour
1 3/4 c. milk
1 tsp. curry powder
3 hard-cooked eggs, diced

Drain crab meat and flake. Mash potatoes; add egg, 3 tablespoons butter, 3/4 teaspoon salt, and pepper, mixing well. Shape into 8 balls 2 inches in diameter. Roll in crumbs. Place in greased custard cups or muffin tins, pressing up sides to form baskets 1/4 inch thick. Bake in 400-degree oven for 20 minutes. Melt remaining butter in saucepan. Add flour and remaining salt, blending well. Stir in milk gradually. Cook over low heat, stirring constantly, until thickened. Add curry

powder, hard-cooked eggs, and crab meat. Heat through. Spoon into potato baskets. Serve hot. Yield: 8 servings.

Jody Weitzel, City Coun. Rep.
Preceptor Lambda XP369, Wooster, Ohio

CREOLE CRAB GUMBO

4 tbsp. butter
1/2 c. sliced onions
4 tbsp. flour
1 lb. crab meat
1 lb. okra, sliced
5 c. canned tomatoes
1 c. diced green pepper
2 cloves of garlic, crushed
1 tsp. nutmeg
2 tsp. salt
Freshly ground pepper

Melt butter in kettle. Saute onions in butter for 10 minutes. Blend in flour; cook, stirring, until browned. Add crab meat, okra, tomatoes, green pepper, garlic, nutmeg, salt, pepper to taste, and 2 cups water. Mix well. Bring to a boil. Reduce heat; simmer, covered, for 1 hour. Yield: 6 servings.

Lona Tipton, Sigma Tau No. 5084
Sacramento, California

GOURMET CRAB CASSEROLE

2 cans crab meat, drained
1 lg. can mushrooms, drained
4 hard-cooked eggs, chopped
1/4 c. minced onions
1/2 c. slivered toasted almonds
2 pimentos, chopped
1/2 c. chopped green pepper
1/2 c. butter
2/3 c. flour
1 tsp. salt
2 2/3 c. milk
1 c. shredded Cheddar cheese
2 c. Croutons

Combine crab meat, mushrooms, eggs, onions, almonds, pimentos, and green pepper; mix well. Melt butter in saucepan. Stir in flour and salt, blending well. Add milk gradually, mixing well. Place over medium heat, stirring constantly, until thickened and bubbly. Place crab meat mixture in buttered casserole. Add white sauce, stirring gently. Sprinkle cheese over top. Sprinkle with Croutons. Bake at 325 degrees for 30 minutes.

Croutons

2 tbsp. melted butter
3 bread slices, cubed

Combine butter and bread cubes, tossing to coat evenly. Place on cookie sheet. Bake at 325 degrees for 15 minutes or until toasted.

Ruth C. Hartkopf
International Honorary Member, BSP
Idaho Falls, Idaho

CRAB MEAT HORS D'OEUVRES

1 lg. can crab meat
1 jar Old English cheese
1/2 c. soft butter
2 tbsp. mayonnaise
1/2 tsp. garlic salt
1/2 tsp. seasoned salt
English muffins

Combine crab meat, cheese, butter, mayonnaise, garlic salt, and seasoned salt in bowl; blend well. Spread mixture on English muffins. Place on cookie sheet. Cut each in half. Broil 4 inches from source of heat for 8 minutes or until cheese melts. Serve hot.

Mrs. Robert Long, Pres.
Preceptor Tau XP607, Holland, Michigan

DEVILED CRAB CAKES

1 tbsp. butter
1 med. onion, chopped
1 sm. green pepper, chopped
1 recipe thick cream sauce
1/2 tsp. thyme
1 tsp. minced parsley
1 tsp. celery flakes
1 can crab meat, drained
Salt and pepper to taste
Cracker meal
1 egg, beaten

Melt butter in skillet. Saute onion and green pepper in butter until soft and transparent. Combine onion mixture, cream sauce, thyme, parsley, celery flakes, crab meat, salt, and pepper; mix thoroughly. Add enough cracker meal to make of mashed potato consistency, mixing well. Refrigerate, covered, for several hours. Shape mixture into small patties. Dip each patty into egg; coat with cracker meal. Fry in small amount of fat until brown. Serve hot. Yield: 7-10 servings.

Dorothy Bell, Pres., Beta Psi No. 4254
Albemarle, North Carolina

HOT CRAB MEAT CANAPES

1/2 lb. crab meat, drained
1 tbsp. dry sherry
1 tsp. salt
1/8 tsp. white pepper
1 tbsp. chopped fresh dill
1 tbsp. butter
1 tbsp. flour
1 egg yolk
1 c. light cream
6 slices home-style bread

Combine crab meat, sherry, salt, white pepper, and dill in large bowl, mixing well. Melt butter in small skillet; add flour, blending well. Beat egg yolk and cream in small bowl. Add cream mixture to flour mixture, stirring briskly with wire whisk. Place over low heat, stirring constantly, until thickened. Do not boil. Pour sauce over crab meat mixture; blend thoroughly. Correct seasoning, if necessary. Cut each bread slice into 4 rounds. Place on cookie sheet. Broil on 1 side only, 4 inches from source of heat, until lightly toasted. Spread untoasted side of each round with crab meat mixture, mounding slightly. Serve hot. Yield: 24 canapes.

Virginia Thomason, Cor. Sec.
Gamma Gamma No. 4148, Decatur, Georgia

SAN FRANCISCO SOLE SUPERB

2 lb. sole fillets
Salt
Dash of white pepper
2 tbsp. butter or margarine
1/2 c. chopped onion
1   8 3/4-oz. can seedless
   green grapes
1/4 c. dry white wine
3/4 c. half and half
1 egg yolk, beaten
1 tbsp. flour
Dash of nutmeg
Paprika

Remove skin from fillets; sprinkle both sides with salt and white pepper. Roll fillets; secure with wooden picks. Melt butter in 10-inch frypan. Add onion; cook until tender. Place fillets in frypan. Drain grapes, reserving 1/4 cup liquid; pour reserved liquid and wine over fillets. Cover; simmer for 8 to 10 minutes or until fish flakes easily. Place fillets on ovenproof serving platter; remove wooden picks. Keep warm. Combine half and half, egg yolk, flour, 1/4 teaspoon salt, and nutmeg; add to hot liquid gradually. Cook until thickened, stirring constantly. Add grapes. Pour sauce over fillets; sprinkle with paprika. Broil about 5 inches from source of heat for 4 to 5 minutes or until lightly browned. Garnish with additional grapes and watercress if desired. Yield: 6 servings.

CHILLED LOBSTER SOUFFLE

5   10-oz. packages frozen
   rock lobster-tails
3 tbsp. margarine
1/4 c. all-purpose flour
1/4 tsp. pepper
1 tsp. salt
Dash of paprika
2 c. milk
1   10 1/2-oz. can beef broth
2 env. unflavored gelatin
6 tbsp. sherry

4 egg whites
3 c. heavy cream

Fold 30-inch length of foil, 12 inches wide, in half lengthwise. Wrap around outside of 7-cup china souffle dish so that collar stands 3 inches high above rim. Fasten with cellophane tape. Lightly grease inside surface of foil collar only. Prepare lobster-tails according to package directions; drain and cool. Melt margarine in saucepan over low heat; stir in flour, pepper, salt, and paprika until blended. Add milk gradually, stirring constantly. Cook, stirring, until smooth and thickened. Remove from heat; cool. Remove meat from lobster shells, reserving 2 shells for garnish. Cut lobster meat into bite-sized pieces into 3-quart bowl, reserving 1 cup chopped lobster. Pour broth into small saucepan; sprinkle with gelatin. Heat, stirring, until gelatin is dissolved. Remove from heat; stir in sherry. Combine gelatin mixture, white sauce, and lobster meat. Chill until slightly thickened. Beat egg whites until stiff. Beat cream until soft peaks form. Fold egg whites and whipped cream into gelatin mixture; place enough lobster mixture in souffle dish to come to rim. Add reserved lobster; add remaining lobster mixture. Cover with plastic wrap; chill overnight.

Sherry Aspic

1 10 1/2-oz. can beef consomme
2 tbsp. unflavored gelatin
1/2 c. sherry
1/4 c. snipped parsley

Combine consomme and gelatin in small saucepan; stir over low heat until gelatin is dissolved. Remove from heat; stir in sherry. Pour into 9 x 5 x 3-inch loaf pan. Chill until set. Cut congealed sherry mixture into 40 to 50 small cubes. Peel foil collar off souffle gently. Press snipped parsley into exposed side of souffle. Pile congealed cubes in center of souffle. Place reserved lobster shells on each side for garnish.

Patricia Smalley, Treas.
Epsilon Lambda No. 5438
Colorado Springs, Colorado

ROCK LOBSTER AMERICAINE

5 9-oz. packages frozen South
   African rock lobster-tails
2 tbsp. butter
2 tbsp. olive oil
1 clove garlic, chopped
2 onions, minced
2 carrots, minced
1/4 c. brandy
1 c. tomato sauce
2 c. canned tomatoes, chopped
1 c. white wine
1/2 tsp. crumbled basil
Salt and pepper to taste

Cut lobster-tails through shell into 1-inch crosswise slices with sharp knife. Heat butter and oil. Add garlic, onions, and carrots; saute for 5 minutes. Add lobster pieces and remaining ingredients; cover tightly. Cook over low heat, stirring occasionally, for about 20 minutes. Yield: 12 servings.

Photograph for this recipe on page 82.

VICHYSSOISE ROCK LOBSTER IN THE SHELL

5 9-oz. packages frozen South African
   rock lobster-tails
2 cans frozen cream of potato soup,
   thawed
1/2 c. light cream
2 tbsp. sherry
1/4 c. frozen chopped chives
1 1/2 tsp. paprika
1 1/2 c. grated mozzarella cheese

Drop lobster-tails into boiling, salted water; cook for 2 to 3 minutes after water reboils. Drain immediately; drench with cold water. Cut away underside membrane. Remove lobster from shells; cut in 1/2-inch crosswise slices. Reserve shells. Combine lobster, soup, cream, sherry, chives, and paprika; heat through. Spoon into reserved shells; sprinkle with cheese. Place on broiler pan. Broil until bubbly and golden; serve at once. Yield: 12 servings.

Photograph for this recipe on page 82.

LOBSTER IMPERIAL

3/4 c. butter
1 c. flour
3 c. milk
2 c. cream
6 c. diced lobster meat
2 c. finely chopped celery
4 cans mushrooms, drained
Salt to taste
2 cans drained pimento, chopped
1 tbsp. sugar
1 tbsp. hot sauce
1 tbsp. Worcestershire sauce
1 tbsp. onion juice
1/2 tsp. nutmeg
3 eggs, beaten
Buttered crumbs
Grated cheese

Melt butter in double boiler; stir in flour until bubbly. Add milk and cream gradually. Cook, stirring constantly, until smooth and thickened. Pour cream sauce into large bowl. Saute lobster meat, celery, and mushrooms separately in additional butter; add to cream sauce. Season with salt. Add pimento, sugar, hot sauce, Worcestershire sauce, onion juice, and nutmeg to cream sauce. Stir in eggs. Spoon lobster mixture into 2 large greased casseroles. Top with crumbs and cheese. Bake at 350 degrees until heated through and bubbly.

Mrs. Allie Ahern
International Honorary Member, BSP
Halifax, Nova Scotia, Canada

CURRIED ROCK LOBSTER AND EGGS ON CALIFORNIA SPAGHETTI

4   9-oz. packages frozen South
    African rock lobster-tails
6 tbsp. butter or margarine
6 tbsp. flour
1 1/2 tsp. salt
1/4 tsp. pepper
1/2 tsp. garlic powder
1 1/2 tbsp. curry powder
4 c. milk
8 hard-cooked eggs, sliced
1 1/2 lb. thin spaghetti
1 1/2 c. sliced ripe pitted olives
3 tbsp. chopped pimento
3 c. grated Cheddar cheese

Drop lobster-tails into boiling, salted water; cook for 2 to 3 minutes after water reboils. Drain immediately; drench with cold water. Cut away underside membrane. Remove lobster from shells; dice. Melt butter in large saucepan; stir in flour, salt, pepper, garlic powder, and curry powder. Stir in milk gradually; cook over low heat, stirring constantly, until sauce bubbles and thickens. Stir in lobster and eggs. Cook spaghetti according to package directions; drain. Toss with olives, pimento, and cheese while hot. Pour spaghetti mixture into a serving dish; top with hot lobster mixture. Yield: 12 servings.

Photograph for this recipe on page 82.

LOBSTER-TAILS CANTONESE

1/3 c. Chinese black beans
2 cloves of garlic
1/4 c. peanut oil
1 tsp. salt
4   6 to 8-oz. lobster-tails
1/4 lb. ground lean pork
1 onion
1 green pepper
1 c. chicken broth
Soy sauce to taste
1 tbsp. cornstarch
2 egg whites, slightly beaten
Hot rice
Fresh parsley

Soak beans in warm water for 2 minutes. Rinse several times to remove thin black coating. Mash beans and garlic together; set aside. Heat oil and salt in large skillet. Remove lobster meat from shells; cut into 1-inch pieces. Combine lobster meat and pork in hot skillet. Cook, stirring, for 3 minutes or until lightly browned. Cut onion and green pepper into 1-inch squares. Add bean mixture, onion, green pepper, broth, and soy sauce to lobster mixture; mix well. Cook over high heat for 2 minutes. Combine cornstarch and 1 tablespoon water; stir into bean mixture. Cook, stirring, until thickened. Add egg whites to lobster mixture gradually, stirring constantly. Serve over hot rice; garnish with parsley.

Marsha McBride, Delta Chap.
Blackfoot, Idaho

PAELLA

1   10 1/2-oz. can chicken broth
1/8 tsp. powdered saffron
8 chicken legs, disjointed
Paprika
1/4 c. olive oil
2 tsp. salt
4 chorizo, sliced
2   8-oz. packages frozen
      lobster-tails, thawed
1 clove of garlic, crushed
2 c. chopped green pepper
2 c. chopped onion
1 1/2 c. rice
1 c. dry white wine
1   16-oz. can tomatoes
1 1/2 c. small pimento-stuffed
      olives
1 tsp. capers, chopped
1/2 tsp. coarsely ground pepper
1/2 tsp. oregano leaves

12 littleneck clams or mussels
1/2 c. frozen peas, thawed

Combine chicken broth and saffron; let stand. Sprinkle chicken lightly with paprika; brown well on all sides in hot oil in 12-inch skillet. Sprinkle chicken with 1 teaspoon salt. Add chorizo; cover. Cook over low heat for 30 minutes or until chicken is tender. Remove chorizo and chicken from skillet. Cut lobster-tails in half if large; saute in same skillet until shells turn bright red. Set aside. Drain pan drippings, reserving 1/2 cup in skillet. Add garlic, green pepper, and onion. Cook, stirring occasionally, until vegetables are crisp-tender. Add rice; saute until opaque. Stir in saffron mixture, wine, tomatoes, olives, capers, pepper, oregano and remaining salt. Cover; cook over low heat for 15 minutes or until liquid is almost absorbed. Stir with fork. Arrange chorizo, chicken, and lobster over rice, pressing into rice. Arrange clams over rice so that shells touch edge of skillet. Sprinkle peas over rice. Cover; cook over low heat for 15 minutes or until clams open and rice is tender.

SALMON PARTY BALL

1   1-lb. can salmon
1   8-oz. package cream cheese
1 tbsp. lemon juice
2 tsp. grated onion
1 tsp. prepared horseradish
1/4 tsp. salt
1/4 tsp. liquid smoke
1/2 c. chopped pecans
3 tbsp. snipped parsley

Drain and flake salmon; remove skin and bones. Have cream cheese at room temperature. Combine salmon, cream cheese, lemon juice, onion, horseradish, salt, and liquid smoke; mix thoroughly. Chill for several hours. Combine pecans and parsley. Shape salmon mixture into ball; roll in pecan mixture. Chill well. Serve with assorted crackers.

Dorothy F. Harding, Delta Delta No. 4830
Richland, Washington

SALMON PUFFS

1   7 1/2-oz. can pink salmon
1/2 egg
1/4 c. minced onion
1/4 c. flour
3/4 tsp. baking powder
Salad oil

Drain and flake salmon; remove skin and bones. Combine with egg and onion until well blended. Mix flour and baking powder; stir into salmon mixture. Shape into small balls. Fry in hot oil for 5 minutes; drain on paper toweling. Serve with wooden picks or cocktail forks. Yields: 4-6 servings.

Jo Fowler, Treas., Beta Sigma No. 3041
Fort Morgan, Colorado

MAINE-SCALLOPED OYSTERS

1 can oysters
2 c. cracker crumbs
1 tsp. grated onion
1/3 c. melted butter
3/4 c. milk
Salt and pepper to taste
Paprika to taste

Drain oysters; reserve juice. Combine cracker crumbs, onion, and melted butter. Arrange half the oysters in greased 8-inch baking dish. Top with half the crumb mixture. Repeat layers. Add 1/4 cup reserved juice to milk; pour over layers. Sprinkle with salt, pepper, and paprika. Bake at 425 degrees for 20 minutes. Yield: 4 servings.

Jackie Fortunato, VP, Zeta No. 1223
Augusta, Maine

OYSTER-MUSHROOM CASSEROLE

1 pt. oysters
1/2 lb. fresh mushrooms, sliced
1 tbsp. minced onion
1/2 c. butter, melted
1 1/2 c. bread crumbs
1/2 tsp. salt

1/4 tsp. pepper
1/2 tsp. rosemary or thyme
1 tbsp. Worcestershire sauce
2 tbsp. cream

Drain oysters, reserving 1/4 cup liquor. Saute mushrooms and onion in 2 tablespoons butter in skillet until transparent; add oysters. Combine crumbs, salt, pepper, rosemary, Worcestershire sauce, remaining butter, cream and reserved oyster liquor. Arrange layers of crumb mixture and oyster mixture in greased baking dish, ending with crumbs on top. Dot with additional butter. Bake at 350 to 375 degrees for 30 minutes.

Rebecca F. Gross
International Honorary Member, BSP
Lock Haven, Pennsylvania

SEVICHE DE CORVINA

1 lb. corbina or whitefish
   fillets
1/2 c. fresh lime juice
2 firm tomatoes, minced
1 med. onion, minced
1 or 2 hot peppers, minced
1 green pepper, minced
1 clove of garlic, minced
1 sprig of parsley, minced (opt.)
Salt and pepper to taste
2 or 3 drops of hot sauce

Skin and fillet corbina; chop fine. Place corbina in glass bowl; add remaining ingredients. Toss gently to blend; chill for 6 hours or overnight. Serve with saltines.

Sue Bradley, Rec. Sec., Xi Kappa Pi X3163
Odessa, Texas

SEAFOOD IMPERIAL

3 env. vegetable broth mix
2 1/4 c. rice, cooked
1 tsp. chopped parsley
3 cans frozen cream of shrimp soup
2 c. milk
3 tsp. lemon juice
1/4 tsp. nutmeg

3 cans lobster
3 lb. shrimp, cooked
3 cans mushrooms
4 c. bread crumbs
1 can toasted slivered almonds

Dissolve vegetable broth in 3 cups boiling water; pour over rice in large bowl. Stir in parsley; set aside. Combine soup and milk in top of double boiler; place over simmering water. Heat, stirring occasionally, until soup is thawed. Stir in lemon juice and nutmeg; blend until mixture is smooth. Combine lobster, shrimp and mushrooms with rice mixture; pour soup mixture over all. Blend thoroughly. Pour into two 3-quart baking dishes. Top with crumbs and almonds. Bake at 350 degrees for 1 hour. Yield: 16 servings.

Joyce Kopsack, Pres., Xi Beta No. 788
Pittsford, Vermont

NEVADA-STYLE ROUNDUP CASSEROLE

1 7-oz. can light chuck tuna
    in oil
Prepared biscuit mix
1 med. onion, chopped
1/2 med. green pepper, cut into
    narrow strips
2 tbsp. butter or cooking oil
2 cubes chicken bouillon
1 lg. whole broiled chicken
    breast, cubed
1 lb. shrimp, cooked
2 c. cooked rice
Salt to taste
Dash of coarsely ground pepper
1 tsp. curry powder
1 tbsp. sliced pimento
2 tbsp. wine (opt.)

Combine tuna with enough biscuit mix to make pie crust consistency; add water, if needed. Saute onion and green pepper in butter in small skillet over medium heat; remove from heat. Combine bouillon cubes with 2 cups boiling water; stir to dissolve cubes. Arrange chicken, shrimp and rice in baking dish; stir in salt, pepper, curry powder, pimento and wine. Add onion mixture and bouillon; blend carefully with wooden spoon. Roll out dough; arrange over shrimp mixture. Cut steam vents in dough. Bake in preheated oven at 350 degrees for 20 minutes or until heated through and top is golden. Serve immediately. Yield: 4 servings.

Lillian G. Barnum
International Honorary Member, BSP
Las Vegas, Nevada

BROILED SHAD ROE

Canned shad roe
Melted butter
Lemon juice
Paprika
Toast
Chopped parsley
Lemon slices

Drain shad roe; separate into small pieces. Pat dry with paper toweling; place in greased shallow baking pan. Brush with butter; sprinkle with lemon juice and paprika. Broil 3 to 4 inches from source of heat for 10 minutes; baste frequently with additional butter. Serve on toast; garnish with parsley and lemon slices.

Mrs. Warren G. Magnuson
International Honorary Member, BSP
Washington, D. C.

MARINATED SHRIMP

1 pkg. garlic salad dressing mix
1 pkg. onion salad dressing mix
1 pkg. Italian salad dressing mix
2 or 3 med. onions
1 7-oz. can jalapeno
    peppers
5 lb. cleaned shrimp, cooked

Prepare salad dressings according to package directions. Slice onions; separate into rings. Chop peppers. Combine all ingredients in large bowl; marinate overnight in refrigerator.

Mrs. Grace Young, Pres., Nu Delta No. 7084
Austin, Texas

SHRIMP JAMBALAYA

2 tsp. salt
1 tsp. hot sauce
1 bay leaf
1 stalk celery with leaves
1 lb. shrimp
1/4 c. butter
1/2 c. chopped onion
1/2 c. chopped green pepper
1 garlic clove, minced
1 c. rice
1 1-lb. can tomatoes
3/4 c. bouillon
1 1/2 c. diced cooked ham

Place 3 cups water, 1 teaspoon salt and 1/2 teaspoon hot sauce in saucepan; add bay leaf and celery. Bring to a boil. Add shrimp; bring to a boil. Cook for 5 minutes. Drain shrimp; cool quickly. Shell; devein. Melt butter in large skillet. Add onion, green pepper and garlic; cook until onion is tender but not brown. Stir in rice, tomatoes, bouillon, and remaining salt and hot sauce. Bring to a boil; reduce heat. Cover skillet. Simmer for 20 minutes. Add ham and shrimp; cover. Cook until liquid is absorbed. Yield: 4-6 servings.

Photograph for this recipe on page 128.

RALPH'S CURRY

1 med. onion, finely chopped
1 clove of garlic, chopped
2 tbsp. butter
1 c. applesauce
1 c. green peas
1 pkg. raisins
1 to 2 tbsp. curry powder
1/2 tsp. turmeric
1/2 lb. cleaned shrimp
1 tbsp. soy sauce
1 tbsp. lemon juice
Hot sauce to taste

Saute onion and garlic in butter in large skillet until tender. Add applesauce, peas, raisins, curry powder, and turmeric. Simmer for 1 hour, stirring frequently. Add shrimp; simmer for about 30 minutes. Stir in soy sauce, lemon juice, and hot sauce. Serve over hot rice with desired condiments. Yield: 3-4 servings.

Mrs. Karen Warren, Coun. Pres.
Mu Zeta No. 3984, Big Spring, Texas

SHRIMP AND ARTICHOKE BAKE

1 lb. fresh shrimp
2 9-oz. packages frozen
   artichoke hearts
1/2 c. butter
1/2 c. flour
1 1/2 c. milk
1/4 c. dry white wine
1 1/2 c. shredded Gruyere cheese
1/4 tsp. salt
1/4 tsp. white pepper
Paprika or fresh dill

Cook shrimp in boiling, salted water to cover for 25 minutes. Shell and devein. Prepare artichoke hearts according to package directions. Melt butter in medium saucepan over medium heat; stir in flour until smooth. Remove from heat. Stir in milk and wine gradually. Return to low heat; cook, stirring constantly, until mixture is thickened and just comes to a boil. Stir in cheese, salt, and pepper; cook until cheese melts. Remove from heat. Arrange artichoke hearts around edge of greased 9-inch baking dish; place shrimp in center. Pour cheese sauce over artichoke hearts and shrimp. Sprinkle with paprika. Bake at 350 degrees for 25 minutes or until cheese sauce is hot and bubbly.

Billie Bergman, Gamma Omicron Chap.
Milwaukie, Oregon

SHRIMP CASSEROLE HARPIN

2 lb. large fresh shrimp,
   cleaned
1 tbsp. lemon juice
3 tbsp. salad oil
3/4 c. rice
2 tbsp. butter or margarine
1/4 c. minced green pepper

1/4 c. minced onion
1 tsp. salt
1/8 tsp. pepper
1/8 tsp. mace
Dash of cayenne pepper
1 can tomato soup
1 c. heavy cream
1/2 c. slivered almonds
1/2 c. sherry
Paprika to taste

Cook shrimp in boiling salted water for 5 minutes; drain. Place shrimp in 2-quart casserole; sprinkle with lemon juice and oil. Cook rice according to package directions. Melt butter in 10-inch pan; add green pepper and onion. Saute for 5 minutes. Add rice, salt, pepper, mace, cayenne pepper, tomato soup, cream, half the almonds, and sherry. Pour rice mixture over shrimp. Top with remaining almonds; sprinkle with paprika. Bake at 350 degrees for about 55 minutes or until bubbly. Yield: 6 servings.

Katie H. Harper, City Coun., Xi Kappa X1089
Raleigh, North Carolina

TOOIE'S SHRIMP DELIGHT •

1 carton sour cream
Dash of hot sauce
1 lb. boiled shrimp, peeled
Cayenne pepper to taste
Lemon juice to taste
Worcestershire sauce to taste
1/2 loaf sliced white bread
Paprika

Blend sour cream and hot sauce together. Mince 4 shrimp; add to sour cream mixture. Add seasonings. Add remaining whole shrimp to sauce. Let marinate for several hours or overnight. Cut each bread slice into 6 sections; toast until lightly browned. Spoon shrimp and sauce over bread sections; sprinkle with paprika. May add chopped onion, horseradish or garlic powder to sauce if desired.

Evelyn Cormier, Dir., Pi No. 1609
New Orleans, Louisiana

SEAFOOD BRUNCH SPECIAL

1/2 lb. fresh or frozen shrimp, cleaned
1/2 lb. fresh or frozen crab meat
1 c. medium white sauce, heated
1/2 c. cooked peas
1/4 c. halved pimento-stuffed olives
1/8 tsp. hot pepper sauce
Pinch of curry powder
3 c. cooked rice
1/2 c. shredded Cheddar cheese
2 tsp. prepared mustard
1 egg, slightly beaten
1/2 c. dry bread crumbs
2 tbsp. melted butter
1/8 tsp. salt

Thaw frozen shrimp and crab meat. Rinse shrimp; drain on paper towels. Cook according to package directions. Drain crab meat; remove any remaining shell or cartilage. Add shrimp and crab meat to white sauce. Stir in peas, olives, pepper sauce, and curry powder. Combine rice, cheese, mustard and egg; form into 6 firm balls. Combine crumbs, butter and salt in pie pan. Roll rice balls in crumb mixture, turning to coat. Place on greased cookie sheet; flatten slightly. Shape into nests. Bake at 350 degrees for 15 minutes or until firm and lightly browned. Fill nests with hot seafood mixture. Yield: 6 servings.

SHRIMP DE JONGHE

2 cloves of garlic, minced
1/3 c. chopped parsley
1/2 tsp. paprika
Dash of cayenne pepper
2/3 c. sherry
1 c. melted butter
2 c. soft bread crumbs
5 to 6 c. cleaned cooked shrimp

Add garlic, parsley, paprika, cayenne pepper, and sherry to melted butter; mix well. Add bread crumbs; toss until well mixed. Place shrimp in 11 x 7 x 1 1/2-inch baking dish; spoon bread dressing over shrimp. Bake in 325-degree oven for 20 to 25 minutes or until crumbs are browned. Sprinkle with additional chopped parsley; serve. Yield: 6-8 servings.

Mary E. Hawkins, Alpha Omega No. 6489
Washington, D. C.

SHRIMP PÂTE

3   10-oz. packages frozen cooked
     shrimp
3/4 c. soft butter
1/2 c. mayonnaise
1 tbsp. Worcestershire sauce
1 tbsp. lemon juice
1/2 tsp. anchovy paste
1/4 tsp. pepper
1/4 tsp. hot sauce
Dash of cayenne pepper
Dash of curry powder

Process shrimp through food grinder using fine blade. Combine all ingredients except shrimp; cream with wooden spoon to form smooth paste. Add ground shrimp. Press mixture, 1/3 at a time, into lightly greased mold. Refrigerate for at least 8 hours or overnight. Unmold on serving plate. May garnish with additional whole shrimp and watercress if desired. Serve with crackers. Keeps well in refrigerator or freezer.

Rowena Conner, Pres., Xi Kappa X837
Roswell, New Mexico

SHRIMP COCKTAIL FRITTERS

1 lb. fresh shrimp, cooked
1 c. flour
1 tsp. baking powder
1/2 tsp. salt
Pepper to taste
2 eggs, beaten
Milk
1 sm. onion, minced
1 tbsp. minced parsley
Dash of hot sauce

Shell and devein shrimp; cut into small pieces. Sift dry ingredients together; add eggs and enough milk to make thick batter. Add onion, parsley, hot sauce and shrimp. Beat well. Drop by spoonfuls into deep hot fat in skillet; cook until evenly browned. Serve hot on cocktail picks.

Jeannette E. Bumpers, Ext. Off.
Omicron No. 7412, Mobile, Alabama

SHRIMP TARTS

10 slices white bread
6 tbsp. butter
2 tbsp. flour
1 c. chicken or turkey stock
Salt and pepper to taste
1/4 lb. small cooked shrimp, shelled
1 tbsp. chopped parsley

Preheat oven to 400 degrees. Remove crusts from bread; roll bread out flat with rolling pin. Cut 1 circle from each slice with 3-inch pastry cutter. Press bread circles into greased muffin cups; brush with 4 tablespoons melted butter. Bake at 400 degrees for 10 to 15 minutes or until bread is crisp and lightly browned. Remove and cool. Melt remaining butter; add flour. Cook for 2 minutes. Stir in stock; bring to a boil, stirring constantly. Cook for 3 minutes, stirring, until thickened. Season with salt and pepper. Chop shrimp; add shrimp and parsley to sauce. Mix well; cool slightly. Spoon sauce into bread cups. Serve warm or cold.

Elisa Procopio, Corr. Sec.
Ohio Epsilon Alpha No. 2140, Youngstown, Ohio

SISSY CIOPPINO

4 med. onions, quartered
2 garlic cloves, chopped
1 lg. bunch parsley, chopped
4 tbsp. oil
1/2 tsp. salt
1/2 tsp. pepper
1 qt. solid-pack tomatoes
4 med. potatoes, quartered
8 oz. fresh or canned crab
10 oz. fresh or canned shrimp
1   6-oz. jar marinated artichoke
   hearts
1/4 c. sherry

Saute onions, garlic, and parsley in oil in large kettle until onions are transparent; add salt, pepper, 1 cup boiling water, tomatoes and potatoes. Cook over medium heat until potatoes are tender; add crab, shrimp, artichoke hearts and sherry. Simmer, covered, until heated through; serve in large bowls with hot French bread. Yield: 4 servings.

Gwen Handa, Pres., Xi Upsilon No. 475
San Jose, California

ALMOND FISH FILLETS

2 lb. frozen fish fillets
Butter
Salt and pepper to taste
1/2 c. water
2 tbsp. flour
1/2 c. milk
1/2 c. slivered blanched toasted
   almonds

Thaw fillets until easily separated. Melt 4 tablespoons butter in skillet. Sprinkle fillets with salt and pepper; place in butter. Add water. Cover pan; simmer for about 10 minutes or until fish flakes easily. Remove fillets carefully to heatproof serving platter. Cook liquid left in pan until reduced by about 1/3. Cream 2 tablespoons butter and flour together. Add butter mixture and milk to liquid in pan. Simmer, stirring occasionally, until thickened. Sprinkle almonds around fillets. Pour sauce over fillets; heat through in oven. Garnish with parsley. Serve immediately. Yield: 6 servings.

GOURMET FILLET OF SOLE

    1 1/2 lb. fillet of sole
    2 tbsp. finely chopped onion
    2 tbsp. chopped parsley
    1/2 c. dry wine
    1/2 can cream of celery soup
    1/2 c. grated Parmesan cheese

Arrange sole in skillet; top with onion and parsley. Pour wine over all. Simmer, covered, for 10 minutes; baste frequently. Transfer sole and vegetables carefully to shallow baking dish. Stir soup into 1/4 cup of pan juices; heat through. Pour over sole; sprinkle with grated cheese. Broil 4 to 5 inches from source of heat until lightly browned and cheese is melted. Yield: 5-6 servings.

Della Gould Emmons
International Honorary Member, BSP
Tacoma, Washington

TUNA LOAF WITH DILL SAUCE

    2 c. milk
    3 c. 1/4-in. soft white bread
      cubes
    2 7-oz. cans tuna, drained and
      flaked
    4 eggs, slightly beaten
    1/4 c. finely chopped onion
    1 tbsp. chopped parsley
    1 tbsp. lemon juice
    1 tsp. salt
    1 tsp. paprika

Combine milk and bread cubes in saucepan; bring to gentle simmer. Remove from heat; beat until smooth. Combine remaining ingredients in mixing bowl; stir in milk mixture. Pour into greased 9 x 5 x 3-inch loaf pan. Bake at 325 degrees for 55 minutes or until set. Let loaf cool in pan for 10 minutes before serving.

Dill Sauce

2 tbsp. butter
2 tbsp. flour
1/2 tsp. salt
Dash of paprika
1 c. milk
1/3 c. finely diced dill pickles
2 tbsp. dill pickle juice
1 tbsp. chopped pimento

Melt butter in skillet; blend in flour, salt and paprika. Add milk gradually. Cook, stirring constantly, until thick and smooth. Stir in pickles, juice, and pimento; heat through. Place loaf on heated serving platter; pour sauce over loaf. Garnish with lemon slices and watercress. Slice to serve. Yield: 6 servings.

CRUNCHY TUNA CASSEROLE

1/4 c. cashew nuts, crushed
1 can Chinese noodles
1 c. diced celery
1 8-oz. can water chestnuts
1 can tuna
1 can mushroom soup
2 green onions, cut up

Combine all ingredients with 1/4 soup can water; blend well. Pour into greased casserole. Bake at 375 degrees for 30 minutes or until heated through and bubbly. Yield: 6 servings.

Gladys Gardner Jenkins
International Honorary Member, BSP
Iowa City, Iowa

TUNA SPECIAL

1 7-oz. can tuna
1 can mushroom soup
1 can celery soup
1 sm. can peas and carrots
1/2 c. milk
Salt and pepper to taste
1/2 tsp. mustard
1 1/2 c. potato chips

5 tomato slices
1/2 c. grated cheese

Combine tuna, soups, peas and carrots, milk, salt, pepper, mustard, and potato chips; blend well. Pour into greased baking dish; top with tomato slices. Sprinkle with cheese. . Bake at 325 degrees for 1 hour. Yield: 8 servings.

Mrs. Z. W. Dean
International Honorary Member, BSP
Calgary, Alberta, Canada

VEGETABLES

ARTICHOKE NIBBLES

2 6-oz. jars marinated artichoke
   hearts
1 sm. onion, finely chopped
1 clove of garlic, minced
4 eggs, beaten
1/4 c. fine dry bread crumbs
1/4 tsp. salt
1/8 tsp. pepper
1/8 tsp. oregano
1/8 tsp. hot sauce
1/2 lb. sharp Cheddar cheese,
   shredded
2 tbsp. minced parsley

Drain marinade from 1 jar of artichokes into frying pan. Drain remaining artichokes. Chop artichokes; set aside. Add onion and garlic to frying pan; saute for 5 minutes or until onion is soft. Combine eggs, crumbs, salt, pepper, oregano, and hot sauce, mixing well. Stir in cheese, parsley, artichokes, and onion mixture; blend well. Turn into greased 7 x 11-inch baking pan. Bake at 325 degrees for 30 minutes or until set when lightly touched. Let cool in pan; cut into 1-inch squares. Serve cold or warm. Yield: 6 dozen.

Dorothy Nalls, Pres., Xi Xi Lambda X3270
San Jose, California

155

ARTICHOKES WITH CROUTONS

2   9-oz. packages frozen
    artichoke hearts
3/8 c. butter
1 1/2 tbsp. lemon juice
1/8 tsp. salt
Dash of pepper
1 bread slice, cubed

Cook artichoke hearts according to package directions. Drain well. Place in serving dish. Combine 1/4 cup butter, lemon juice, salt, and pepper in saucepan. Heat through, stirring to blend. Pour butter mixture over artichokes. Melt remaining butter in small skillet. Add bread cubes; saute until lightly browned and toasted. Sprinkle toasted cubes over artichoke mixture. Yield: 8 servings.

Kay Dale, Serv. Chm.
Upsilon Upsilon No. 5734, Abilene, Texas

ASPARAGUS MASQUERADE

3 tbsp. flour
3/4 c. butter, melted
1 1/2 c. milk
8 oz. Old English cheese, shredded
1 1/2 c. cracker crumbs
1 lg. can asparagus spears, diced
4 oz. sliced almonds

Combine flour and 1/4 cup melted butter in medium saucepan; place over low heat, blending well. Add milk; mix well. Cook, stirring constantly, until sauce begins to thicken. Add cheese; stir until cheese is melted and thoroughly blended. Remove from heat. Combine cracker crumbs and remaining butter in bowl, mixing well. Pour 1/3 of the mixture into 1 1/2-quart baking dish. Place half the asparagus spears over crumbs. Sprinkle with half the almonds. Pour half the sauce over. Repeat layers. Top with remaining crumbs. Bake at 450 degrees for 15 minutes or until heated through and lightly browned. Yield: 6-8 servings.

Janice Head, Pres., Iota Omega No. 7017
Saint Louis, Missouri

PEGGY'S RANCH STYLE FRIJOLES

2 lb. pinto beans
2 tsp. salt
1/2 tsp. pepper
2 lg. onions
4 cloves of garlic
1 can roasted green chilies
1 can taco sauce
1/2 tsp. cumino seed
1 can tomatoes

Soak beans in cold water to cover overnight. Drain, rinse, and place in saucepan. Add water to 2-inch depth. Add salt and pepper; bring to a boil. Cook for 1 hour, adding water as necessary. Dice onions and garlic; chop green chilies. Combine garlic, onions, chilies, taco sauce, cumino seed, and tomatoes, mixing well. Stir tomato mixture into beans. Simmer for 1 hour and 30 minutes or until beans are tender.

Mrs. Barry Goldwater
International Honorary Member, BSP
Scottsdale, Arizona

SWEET-SOUR BAKED BEANS

8 slices bacon, diced
2 onions, chopped
1/2 c. (packed) brown sugar
1/2 c. cider vinegar
1 tsp. dry mustard
1 tsp. salt
1   15-oz. can pork and beans in
    tomato sauce
1 can kidney beans, drained
2 cans butter beans, drained

Fry bacon until crisp. Add onions, brown sugar, vinegar, dry mustard and salt, mixing well. Simmer, covered, for 20 minutes. Combine pork and beans, kidney and butter beans in large casserole. Pour sauce over. Mix gently. Bake at 350 degrees for 1 hour. Yield: 8-10 servings.

Mrs. Katherine Kraemer, Pres.
Beta Eta No. 3397, Merrill, Wisconsin

GREEN BEANS PAPRIKA

1   9-oz. package frozen whole
    green beans
1/4 c. butter
3/4 c. thinly sliced onions
1 tsp. paprika

Place beans in 2-quart saucepan containing small amount of salted water; cover. Cook for 10 minutes; drain. Melt butter in saucepan; saute onions in butter until tender. Stir in paprika. Place beans in warm serving dish; top with onion rings. Pour butter sauce over beans. Three-fourths pound fresh beans may be substituted for frozen beans; cook for 20 minutes. Yield: 4 servings.

Photograph for this recipe on page 123.

TANGY GREEN BEANS

1 can whole green beans
2 strips bacon
3 tbsp. butter
3 tbsp. vinegar
1 tsp. salt
1 tsp. paprika
1 tsp. chopped parsley
1 tsp. onion juice

Drain beans. Cut bacon strips in half. Wrap 5 to 6 beans with each bacon strip, fastening with wooden picks, making bundles. Place bundles on rack in broiler pan. Broil 4 inches from source of heat until bacon is crisp and lightly browned. Place bean bundles in serving dish. Combine butter, vinegar, salt, paprika, parsley, and onion juice in saucepan, stirring well. Bring to a boil. Pour over beans to serve.

Barbara Davis, Corr. Sec.
Beta Theta Chap., Laurel, Mississippi

ORIENTAL GREEN BEANS

1   1-lb. can cut green beans
2 tbsp. cornstarch
3 tbsp. sugar

3 tbsp. vinegar
1 tbsp. soy sauce
1/4 c. sweet pickle relish
1 c. pineapple tidbits
1 1/2 c. cooked shrimp

Drain beans, reserving 1/2 cup liquid. Pour reserved liquid in saucepan. Add cornstarch, sugar, vinegar, soy sauce, and pickle relish; blend thoroughly. Cook, stirring constantly, until thickened and bubbly. Drain pineapple. Add to sauce. Stir in beans and shrimp, mixing well. Heat through. Serve over rice or Chinese noodles, if desired. Yield: 4-6 servings.

Dr. Donna M. Stoddard
International Honorary Member, BSP
Lakeland, Florida

LUSCIOUS SPINACH CASSEROLE

2 pkg. frozen spinach
3/4 c. sour cream
1/2 pkg. dry onion soup mix
1 can drained water chestnuts,
    sliced

Cook spinach according to package directions; drain well. Place spinach in greased casserole; stir in sour cream, soup mix and water chestnuts. Bake at 275 degrees for about 30 minutes or until bubbly. Yield: 8 servings.

Theresa Anonsen, Xi Alpha Upsilon X882
Galveston, Texas

DIFFERENT SPINACH CASSEROLE

2 No. 303 cans spinach, drained
1 pt. sour cream
1 pkg. dry onion soup mix
Crushed potato chips

Combine all ingredients except potato chips; spoon into greased 1 1/2-quart casserole. Cover with potato chips. Bake at 350 degrees for 40 minutes. Yield: 8 servings.

Dona Trumble, VP
Xi Epsilon Epsilon X3696, Clinton, Missouri

MARINATED BRUSSELS SPROUTS

2 10-oz. packages frozen
  Brussels sprouts
1/2 c. tarragon vinegar
1/2 c. cooking oil
1/4 tsp. garlic powder
1 tbsp. sugar
2 dashes of hot sauce
2 tbsp. thinly sliced green
  onions and tops

Cook Brussels sprouts according to package directions; drain and cool. Combine vinegar, oil, garlic powder, sugar, and hot sauce, blending well. Add Brussels sprouts and onions; toss lightly. Chill, covered, for 8 hours. Toss 4 or 5 times while chilling. Yield: 20 servings.

Elizabeth L. Quigley, Pres.
Xi Epsilon Omicron X3900, Ballwin, Missouri

DILLED BRUSSELS SPROUTS

1 10-oz. package frozen Brussels
  sprouts
1/2 c. Italian salad dressing
1 sm. clove of garlic, minced
2 tbsp. finely chopped onion
1 tsp. dried parsley flakes
1/2 tsp. dried dillweed

Cook Brussels sprouts according to package directions; drain. Cut large pieces in half. Combine salad dressing, garlic, onion, parsley, and dillweed. Pour over warm Brussels sprouts. Marinate, covered, in refrigerator for several hours or overnight. Drain and serve with cocktail picks.

Nicole Van Brocklen, Gamma Gamma No. 6344
Sierra Vista, Arizona

BROCCOLI CASSEROLE

2 pkg. frozen chopped broccoli
1/2 c. chopped celery
1/2 c. chopped onion
2 tbsp. cooking oil
1 can cream of chicken soup
1/2 c. milk
1 8-oz. jar Cheez Whiz
2 c. cooked rice
Chinese noodles

Cook broccoli according to package directions until crisp-tender. Drain. Saute celery and onion in oil in skillet for 10 minutes. Combine soup, milk, and Cheez Whiz in bowl, blending thoroughly. Add rice, stirring well. Combine broccoli and rice mixture, mixing gently. Place in greased casserole. Top with Chinese noodles. Bake at 350 degrees for 20 minutes or until bubbly and lightly browned. Yield: 10-12 servings.

Mrs. William Ireland
International Honorary Member, BSP
Calgary, Alberta, Canada

CRISPY CARROT CASSEROLE

4 c. sliced carrots
1/4 c. butter
1 sm. onion, chopped
1 c. diced Velveeta cheese
Crushed potato chips

Cook carrots in small amount of water for 5 minutes until tender-crisp; drain. Place carrots in greased casserole. Dot with butter. Stir in onion; sprinkle with cheese. Top with crushed potato chips. Bake at 350 degrees for 30 minutes. Yield: 6-8 servings.

Dorothy Sielert, Treas., Xi Alpha Psi Chap.
Ames, Iowa

BAKED CARROT PUFF

2 lb. pared carrots, sliced
1/2 c. water
1/2 tsp. salt
6 tbsp. butter
3/4 c. graham cracker crumbs
Dash of ground ginger
2 eggs, separated
1/4 c. (packed) light brown sugar
1/4 c. fine dry bread crumbs

Preheat oven to 375 degrees. Combine carrots, water, and salt in heavy 3-quart pan.

Bring to a boil; reduce heat to medium. Cook for 15 minutes or until carrots are tender. Drain liquid; mash carrots. Combine carrots, 4 tablespoons butter, graham cracker crumbs, and ginger; blend until smooth. Beat in egg yolks; cool. Beat egg whites until stiff peaks form; fold into carrot mixture. Spoon into 3-quart buffet casserole. Combine remaining butter, brown sugar and bread crumbs. Sprinkle over carrot mixture. Bake for 40 minutes. Yield: 6-8 servings.

Leah A. Boreing, Preceptor Gamma Chap.
Billings, Montana

BUFFET CHEESE-SCALLOPED CARROTS

12 pared sliced carrots
1 sm. onion, minced
1/4 c. butter
1/4 c. flour
1 tsp. salt
1/4 tsp. dry mustard
2 c. milk
1/8 tsp. pepper
1/4 tsp. celery salt
1/2 lb. sliced process Cheddar
   cheese
3 c. fresh buttered bread crumbs

Preheat oven to 350 degrees. Cook carrots in boiling salted water until tender; drain. Saute onion in butter in saucepan for 2 to 3 minutes. Stir in flour, salt, mustard, and milk. Cook, stirring, until smooth and thickened. Add pepper and celery salt. Arrange layers of carrots and cheese in greased 2-quart casserole. Pour sauce over layers; top with crumbs. Bake for 25 minutes or until golden. Yield: 8 servings.

Dorothy Burns, Pres., Eta Mu No. 6595
Muscatine, Iowa

SWEET AND SOUR CARROTS

2 10-oz. packages frozen carrot
   nuggets

4 thin orange slices
4 thin lemon slices
1 8 3/4-oz. can pineapple
   tidbits, drained
2 tbsp. pineapple juice
1/4 c. (packed) brown sugar
2 tsp. cornstarch
1/4 c. nut halves

Thaw carrot nuggets; place in casserole. Combine orange slices, lemon slices, pineapple, pineapple juice, brown sugar, and cornstarch. Spoon over carrots in casserole. Top with nut halves. Bake at 350 degrees for 15 minutes.

Donna Baker, Pres., Gamma Sigma No. 4243
Anacortes, Washington

CAULIFLOWER CASSEROLE

1 sm. cauliflower
1/2 sweet red pepper
1/2 sweet green pepper
1 c. sliced celery
1 green onion, chopped
3 tbsp. butter
3 tbsp. flour
1 tsp. salt
1 1/2 c. milk
2/3 c. bread crumbs
1/2 c. grated cheese

Separate cauliflower into flowerets. Cook in boiling salted water in saucepan for about 7 minutes. Cut peppers into strips. Add vegetables to cauliflower; cook for about 3 minutes. Drain vegetables. Melt butter in double boiler; stir in flour and salt. Cook until bubbly. Add milk gradually; cook, stirring, until thick. Combine vegetables and cream sauce in shallow medium casserole. Sprinkle with bread crumbs and cheese. Bake at 350 degrees for about 20 minutes or until bubbly. Yield: 5 servings.

Marjorie L. Ball
International Honorary Member, BSP
St. John's, Newfoundland, Canada

CORN FRITTERS

1 c. flour
2 tsp. baking powder
1 tsp. salt
2 c. corn, cut from cob
2 eggs
2 tbsp. melted fat
Oil

Mix dry ingredients; sift. Place corn in bowl; add eggs. Add fat; stir well. Stir in dry ingredients; beat until mixed. Drop by spoonfuls into deep oil at 365 degrees; cook for 4 minutes or until golden brown. Drain; serve warm. Canned cream-style corn or canned whole kernel corn mixed with 1/2 cup cream may be substituted for fresh corn. Yield: 10-12 servings.

Cecilia Davis, Beta Sigma No. 4834
Jal, New Mexico

PETER PANCHO SAUCE

1 tbsp. butter
1 tbsp. flour
1 1/2 c. milk
1/2 c. smooth peanut butter
1/4 lb. process American cheese, grated
Hot cooked cauliflower

Melt butter in saucepan; blend in flour quickly. Stir in milk gradually. Bring to a boil, stirring constantly; boil for 1 minute. Add peanut butter and cheese, stirring until melted and blended. Serve over cauliflower.

Peter Panamanian Sauce

2 tbsp. chopped celery
2 tbsp. chopped onion
1 tbsp. butter
1 tbsp. flour
1 1/2 c. milk
1/2 c. crunchy peanut butter
Hot cooked sweet potatoes

Saute celery and onion in butter until crisp-tender; blend in flour quickly. Stir in milk gradually. Bring to a boil, stirring constantly; boil for 1 minute. Add peanut butter, stirring until melted and blended. Serve over sweet potatoes.

DUTCH-SCALLOPED CORN

1/2 green pepper, chopped
1/2 c. finely chopped onion
3 tbsp. butter
2 tbsp. flour
1 tsp. salt
1/4 tsp. paprika
1/4 tsp. dry mustard
1 c. milk
1/2 c. dry bread cubes
2 c. whole kernel corn
1 egg, beaten
1 6-oz. can sm. oysters, drained
1/2 c. buttered cracker crumbs

Cook green pepper and onion in 2 tablespoons butter for 5 minutes. Add flour and seasonings; stir until blended. Add milk; cook until thickened, stirring constantly. Brown bread in remaining butter; add to sauce. Add corn, egg, and oysters; mix well. Turn into greased 1-quart baking dish; cover with cracker crumbs. Bake in 400-degree oven for 20 minutes. Yield: 6 servings.

Ardell Smith, Pres., Xi Omicron X2490
Powell, Wyoming

EASY CORN SCALLOP

1 17-oz. can cream-style corn
2 eggs, beaten
1/2 c. crushed soda crackers
1/4 c. melted butter or margarine
1/4 c. evaporated milk
1/4 c. finely shredded carrot
1/4 c. chopped green pepper
1 tbsp. chopped celery
1 tsp. chopped onion
6 drops of hot sauce
1/2 tsp. sugar
1/2 tsp. salt
1/2 c. shredded Cheddar cheese
Paprika

Preheat oven to 350 degrees. Combine all ingredients except cheese and paprika; mix thoroughly. Turn into greased 8 x 8 x 2-inch baking dish. Top with cheese; sprinkle with paprika. Bake for 30 minutes or until golden brown and set. Yield: 6-8 servings.

Mrs. Eva Curcio, Pres., Preceptor Beta XP357
Vineland, New Jersey

GRILLED FRESH CORN ON THE COB

6 ears of corn
Salt to taste
6 tbsp. butter

Remove husks and silks from corn; wash. Place each ear of corn on piece of aluminum foil. Sprinkle with salt; place 1 tablespoon butter on each ear. Wrap corn with foil; seal. Place on grill over coals; cook for about 30 minutes or until corn is tender, turning occasionally.

Photograph for this recipe on page 85.

FRESH VEGETABLE KABOBS

Fresh mushrooms
Fresh cherry tomatoes
Small onions, cut in half
Fresh Brussels sprouts, parboiled
Fresh sliced yellow squash
1 bottle Italian dressing

Marinate mushrooms, tomatoes, onions, Brussels sprouts, and squash in Italian dressing for several hours. Drain vegetables; reserve marinade. Place vegetables on skewers; place on grill over low coals. Cook until vegetables are tender, turning and brushing with reserved marinade occasionally.

Photograph for this recipe on page 85.

CUCUMBER DIP

1 sm. clove of garlic
1 lg. package cream cheese, softened
1 med. cucumber, grated
Mayonnaise

Mash garlic in bowl; remove pulp, leaving juice. Add cream cheese; mix. Add cucumber; mix. Add enough mayonnaise for easy dipping consistency. May be spread on bread for sandwiches, if desired.

Jane Presley, Pres., Xi Iota Phi X2932
Odessa, Texas

EGGPLANT PARMESAN

1 lg. eggplant
1 egg
Milk
1 c. dry bread crumbs
3/4 c. olive oil
1/2 c. grated Parmesan cheese
2 tsp. oregano
2 sm. cans tomato sauce
1/2 lb. sliced mozzarella cheese

Wash eggplant; peel. Cut in 1/2-inch slices. Mix egg with small amount of milk. Dip eggplant in egg mixture; dip in bread crumbs. Saute in olive oil in frypan until golden brown on both sides. Place alternate layers of eggplant, Parmesan cheese, oregano, tomato sauce, and mozzarella cheese in casserole. Bake at 350 degrees for 30 minutes or until sauce is bubbling and cheese is melted. Yield: 6 servings.

Patricia Koson, Nu No. 5860
Keene, New Hampshire

EGGPLANT CASSEROLE

1 lg. eggplant
6 slices bacon
1 med. onion, sliced
Butter
1 can sm. whole tomatoes
1 tbsp. brown sugar
2 tbsp. flour
1/2 tsp. salt
Freshly ground pepper to taste
Bread crumbs
Grated cheese to taste

Peel and slice eggplant; cut into small cubes. Cook in boiling water for several minutes or until soft; drain. Cook bacon until partially done; drain. Cut into small pieces. Saute onion in small amount of butter until tender. Place eggplant, bacon, onion, and tomatoes in bowl; mix lightly. Add brown sugar, flour, salt, and pepper; mix. Place in greased casserole; cover with bread crumbs. Add cheese; dot with butter. Bake at 350 degrees for 30 minutes. Chopped green pepper may be added before baking, if desired. Yield: 6 servings.

Mrs. Grace Grout
International Honorary Member, BSP
Chapleau, Ontario, Canada

MUSHROOM PIE

6 tbsp. butter
2 lb. mushrooms, sliced
Salt and pepper to taste
Juice of 1/2 lemon
6 tbsp. flour
1 c. chicken stock or bouillon
1/2 c. madeira
1/2 c. heavy cream
Pastry for 2-crust pie
1 egg

Heat 4 tablespoons butter in large skillet; add mushrooms. Sprinkle with salt and pepper, and lemon juice. Cover skillet; cook for 10 minutes, shaking pan frequently. Arrange mushrooms in greased baking dish. Add remaining butter and flour to pan juices in skillet. Stir in 1 cup chicken broth gradually; cook, stirring constantly, until sauce is thick and smooth. Stir in madeira and cream. Season with additional salt and pepper if desired. Pour sauce over mushrooms. Fit pastry into pie pan. Spoon filling into bottom crust of pie shell; cover with top crust, fluting edge. Cut slits in top crust for steam vents. Brush with beaten egg. Bake at 450 degrees for 15 minutes. Reduce oven temperature to 350 degrees. Bake for 10 to 15 minutes longer. Yield: 6-8 servings.

Sue Pickell, Pres., Zeta Theta No. 5316
Olathe, Kansas

STUFFED MUSHROOMS

1 pt. fresh mushrooms
1 tbsp. butter
1 tbsp. chopped onion
2 tbsp. dry bread crumbs
1   4 3/4-oz. can chicken spread
2 tsp. mustard
1/4 tsp. Worcestershire sauce

Cover mushrooms with boiling water; let stand for 5 minutes. Remove stems from caps; chop. Melt butter in skillet; saute stems and onion until tender. Add crumbs, chicken spread, mustard and Worcestershire sauce; mix well. Stuff mushroom caps with crumb mixture; place on baking sheet. Place under broiler until heated through; serve.

Coni Chaney, Pres., Omega Chi No. 5908
Chula Vista, California

MARINATED FRESH MUSHROOMS

1 lb. mushrooms
3/4 c. olive oil
3 tbsp. tarragon vinegar
1/2 tsp. salt
Freshly ground pepper
2 tsp. minced parsley
1/2 tsp. minced fresh tarragon

Wash mushrooms; slice lengthwise through stems and caps. Combine remaining ingredients; mix well with mushrooms. Let stand for 5 to 6 hours before serving. Do not chill.

Mrs. Sherry Blunt, Ritual of Jewel
Theta Upsilon No. 6978, Springfield, Missouri

HERBED POTATOES

4 med. potatoes
1/3 c. flour
1/2 tsp. thyme
1/2 tsp. marjoram
1/2 tsp. sage
3/4 tsp. salt
Dash of pepper
4 tbsp. butter
1 bay leaf

Peel and quarter potatoes. Mix flour, thyme, marjoram, sage, salt, and pepper. Dip potatoes in flour mixture; place in greased 1-quart casserole. Dot with butter; place bay leaf on top. Cover tightly. Bake at 450 degrees for 1 hour; remove bay leaf before serving.

Kathryn Irwin, Pres., Kappa Omicron No. 8089
Stroudsburg, Pennsylvania

CURRIED PECAN AND GREEN PEA SHORTCAKES

2 c. biscuit mix
Butter

Milk
2 tbsp. minced onion
3 tbsp. water
1   10-oz. package frozen green peas
Salt
1 c. shelled pecan halves
2 tbsp. flour
1/2 tsp. paprika
1/2 to 1 tsp. curry powder
1/2 c. half and half

Pour biscuit mix into mixing bowl. Prepare according to package directions, using 1/3 cup butter and 2/3 cup milk. Roll out 1/4 inch thick on lightly floured surface; cut into rounds with 3-inch biscuit cutter. Cut centers from half the rounds with 1 1/2-inch cutter or knife. Place uncut rounds on baking sheet; top with cut biscuits. Bake according to package directions. Saute onion in 4 teaspoons butter. Combine onion, water, peas, and 1/2 teaspoon salt in saucepan; cover. Cook over low heat until peas are tender. Stir in pecans; heat through. Set aside; keep warm. Melt 2 tablespoon butter in double boiler; stir in flour, 1/2 teaspoon salt, paprika and curry powder until bubbly. Stir in half and half and 3/4 cup milk gradually. Cook, stirring constantly, until smooth and thickened. Place biscuit shells on serving dish. Spoon sauce into centers; top with pea mixture. Serve immediately. Yield: 4 servings.

NEW POTATO CRISPS

20 sm. new potatoes
4 tbsp. melted butter
6 tbsp. dry breadcrumbs
6 tbsp. grated Swiss cheese

Cook potatoes in boiling water until partially done; drain well. Peel; arrange in shallow casserole. Pour butter over potatoes. Combine crumbs and cheese; sprinkle over casserole. Bake in 300-degree oven for 45 minutes or until brown.

Mildred Bergstrom
International Honorary Member, BSP
Montreal, Quebec, Canada

STUFFED ITALIAN SQUASH

3 med. squash
1 1/2 c. boiling water
1 clove of garlic
1 1/2 tsp. salt
3/4 c. crushed cracker crumbs
2 tbsp. chopped green pepper
2 tbsp. chopped onion
1/4 c. grated Cheddar cheese
1 egg, beaten
3 tbsp. salad oil

Cut squash into halves lengthwise; place in boiling water in saucepan. Add garlic and 1 teaspoon salt. Cover; simmer for 10 minutes. Remove squash from water; scoop out and reserve pulp. Combine all remaining ingredients except oil with reserved pulp; refill squash shells. Pour 1 tablespoon oil into shallow baking pan. Heat remaining oil in large skillet. Fry squash, filling sides down, in hot oil in skillet until browned. Place squash in greased baking pan, filling sides up. Bake at 400 degrees for 30 minutes.

Ann Coleman, Pres.
Beta Alpha Kappa No. 6289, Los Banos, California

ZUCCHINI OMELET

1 med. onion, chopped
2 cloves of garlic, minced
2 tbsp. olive oil
6 med. zucchini
1 tsp. marjoram
1/2 tsp. sweet basil
1/4 tsp. oregano
Salt and pepper to taste
4 eggs
1 1/4 c. grated Romano or
    Parmesan cheese
Paprika to taste

Preheat oven to 350 degrees. Saute onion and garlic in hot olive oil in skillet until limp. Dice unpeeled zucchini; add to onion mixture. Add herbs, salt, and pepper. Stir well; cover. Simmer for 10 to 15 minutes or until zucchini is tender. Cool thoroughly. Beat eggs until fluffy; stir in cheese and zucchini. Pour into greased 8 x 8 x 2-inch pan. Sprinkle with paprika. Bake for 30 minutes or until inserted knife comes out clean. May be served hot or cold. Yield: 8-12 servings.

Mrs. Gladys M. McCarthy
International Honorary Member, BSP
Forest Park, Illinois

SWEET POTATO PUFFS

2 c. mashed cooked sweet
    potatoes
1/2 tsp. salt
1/8 tsp. pepper
1 egg, beaten
Milk
8 lg. marshmallows
1/2 c. crushed corn flakes
Salad oil

Mix mashed potatoes, salt, and pepper. Add egg and enough milk to moisten; mix well. Form into 8 balls with marshmallow in center of each; roll in corn flake crumbs. Fry in deep oil at 390 degrees until brown; drain on absorbent paper. May be placed on greased baking sheet, brushed with melted butter, and baked at 350 degrees for 30 minutes, if desired. Chopped peanuts may be substituted for corn flake crumbs.

Violet Denney, Xi Beta Beta Oregon X2217
Portland, Oregon

SWEET POTATO SOUFFLE

1 c. milk
2 tbsp. butter
2 tbsp. sugar
1/2 tsp. salt
2 c. cooked sweet potatoes,
    mashed
1/4 c. raisins
1/4 c. broken nuts
1 tsp. nutmeg

1 tsp. allspice
2 egg whites
Marshmallows

Scald milk. Add butter, sugar, and salt; stir until butter is melted. Add potatoes, raisins, nuts, and spices. Beat egg whites until stiff peaks form; fold into potato mixture. Place in greased casserole; arrange marshmallows over top. Bake in 350-degree oven for 25 minutes. Yield: 8 servings.

Betty P. Andrews, Beta Lambda Chap.
Portsmouth, Virginia

SWEET POTATO SURPRISE

1   1-lb. 1-oz. can sweet potatoes
1 1/4 c. (packed) brown sugar
1 1/2 tbsp. cornstarch
1/4 tsp. salt
1/8 tsp. cinnamon
1 tsp. shredded orange peel (opt.)
1   1-lb. can apricot halves
2 tbsp. butter
1/2 c. pecan halves

Drain sweet potatoes; place in baking dish. Combine sugar, cornstarch, salt, cinnamon, and orange peel in saucepan. Drain apricots; reserve syrup. Stir 1 cup reserved syrup into cornstarch mixture; cook, stirring, over medium heat until mixture comes to a boil. Add apricots, butter, and pecans; pour over potatoes. Bake at 375 degrees for 25 minutes. Yield: 6 servings.

Connie K. Heineman, Pres.
Phi Delta Iota P1932, Elkhart, Indiana

SWEET POTATOES WITH MERINGUE TOPPING

2 lb. sweet potatoes
2 tbsp. butter or margarine
1/2 c. milk
1/4 tsp. nutmeg
Salt to taste
1/4 tsp. cinnamon

3 egg whites
6 tbsp. sugar

Cook potatoes in boiling water until tender; peel and mash. Add butter, milk, nutmeg, and salt; mix well. Turn into greased casserole; sprinkle with cinnamon. Beat egg whites until soft peaks form; add sugar gradually, beating until stiff peaks form. Spoon over sweet potato mixture. Bake at 400 degrees until meringue is brown.

Photograph for this recipe on page 128.

LOUISIANA YAMS WITH GRAPES

4 med. Louisiana yams, cooked
1/4 c. butter or margarine
1/3 c. (firmly-packed) dark
    brown sugar
1/2 tsp. grated lemon peel
2 tbsp. lemon juice
1 1/2 c. halved dark grapes,
    seeded

Peel yams; cut into large slices. Melt butter in large skillet; stir in sugar, lemon peel and juice. Heat until blended and bubbling. Add yams and grapes. Cook, partially covered, over medium heat for 8 to 10 minutes, turning yams once. Serve hot.

BREADS

EASY BREADSTICKS

1 c. butter
1 clove of garlic, crushed
1 loaf day-old bread
Grated Parmesan cheese
Cayenne pepper

Melt butter; stir in garlic. Cut bread into 4-inch strips; brush all sides of bread with butter mixture. Place on cookie sheet. Bake in 275-degree oven for 1 hour and 30 minutes, turning bread every 15 minutes; sprinkle with cheese and cayenne pepper. Store in airtight container; bread sticks will keep for a month.

Cherry Corman, Yearbook Chm.
Alpha Delta Phi No. 7411, Eagle Lake, Texas

GREAT CAESAR'S TOAST

1 egg, beaten
1/4 c. Caesar salad dressing
1 can refrigerator crescent
    dinner rolls
2 c. herb-seasoned stuffing mix,
    coarsely crushed
1/3 c. grated Parmesan cheese

Combine egg and salad dressing in small mixing bowl. Unroll crescent dough; separate into 8 triangles. Cut each triangle in half, forming 16 triangles. Dip each triangle into salad dressing mixture; dip in crushed stuffing mix, coating both sides. Place 1 inch apart on ungreased cookie sheets; sprinkle with cheese. Bake at 375 degrees for 13 to 15 minutes or until golden brown.

Ellen Wilbert, Pres., Xi Beta Lambda X1997
Derby, Kansas

THELMA THOMPSON SLAYDEN'S MEAL PATTIES

1 c. flour
2 c. white cornmeal
1/2 c. sugar
2 tbsp. baking powder
Pinch of salt
1 c. milk
1 1/2 c. melted butter
2 eggs, beaten

Mix flour, cornmeal, sugar, baking powder, and salt. Add milk, butter, and eggs; mix well. Drop by spoonfuls onto hot, greased griddle; cook until brown on both sides. May be baked in oven, if desired.

Thelma Slayden
International Honorary Member, BSP
Atlanta, Georgia

SALLIE EARLE'S BUTTERMILK BISCUITS

2 c. all-purpose flour
1/2 tsp. soda
2/3 tsp. salt
3 tbsp. shortening
3/4 c. buttermilk

Sift dry ingredients together; cut in shortening with two forks. Add buttermilk all at once; mix well. Knead lightly on floured surface; roll out to 1/2-inch thick circle. Cut with biscuit cutter; place on lightly greased baking sheet. Bake at 450 degrees for 12 minutes or until brown. Yield: 12 biscuits.

Dr. Herberta Ann Leonardy
International Honorary Member, BSP
Miami, Florida

BLENDER BREAD

1 c. milk
1 pkg. dry yeast
1/4 c. oil
1 egg
1 tsp. salt
2 tbsp. sugar
3 c. flour

Scald milk; cool to lukewarm. Place milk and yeast in blender; let stand for 5 minutes. Cover blender; blend at high speed for 20 seconds. Add remaining ingredients except flour; blend at high speed for 5 seconds. Pour into flour in bowl; mix thoroughly. Cover; let rise for 1 hour and 30 minutes or until doubled in bulk. Stir down. Turn out on lightly floured board; shape into loaf. Place in greased loaf pan; let rise for 45 minutes or until doubled in bulk. Bake at 375 degrees for 45 minutes. May shape into rolls, if desired. May use 1 cup lukewarm orange juice instead of milk, omit sugar, and add grated rind of 1/4 orange and 1/2 cup raisins for orange-raisin bread.

Trudy Challis, Eta No. 1172
Montgomery, Alabama

DILLY BREAD

1 pkg. yeast
1/4 c. warm water
1 c. cottage cheese
2 tbsp. sugar
1 tbsp. onion flakes
2 tbsp. dillseed
2 tbsp. butter
1 tsp. salt
1/4 tsp. soda
1 egg
2 1/2 c. flour

Dissolve yeast in warm water. Heat cottage cheese to lukewarm; stir in yeast. Add remaining ingredients; mix well. Let rise in warm place until doubled in bulk. Place in well-greased loaf pan; let rise for 30 minutes. Bake at 350 degrees for 45 minutes.

Mrs. Elender H. Barrett
International Honorary Member, BSP
Albany, Missouri

AIRY CHEESE ROLLS

1 pkg. dry yeast
Sugar
1/4 c. warm water
1 3/4 c. milk, scalded
1 c. shredded sharp cheese
2 tbsp. shortening
1 tsp. salt

4 c. sifted all-purpose flour
1 egg, beaten
1/2 c. cornmeal

Dissolve yeast and 1/2 teaspoon sugar in water. Combine milk, cheese, 1/4 cup sugar, shortening, and salt in large mixing bowl; stir until cheese melts. Cool to lukewarm. Add 2 cups flour; beat at medium speed for 2 minutes. Add egg, yeast mixture, cornmeal, and remaining flour; beat for 2 minutes. Cover; let rise in warm place for about 1 hour and 15 minutes or until doubled in bulk. Stir down; fill greased 2 1/2-inch muffin tins 1/2 full. Cover; let rise in warm place for 45 minutes or until doubled in bulk. Bake at 375 degrees for 15 to 20 minutes. Yield: 2 dozen.

Irene R. Squires, Beta Zeta No. 6931
Terrace, British Columbia, Canada

CARAWAY PUFFS

2 pkg. dry yeast
1/2 c. warm water
2 tbsp. caraway seed
2 c. creamed cottage cheese
1/4 c. sugar
2 tsp. salt
1/2 tsp. soda
2 eggs, slightly beaten
4 2/3 c. flour
Melted butter or margarine

Dissolve yeast in water in mixing bowl; add caraway seed. Heat cheese just until lukewarm. Add cheese, sugar, salt, soda, and eggs to yeast mixture; mix well. Add flour gradually, mixing until dough cleans bowl; let rise in warm place for 1 hour or until doubled in bulk. Stir down; place in 24 large well-greased muffin cups. Cover; let rise for about 45 minutes or until doubled in bulk. Bake in preheated 350-degree oven for 25 minutes or until golden brown and puffs sound hollow when tapped. Remove from cups; brush with butter.

Phyllis Hughes, Pres., Xi Gamma Rho No. 3091
Lyons, Kansas

CARAWAY-RYE PAN ROLLS

4 c. unsifted flour
1 c. unsifted rye flour
1 tbsp. sugar
1 tbsp. salt
1 tbsp. caraway seed
1 pkg. dry yeast
1 c. milk
2 tbsp. honey
1 tbsp. margarine
1 egg white

Blend flours together. Combine 1 2/3 cups flour mixture, sugar, salt, caraway seed and yeast in large bowl. Combine milk, 3/4 cup water, honey and margarine in saucepan. Heat over low heat until liquids are lukewarm. Margarine does not need to melt. Add to dry ingredients gradually. Beat for 2 minutes at medium speed of electric mixer, scraping bowl occasionally. Add 1 cup remaining flour mixture or enough flour mixture to make thick batter. Beat at high speed for 2 minutes, scraping bowl occasionally. Stir in enough flour mixture to make soft dough. Add additional flour to obtain desired dough if necessary. Turn dough out onto lightly floured board; knead for about 8 to 10 minutes, until smooth and elastic. Place in greased bowl, turning to grease top. Cover; let rise for about 1 hour in warm place, free from draft, until doubled in bulk. Punch dough down; turn out onto lightly floured board. Divide in half; form each half into smooth ball. Cover; let rest for 10 minutes. Form each piece into 12-inch roll; cut into 12 equal pieces. Shape into smooth balls. Place in 2 greased 9-inch round cake pans. Cover; let rise for about 1 hour in warm place, free from draft, until doubled in bulk. Combine egg white and 2 tablespoons water; brush rolls. Bake at 400 degrees for about 25 minutes or until done. Remove from baking pans; cool on wire racks. Yield: 24 rolls.

CRESCENT ROLLS

1/3 c. sugar
1/2 c. shortening
1 tsp. salt
1/2 c. boiling water
1 env. yeast

1/2 c. warm water
1 egg, beaten
3 c. flour, sifted
Butter

Cream sugar, shortening, and salt in bowl. Stir in boiling water; cool. Dissolve yeast in warm water; stir in egg. Stir into sugar mixture; stir in flour. Let stand for 1 hour. Beat well; cover with cloth. Place in refrigerator; let rise until doubled in bulk. Remove from refrigerator; punch down. Divide in half. Roll out on floured surface into 8-inch circles; cut each circle into 6 or 8 pie-shaped wedges. Place pat of butter on wide end of each wedge; roll towards point. Place on greased cookie sheet, point side down; let rise for about 2 hours. Bake at 400 degrees for 8 to 10 minutes.

Mrs. Leon D. Pryor, Rho No. 1322
Raleigh, North Carolina

MOTHER ADINE MATTSON'S SWEDISH RYE BREAD

1 env. dry yeast
1 tsp. sugar
8 1/2 to 9 c. flour
2 1/2 tsp. salt
2 1/2 c. rye flour
1/4 c. lard or shortening
3/4 c. molasses
2 tsp. caraway seed
1/2 c. (packed) brown sugar

Dissolve yeast and sugar in 1/4 cup warm water. Mix 1 1/2 cups warm water and 2 cups flour; stir in yeast and 1/2 teaspoon salt. Let rise for about 1 hour or overnight. Mix rye flour with 2 cups hot water. Add lard, molasses, caraway seed, remaining salt, and brown sugar. Stir in yeast mixture; add enough remaining flour to make stiff dough. Let rise until doubled in bulk. Shape into 4 loaves; place in greased loaf pans. Let rise until doubled in bulk. Bake at 325 degrees for 1 hour.

Elwill M. Shanahan
International Honorary Member, BSP
Topeka, Kansas

ENGLISH SALLY LUNN

1 1/2 c. milk
2 pkg. dry yeast
1/2 c. very warm water
2 tbsp. sugar
1 1/2 tsp. salt
2 eggs
1/4 c. soft shortening
5 1/2 c. flour

Scald milk; cool to lukewarm. Dissolve yeast in very warm water in mixing bowl. Stir in milk and remaining ingredients; beat until smooth. Cover; let rise for 1 hour. Beat down; pour into 10-inch tube pan. Let rise for 45 minutes or until dough is within 1 inch of top of pan. Bake at 350 degrees for 45 to 50 minutes; serve hot.

Carol J. Mick, Ohio Lambda Tau No. 5625
Weirton, West Virginia

SWISS OATMEAL BREAD

1 1/2 c. milk
1/4 c. (packed) brown sugar
1 tbsp. salt
3 tbsp. butter
1/2 c. lukewarm water
2 pkg. yeast
2 c. rolled oats
1 c. grated Swiss cheese
4 c. (about) flour

Scald milk; stir in sugar, salt, and butter. Cool until lukewarm. Place water in large bowl. Add yeast; stir until dissolved. Stir in milk mixture, oats, cheese, and half the flour; beat until blended. Add enough remaining flour to make soft dough; knead on floured surface for 10 minutes. Place in greased bowl; turn to grease top. Cover; let rise for 1 hour. Punch down; turn onto floured board. Divide in half; shape into loaves. Place in 2 greased 9 x 5 x 3-inch loaf pans; cover. Let rise for 1 hour or until doubled in bulk. Bake at 375 degrees for 35 to 40 minutes.

Mary L. Herr, Xi Epsilon Chi No. 2744
Granite City, Illinois

HERBED PINWHEELS

1 c. softened butter
1/4 c. chopped parsley
1/2 tsp. oregano leaves
1/4 tsp. tarragon leaves
1/4 tsp. ground thyme
1/8 tsp. pepper
4 c. sifted all-purpose flour
2 tbsp. baking powder
2 tsp. salt
2/3 c. vegetable shortening
1 1/2 c. milk
1 egg

Whip butter with parsley, oregano, tarragon, thyme, and pepper; let stand for 1 hour to blend flavors. Mix flour, baking powder, and salt in bowl; cut in shortening until mixture resembles coarse meal. Stir in milk. Knead for about 10 times on floured board; divide in half. Roll out each half into 12 x 10-inch rectangle; spread half the herb mixture on each rectangle. Roll up each rectangle from 12-inch side as for jelly roll; seal edge. Cut each roll into 1/2-inch slices; place, cut side down, in ungreased muffin pans. Beat egg with 2 tablespoons water; brush over pinwheels. Bake in 425-degree oven for 10 to 15 minutes or until golden brown.

Photograph for this recipe on page 3.

LINDA'S RYE BREAD

1 tbsp. yeast
1 tsp. sugar
3/4 c. lukewarm water
1/2 c. (packed) brown sugar
1/2 c. molasses
1 tbsp. salt
1/2 c. shortening
2 c. hot water
2 c. cool water
2 c. rye flour
8 to 10 c. flour
2 tbsp. aniseed

Mix yeast, sugar, and lukewarm water; let stand for 10 minutes. Mix brown sugar, molasses, salt, and shortening in large bowl. Add hot water; stir until shortening is melted. Stir in cool water. Add rye flour; mix. Add enough flour to make stiff dough; stir in aniseed. Knead on floured surface until smooth and elastic. Place in greased bowl; turn to grease top. Let rise until doubled in bulk. Punch down; let rise until doubled in bulk. Form into 4 loaves; place on greased cookie sheet. Let rise until doubled in bulk. Bake at 400 degrees for 45 to 60 minutes or until done.

Linda Thompson, VP, Alpha Eta No. 7719
Carrot River, Saskatchewan, Canada

FRENCH BREAD

1 env. dry yeast
1 1/2 c. very warm water
2 tbsp. sugar
1 1/2 tsp. salt
1 tbsp. soft shortening
4 c. flour
1/4 c. melted margarine
1 egg white, beaten
Sesame seed

Sprinkle yeast into 3/4 cup very warm water; stir until dissolved. Combine remaining water, sugar, and salt in large bowl. Add shortening and yeast mixture; mix well. Add 3 cups flour; mix well. Add remaining flour; mix well. Let stand for 50 minutes, stirring every 10 minutes. Turn out on lightly floured surface; divide in half. Shape into 2 balls; let rest for 10 minutes. Roll each ball into 12 x 9-inch rectangle; roll from 12-inch side as for jelly roll. Seal edge. Place on greased baking sheet; cut across top of each roll 5 times. Brush with margarine, then with egg white; sprinkle with sesame seed. Cover with cloth; let rise for 1 hour and 30 minutes. Bake at 375 degrees for 30 to 35 minutes.

Joyce Emerson, Delta Theta No. 2930
Lexington, Missouri

HEIRLOOM BREAD

4 c. flour
2 tsp. baking powder

1 1/2 tsp. soda
2 tsp. salt
2 tsp. cinnamon
1/2 tsp. nutmeg
1/2 tsp. ground cloves
2 c. sugar
1 c. margarine
4 eggs
1 tsp. lemon extract
1 tsp. vanilla
2 c. canned applesauce
2/3 c. chopped nuts
1/2 c. currants

Combine first seven ingredients; sift. Cream sugar and margarine until fluffy; beat in eggs, flavorings, and applesauce. Add to dry ingredients; blend until smooth. Stir in nuts and currants; turn into 2 greased 9 x 5 x 3-inch loaf pans. Bake in 300-degree oven for 55 to 60 minutes. Cool for at least 4 hours before slicing.

Carolina Warren, Honorary Member
Xi Alpha Pi X1364, Carrollton, Missouri

NECTARINE-NUT LOAF

2 to 3 fresh nectarines
1/2 c. shortening
1 c. sugar
2 eggs
1 tsp. vanilla
2 1/2 c. sifted all-purpose flour
2 1/2 tsp. baking powder
1 tsp. salt
1/2 c. chopped pecans

Blanch nectarines; remove peels. Mash enough fruit to measure 1 cup. Cream shortening with sugar; mix in eggs and vanilla. Sift flour with baking powder and salt; add to creamed mixture alternately with mashed nectarines, mixing well after each addition. Mix in pecans. Turn into greased and floured 9 x 5 x 3-inch loaf pan. Bake in 350-degree oven for about 1 hour. Cool in pan for 10 minutes; remove. Cool completely on rack. Wrap and store overnight for best slicing.

CROWN ROLLS

1 recipe butterhorn roll dough
Melted butter
1/2 c. sugar
1 tsp. cinnamon
1/2 c. raisins
1/2 c. chopped walnuts

Shape dough into golf ball-sized balls; dip in melted butter. Mix remaining ingredients; dip balls in sugar mixture. Place in well-greased angel food cake pan in staggered layers, leaving as much space between balls as possible for rising; sprinkle remaining sugar mixture over top. Cover; let rise for 1 hour. Bake at 350 degrees for 1 hour. Remove from pan; serve hot.

Mrs. Lawrence Stavig
International Honorary Member, BSP
Sioux Falls, South Dakota

ALMOND-FILLED STOLLEN

1 3/4 c. mixed glace fruits
Rum
2 env. dry yeast
Sugar
1 1/2 c. milk
2 1/2 tsp. salt
1 1/4 c. butter
2 tsp. grated lemon rind
1 tsp. almond extract
6 1/2 to 8 c. flour
5 eggs, beaten
1/3 c. slivered almonds
1 c. almond paste
2 tbsp. whipping cream
Egg yolk
Sifted powdered sugar

Combine glace fruits with 1/2 cup rum; let stand for several hours or overnight. Dissolve yeast in 1/2 cup very warm water; add 2 teaspoons sugar. Scald milk; stir in 2/3 cup sugar, salt, butter, lemon rind, almond extract, and 2 tablespoons rum. Cool to lukewarm. Stir in yeast mixture and 4 cups flour; blend well. Let rise in warm place for about 30 minutes or until blistery. Stir in 4 eggs and enough remaining flour to make soft but not sticky dough; turn out onto floured board. Drain fruits; reserve rum. Knead all but 1/2 cup fruits into dough; knead in slivered almonds until smooth and elastic, adding flour, as necessary, to prevent sticking. Place in greased bowl; let set in warm place for 1 hour and 30 minutes or until doubled in bulk. Divide dough in thirds; roll each third on floured board into circle about 3/4 inch thick. Mix almond paste, cream, and remaining egg; spread on each circle. Fold dough over, not quite lining up edge. Beat egg yolk with 2 teaspoons water; brush on almond filling. Place on greased cookie sheet; let rise until doubled in bulk. Bake at 375 degrees for 35 minutes. Mix reserved rum and enough powdered sugar for glaze; spread on warm stollen. Garnish with remaining fruits and additional almonds.

Mrs. Harvey Binsfield, Corr. Sec.
Xi Mu Delta No. 2892, Merced, California

DESSERTS

BLUEBERRY CAKE

1/4 c. vegetable shortening
1 c. sugar
1/4 tsp. salt
2 eggs
1 c. milk
2 c. sifted flour
4 tsp. baking powder
1/2 tsp. vanilla
Dash of nutmeg
2 c. blueberries

Combine shortening, sugar, and salt in bowl; beat with electric beater until creamy. Add eggs, beating until frothy. Add milk; beat until smooth. Sift flour and baking powder together; add to milk mixture. Add vanilla and nutmeg. Fold in blueberries carefully; pour into prepared cake pan. Bake for 30 minutes at about 425 degrees.

Hon. Margaret Chase Smith
International Honorary Member, BSP
Washington, D. C.

APRICOT NECTAR CAKE

1 box yellow cake mix
1 pkg. lemon gelatin
3/4 c. apricot nectar
1 c. vegetable oil
4 eggs
1 tsp. lemon extract
1/2 box confectioners' sugar
Lemon juice

Combine first 6 ingredients in bowl; beat for 4 minutes. Pour into well-greased and floured tube pan. Bake for 1 hour at 325 degrees. Combine confectioners' sugar and enough lemon juice to make a pouring consistency. Turn cake out on plate; pour glaze on top and side of cake.

Joan Sue Segal, Hon. Mem.
Alpha Beta No. 2164, Portsmouth, Virginia

CHEESECAKE SUPREME

1 c. sifted all-purpose flour
1/4 c. sugar
1 tsp. grated lemon peel
1/2 c. butter
1 egg yolk, slightly beaten
1/4 tsp. vanilla

Combine first 3 ingredients; cut in butter until mixture is crumbly. Add egg yolk and vanilla; blend thoroughly. Press 1/3 of the pastry on bottom of 9-inch springform pan. Bake in 400-degree oven for about 8 minutes. Attach side to bottom of pan; grease with additional butter. Press remaining pastry 1 3/4 inches up side of pan.

Filling

5 8-oz. packages cream cheese
1/4 tsp. vanilla
3/4 tsp. grated lemon peel
1 3/4 c. sugar
3 tbsp. all-purpose flour
1/4 tsp. salt
1 c. eggs
2 egg yolks
1/4 c. whipping cream

Soften cream cheese at room temperature; beat until creamy. Stir in vanilla and lemon peel. Mix sugar, flour, and salt; blend into cheese mixture gradually. Add eggs and egg yolks, one at a time, beating well after each addition; stir in whipping cream. Turn into crust. Bake at 450 degrees for 12 minutes. Reduce temperature to 300 degrees; bake for 55 minutes longer. Remove from oven; cool for 30 minutes. May be covered with glaze, if desired. Yield: 12 servings.

Judy Glassburn, Pres.
Phi Delta Phi No. P1193, Chillicothe, Ohio

ALMOND-CHOCOLATE CAKE

8 eggs, separated
1 c. sugar
1/2 lb. semisweet chocolate
1 1/2 c. ground walnuts
4 tbsp. unsalted butter, melted

Beat egg yolks well; add 1/2 cup sugar, beating until frothy. Beat egg whites until soft peaks form; add remaining sugar slowly, beating until stiff but not dry. Fold egg yolks and egg whites together. Shred chocolate fine. Fold chocolate and walnuts into egg mixture. Fold in melted butter. Pour batter into 2 greased 9-inch cake tins. Bake at 325 degrees for 45 minutes or until done.

Buttercream Frosting

4 egg yolks
5 tbsp. sugar
1 1/2 tbsp. instant coffee
1/2 lb. unsalted butter

Place egg yolks, sugar, and instant coffee in bowl; beat until frothy. Place in top of double boiler; cook for 5 to 8 minutes, stirring constantly, until thickened. Cool. Whip butter until frothy; add egg yolk mixture. Frost cake top and side. Sprinkle top with additional shredded chocolate; decorate with blanched almonds.

Josephine R. Krieger, Xi Beta Theta No. 2438
Molalla, Oregon

CHOCOLATE ICE CREAM CAKE

1 pkg. angel food cake mix
3 c. whipping cream
1 16-oz. can chocolate syrup
2 tbsp. powdered sugar
1 tsp. vanilla

Prepare and bake cake mix according to package directions; cool. Slice crosswise into 4 layers. Whip cream until soft peaks form. Add remaining ingredients all at once; beat until thick. Do not let mixture separate. Spread between layers and on side and top of cake. Slice. May be frozen for up to 6 months; transfer to refrigerator 1 hour before serving. Yield: 16-20 servings.

Mrs. Lois Keener Thome
International Honorary Member, BSP
Corona, California

CHRISTMAS CAKE

1 lb. butter
2 c. sugar
6 eggs
4 c. flour
1 tsp. baking powder
1/2 c. whiskey
1 lb. chopped pecans
1 lb. white raisins

Combine butter and sugar in bowl; cream until smooth. Add eggs, one at a time, beating well. Sift flour and baking powder together; add to creamed mixture alternately with whiskey. Fold in pecans and raisins. Turn into greased and floured tube pan. Bake at 325 degrees for 1 hour and 30 minutes.

Mrs. L. J. Wathen
Honorary International Member, BSP
Dallas, Texas

FRESH APPLE-BUTTER CAKE

1 c. butter
2 c. sugar
3 eggs
3 c. sifted flour
1 1/2 tsp. soda
1/2 tsp. salt
1 tsp. cinnamon
1/8 tsp. nutmeg
2 tsp. vanilla
3 c. peeled chopped apples
2 c. chopped walnuts

Combine butter and sugar in bowl; cream until smooth. Add eggs, one at a time, beating well after each addition. Sift flour, soda, salt, cinnamon, and nutmeg together; add to creamed mixture. Stir in vanilla. Fold in chopped apples and walnuts. Pour into greased and floured 10-inch tube pan. Bake in 325-degree oven until cake tester inserted in cake comes out clean. Remove to rack. Let stand for 15 minutes. Turn onto cake plate. Glaze, if desired.

Glaze

1 1/2 c. sugar
1/2 c. sherry

Combine sugar and sherry in saucepan. Cook, stirring constantly, until sugar is dissolved. Pour on cake.

Mrs. Roy Zyko, VP, Beta Nu No. 6478
Waterbury, Connecticut

QUICK CAKE

1/3 c. soft butter
1 1/3 c. (firmly packed) brown
   sugar
2 eggs
1/2 c. milk
1 3/4 c. flour
3 tsp. baking powder
1/2 tsp. cinnamon
1/2 tsp. grated nutmeg
1/2 lb. dates, chopped (opt.)

Combine all ingredients in bowl; beat for 3 minutes with wooden spoon. Pour in buttered and floured pan. Bake at 350 degrees for 35 to 40 minutes.

Dr. Vega G. Dawson
International Honorary Member, BSP
Halifax, Nova Scotia, Canada

FRUIT CAKE

4 eggs
1 c. sugar
1 c. flour
2 tsp. baking powder
Dash of salt
1 lb. pecan halves
1 lb. dates, cut up
1 c. maraschino cherries, drained
  and chopped
1 tsp. vanilla

Beat eggs well; add sugar, mixing thoroughly. Sift flour, baking powder and salt together. Add to egg mixture. Add remaining ingredients; mix well. Pour into 3 greased and floured small cake pans or 1 tube pan. Bake at 325 degrees for 1 hour.

Mrs. Ernestine Nobles
International Honorary Member, BSP
Amarillo, Texas

MRS. CRAWFORD'S POUND CAKE

1 stick margarine, room temperature
1/2 c. shortening
2 c. sifted flour
2 tsp. baking powder
4 lg. eggs
1/2 c. milk
1 1/2 c. sugar
1 tsp. vanilla
1/2 tsp. salt

Place all ingredients in large bowl; mix with electric mixer for 20 minutes, scraping down side occasionally. Pour in tube pan. Place in cold oven. Bake at 350 degrees for 1 hour. Turn out on cake stand.

Glaze

1 tbsp. frozen orange juice
2 tbsp. confectioners' sugar

Combine orange juice and confectioners' sugar in bowl; spoon over warm cake.

Mrs. Alice VanLandingham
International Honorary Member, BSP
Morgantown, West Virginia

RAISIN CAKE

1 c. raisins
1 tsp. soda
1 stick margarine
1 c. sugar
1 egg, beaten
1 1/2 c. flour
1 tsp. cinnamon
Dash of nutmeg

Combine raisins and 2 cups water in saucepan; boil for 15 minutes. Add soda and margarine; cool. Add sugar, egg, flour and spices. Pour into square cake pan. Bake at 350 degrees for 1 hour or until done. Cut in squares to serve. Batter may be poured in large baking dish and sprinkled with cinnamon. Cut into size and shape as desired for cookies.

Gladys Pyle
International Honorary Member, BSP
Huron, South Dakota

BOURBON POUND CAKE

1 lb. butter or margarine
3 c. sugar
8 eggs, separated
3 c. sifted flour
2 tsp. vanilla
2 tsp. almond extract
1/3 c. bourbon
1/2 c. chopped pecans

Combine butter and 2 cups sugar in bowl; cream until light and fluffy. Add egg yolks, one at a time, beating thoroughly after each addition. Add flour alternately with flavorings and bourbon in thirds, beating until smooth after each addition. Beat egg whites until soft peaks form; add remaining sugar gradually, beating until stiff. Fold egg yolk mixture into meringue gently. Sprinkle pecans in bottom of well-buttered 10-inch tube pan. Turn batter into pan. Bake at 350 degrees for 1 hour and 30 minutes. Pecans may be folded into cake batter, if desired.

Olive White, Pres., Alpha Beta Tau No. 6891
Boerne, Texas

PINEAPPLE POLYNESIAN TORTE

2   13 1/4-oz. cans pineapple
    tidbits
1   1-lb. 1-oz. package pound cake
    mix
1/2 c. sugar
3 tbsp. cornstarch
1/8 tsp. salt
1 egg, beaten
1 tbsp. butter
1/4 tsp. grated lemon peel
1 tbsp. lemon juice
2   2-oz. envelopes whipped
    topping mix

Drain pineapple, reserving syrup. Prepare cake mix according to package directions. Turn into greased 9-inch springform pan. Bake at 350 degrees for about 50 minutes or until cake tests done. Cool. Split cake into 3 layers. Combine reserved pineapple syrup, sugar, cornstarch, and salt. Cook, stirring constantly, until mixture boils and thickens. Stir small amount of hot mixture into egg. Blend into remaining cooked mixture. Stir briskly; cook for 1 minute longer over low heat. Remove from heat. Blend in butter, lemon peel, lemon juice, and pineapple. Cool. Prepare topping mix according to package directions. Spread pineapple mix-

ture between layers and on top of cake, piping edges with whipped topping.

FILBERT TORTE WITH STRAWBERRY WHIPPED CREAM

Graham cracker crumbs
2 c. sugar
1/2 tsp. ground allspice
1 lb. filberts, ground
1 tsp. grated lemon peel
6 eggs, separated
1/4 tsp. salt
1 tbsp. light corn syrup
1 tsp. water
1 egg white, slightly beaten

Grease 9-inch 6 1/2-cup ring pan; sprinkle with graham cracker crumbs. Set aside. Mix sugar and allspice together; mix in filberts and lemon peel with tossing motion. Beat egg yolks until thick and lemon colored; blend into filbert mixture, working in well with hands. Beat egg whites until frothy; add salt. Beat until stiff but not dry; fold into filbert mixture. Turn into prepared ring pan. Bake at 350 degrees for 35 to 40 minutes or until cake tests done. Cool for 5 minutes. Loosen cake with spatula; turn out onto ungreased baking sheet. Blend corn syrup and water; brush over top of torte. Brush entire torte with egg white. Bake for 5 minutes longer. Cool; place torte on serving plate.

Strawberry Whipped Cream

2 pt. fresh strawberries
1 1/2 c. heavy cream
3 tbsp. kirsch

Slice strawberries, reserving 1 cup for garnish. Whip cream until stiff, adding kirsch gradually. Fold in sliced strawberries. Mound in center of torte; garnish with reserved strawberries.

Photograph for this recipe on page 135.

EGGNOG MOLD

3 env. unflavored gelatin
1/2 c. water

5 c. dairy eggnog
1 tsp. grated lemon rind
1/4 tsp. salt
1 c. whipping cream
Cranberry-Orange Sauce

Soften gelatin in water. Pour 2 cups eggnog in 3-quart saucepan; heat to simmering. Add gelatin; stir until gelatin is dissolved. Add remaining eggnog, lemon rind, and salt. Chill until mixture begins to thicken. Whip cream until stiff; fold into eggnog mixture. Turn into a 7-cup mold. Chill until firm. Unmold onto chilled plate; top with about 1/2 cup Cranberry-Orange Sauce. Serve with remaining sauce.

Cranberry-Orange Sauce

2 c. sugar
1/2 c. water
6 tbsp. frozen concentrated
  orange juice
2 c. cranberries
2 tbsp. water
1 tbsp. cornstarch
4 to 5 drops of angostura bitters

Combine sugar, water, and orange juice in 2-quart saucepan; heat until sugar is dissolved. Add cranberries; cook for about 5 minutes. Combine water and cornstarch in a small bowl; stir into cranberry mixture. Cook until slightly thickened and clear. Stir in bitters; chill.

Photograph for this recipe on page 46.

LEMON FLUFF

2 env. unflavored gelatin
8 eggs, separated
1 1/2 c. sugar
Grated rind of 4 lemons
Juice of 4 lemons
1 pt. whipping cream

Soften gelatin according to package directions; dissolve over hot water. Beat egg yolks until thick and lemon colored; add 1 1/4 cups sugar gradually, beating constantly.

Add lemon rind; add lemon juice gradually, beating constantly. Add gelatin; mix well. Beat egg whites until stiff peaks form, adding remaining sugar gradually; fold into gelatin mixture. Whip cream until stiff; fold into gelatin mixture. Place in mold; chill for at least 4 hours. Unmold; garnish with strawberries or mandarin orange sections. Yield: 12 servings.

Mrs. Edmund McKenzie
International Honorary Member, BSP
Swift Current, Saskatchewan, Canada

JAM CAKE

1 1/2 c. sugar
2/3 c. butter
3 eggs, separated
3 c. cake flour
1 tsp. cinnamon
1/2 tsp. cloves
1/2 tsp. nutmeg
1 c. buttermilk
1 tsp. soda
1 c. favorite jam

Cream sugar, butter, and egg yolks together. Sift flour, cinnamon, cloves, and nutmeg together at least twice. Add buttermilk to creamed mixture alternately with flour mixture. Combine soda and 1 1/2 tablespoons warm water. Add to flour mixture. Add jam; fold in stiffly beaten egg whites. Pour into tube pan. Bake at 350 degrees until done.

Caramel Icing

2 c. (firmly packed) light brown
  sugar
1/2 c. cream
1/2 c. butter
1 tsp. vanilla

Combine sugar, cream, and butter in saucepan. Bring to a boil over low heat; cook until soft ball forms in water. Add vanilla; beat until of spreading consistency.

Andree Frady, Rec. Sec., Xi Mu Delta X3554
Denton, Texas

water. Stir until gelatin is dissolved. Pour evaporated milk in ice tray; freeze until ice crystals form around edge of tray. Pour milk into cold bowl; whip until thick. Add to gelatin mixture. Pour in desired mold. Chill until firm.

Mrs. Helen Holt
International Honorary Member, BSP
Georgetown, D. C.

LEMON ICEBOX CAKE

1 tbsp. unflavored gelatin
8 eggs, separated
1 1/4 c. sugar
9 tbsp. lemon juice
1 box vanilla wafers
Serve with whipped cream

Soften gelatin in 2/3 cup cold water. Beat egg yolks well in top of double boiler; stir in 3/4 cup sugar and lemon juice. Place over boiling water; cook until thickened, stirring constantly. Stir in gelatin until dissolved. Chill until thickened. Beat egg whites until stiff, adding remaining sugar gradually; fold into gelatin mixture. Line pan with vanilla wafers; pour in half the custard. Add layer wafers; add remaining custard. Refrigerate for 24 hours. Do not freeze. Yield: 12 servings.

Nellie Cline Steenson
International Honorary Member, BSP
Pocatello, Idaho

LEMON ANGEL RING

1   9-in. angel food cake
1 No. 2 can lemon pie filling
1/2 pt. heavy cream, whipped
1/4 c. crushed lemon drops

Line 9-inch tube pan with waxed paper. Remove brown crusts from cake; tear cake into bite-sized pieces. Fold lemon pie filling into whipped cream; fold in candy lightly. Fill pan with alternate layers of lemon mixture and cake, beginning and ending with lemon mixture. Cover. Refrigerate overnight. Unmold on serving platter. Swirl additional whipped cream or dessert topping over top; sprinkle with additional crushed candy. Yield: 10-12 servings.

LEMON SPONGE

1 pkg. lemon gelatin
1/2 c. sugar
4 tbsp. lemon juice
Grated rind of 1 lemon
1/8 tsp. salt
1 can evaporated milk

Combine gelatin, sugar, lemon juice and rind and salt in bowl; add 1 1/4 cups boiling

ANGEL MOUSSE

6 eggs, separated
1 c. sugar
2 oz. brandy
2 oz. rum
1 pt. whipping cream
2 tsp. vanilla
Dash of salt
2 env. unflavored gelatin
Maraschino cherries

Beat egg yolks until light and lemon colored. Add sugar gradually, beating until creamy.

178

Add brandy and rum, mixing well. Beat egg whites until stiff but not dry. Whip cream until stiff. Add vanilla and salt to whipped cream. Soften gelatin in 1/2 cup cold water for 5 minutes. Place over low heat, stirring until dissolved. Mix gelatin with egg yolk mixture. Fold egg whites and whipped cream into gelatin mixture gently. Pour into sherbet glasses. Top with a cherry. Chill for 2 hours or longer. Yield: 12 servings.

Rosemary Kuga, Pres., Zeta Omicron No. 5452
Lake Worth, Florida

LIGHT CHOCOLATE BROWNIES

2/3 c. sifted all-purpose flour
1/2 tsp. baking powder
1/4 tsp. salt
2 sq. semisweet chocolate
1/3 c. butter
2 eggs
3/4 c. sugar
1/2 c. chopped walnuts
1 tsp. vanilla

Sift flour with baking powder and salt. Melt chocolate partially with butter over hot water. Remove from water; stir rapidly until chocolate is entirely melted. Beat eggs until foamy. Add sugar gradually, beating thoroughly. Blend in chocolate. Add flour; mix well. Stir in walnuts and vanilla. Spread in greased 8-inch square pan. Bake at 350 degrees for about 25 minutes. Cool in pan. Cut into small squares. Yield: About 16 brownies.

Photograph for this recipe on cover.

SUGAR COOKIES

3 2/3 c. sifted cake flour
2 1/2 tsp. baking powder
1/2 tsp. salt
2/3 c. butter or shortening
1 1/2 c. sugar
2 eggs
1 tsp. vanilla
4 tsp. milk
Colored sugar or sugar (opt.)

Sift flour with baking powder and salt. Cream butter; blend in sugar gradually. Add eggs, one at a time, beating thoroughly after each addition. Stir in vanilla. Add flour mixture alternately with milk, mixing well after each addition. Chill for 3 to 4 hours or overnight. Roll dough out wafer-thin. Cut with floured 3-inch star cutter. Sprinkle with colored sugar. Place on ungreased baking sheets. Bake at 400 degrees for 5 to 8 minutes or until lightly browned. Cookies may be decorated with gelatin instead of sugar if desired. Bake cookies, then brush lightly with light corn syrup, slightly beaten egg white, or honey while still warm. Sprinkle with flavored gelatin. Yield: 6 dozen.

Photograph for this recipe on cover.

STRAWBERRY CHANTILLY

1 c. flour
1/4 c. (packed) brown sugar
1/2 c. butter
1/2 c. chopped walnuts
2 egg whites
1 c. sugar
2 c. fresh strawberries
1 tbsp. lemon juice
1 c. whipping cream or whipped
   topping mix

Mix flour, brown sugar, and butter until crumbly; stir in walnuts. Place in baking pan. Bake at 300 degrees for 20 minutes, stirring every 5 minutes. Place 2/3 of the mixture in 9 x 13-inch baking dish. Place egg whites, sugar, strawberries, and lemon juice in large, deep bowl; whip with electric mixer at high speed for 10 minutes. Whip cream until stiff; fold into strawberry mixture. Spread over crumb mixture in baking dish; sprinkle with remaining crumb mixture. Freeze for 6 hours or overnight. One 10-ounce package frozen strawberries and 2/3 cup sugar may be substituted for fresh strawberries and 1 cup sugar. Yield: 12-14 servings.

Mrs. Vera Ayling
International Honorary Member, BSP
Moncton, New Brunswick, Canada

MINTED BAVARIAN

1 tbsp. gelatin
2 eggs, separated
3/4 c. sugar
1/8 tsp. salt
1 c. milk
1/2 tsp. peppermint flavoring
1/2 pt. whipping cream
Green food coloring

Soften gelatin in 1/4 cup cold water for 5 minutes. Beat egg yolks; add sugar and salt. Add milk gradually. Cook in double boiler until thick, stirring constantly. Add softened gelatin to hot custard; stir until dissolved. Cool; add flavoring. Beat egg whites until stiff. Whip cream. Fold egg whites and whipped cream into cool custard, blending gently and thoroughly. Tint to desired color with food coloring. Pour into cold damp ring mold; chill until firm. Unmold; fill centre with whipped cream or fruit if desired.

Mrs. Comeron H. Montrose
Honorary International Member, BSP
Windsor, Ontario, Canada

SCOTCH COOKIES

2 lb. dark brown sugar
1 lb. butter, softened
3 lg. eggs, beaten
1   12-oz. bottle dark molasses
3 tbsp. cinnamon
Flour

Cream sugar and butter until fluffy. Add eggs; mix well. Stir in molasses and cinnamon. Add enough flour to make stiff dough. Pull off small sections of dough; roll in floured hands. Place on greased cookie sheet; pat down. Place cookie sheet on bottom shelf of oven. Bake at 300 degrees for 12 minutes, transferring cookie sheet to higher shelf of oven as cookies begin to rise. Cool before removing from cookie sheet.

Grace E. Alt
Honorary International Member, BSP
Baltimore, Maryland

SNOWBALL CAKE

2 env. unflavored gelatin
1 c. sugar
1 No. 2 can crushed pineapple
Juice of 1 lemon
1 pt. whipping cream, whipped
1 loaf angel food cake, thinly
   sliced
1 sm. can flaked coconut
1 sm. jar maraschino cherries

Soften gelatin in 1/4 cup cold water; dissolve in 1 cup boiling water. Add sugar, stirring to dissolve. Add pineapple and lemon juice; chill until partially congealed. Fold in whipped cream; set aside. Arrange layers of cake slices and gelatin mixture in large serving bowl, ending with gelatin mixture on top. Chill overnight. Garnish with coconut and cherries.

Ruby Altizer Roberts
International Honorary Member, BSP
Christiansburg, Virginia

FRUIT COMPOTE

2 c. watermelon balls
2 red unpeeled apples, cut in
   thin wedges
1 cantaloupe, sliced in wedges
2 c. grapefruit sections
2 bananas, sliced diagonally
1   6-oz. can frozen orange
   juice, thawed

Place watermelon balls in center of compote; arrange remaining fruits around watermelon. Spoon orange juice over fruits; chill. Yield: 6 servings.

Photograph for this recipe on page 128.

ORANGE ICEBOX CAKE

1/2 c. sugar
1 tbsp. cornstarch
3 eggs, separated
1 c. orange juice
1 tbsp. butter

Grated rind of 1 orange
2 boxes ladyfingers
Whipped cream or ice cream

Mix sugar, cornstarch, egg yolks, orange juice, and butter in top of double boiler; cook over hot water until thick, stirring constantly. Remove from water; fold in stiffly beaten egg whites and orange rind. Line serving dish with waxed paper. Split ladyfingers; place in single layer over waxed paper. Add half the orange mixture. Add layer of ladyfingers; add remaining orange mixture. Cover; refrigerate for 24 hours. Serve with whipped cream. Yield: 4 servings.

Dr. Florence B. Seibert
International Honorary Member, BSP
Saint Petersburg, Florida

FROSTY NESSELRODE MOUNTAIN

1   8-oz. package cream cheese
1/2 c. mayonnaise
1/2 c. pineapple preserves
1/2 c. raisins
1/2 c. chopped walnuts
1/2 c. candied cherries, halved
1 c. heavy cream, whipped

Soften cream cheese; blend in mayonnaise. Add pineapple preserves, raisins, walnuts, and cherries; mix well. Fold in whipped cream; place in 9 x 5 x 3-inch pan. Freeze for several hours or overnight. Yield: 8-10 servings.

Mary Regina Hayford
International Honorary Member, BSP
Dubuque, Iowa

PUFFY APPLE FRITTERS

1 1/3 c. sifted all-purpose flour
1 tbsp. sugar
2 tsp. baking powder
1/2 tsp. salt
2 eggs, beaten
2/3 c. milk
1 tbsp. salad oil
3 c. small apple cubes

Sift dry ingredients together. Blend eggs, milk, and salad oil together; add dry ingredients all at once. Mix just until moistened. Stir in apple cubes. Drop by spoonfuls into deep 375-degree fat. Fry for about 3 to 4 minutes or until puffy and golden, turning once. Drain on paper towels. Sprinkle with confectioners' sugar, sugar, or cinnamon sugar while warm.

Jean Stutzman, Pres., Mu Alpha No. 5836
St. Anne, Illinois

GINGER PEARS

1   1-lb. 13-oz. can Bartlett pear halves
3 1/2 tbsp. brown sugar
1 tsp. ground ginger
1 tbsp. vinegar

Drain pears, reserving 3/4 cup syrup. Combine reserved syrup, brown sugar, ginger and vinegar in small saucepan. Simmer for 5 minutes, stirring occasionally. Arrange pear halves, hollow sides up, in single layer in baking dish. Pour hot syrup over pears; cool to room temperature. Refrigerate for 2 hours or overnight. Serve as dessert or salad.

Mrs. Orlando A. Petrillo
International Honorary Member, BSP
Elyria, Ohio

PINEAPPLE CHUNK DIPPERS

1   4 1/2-oz. can pineapple chunks
Mint leaves
1 1/2 c. sour cream
1 1/2 c. (packed) brown sugar

Drain pineapple; chill well. Fill shallow bowl with crushed ice. Place pineapple chunks and mint leaves on ice. Place sour cream and brown sugar in small separate bowls next to pineapple. Spear pineapple chunks with wooden picks; dip into sour cream and brown sugar.

Leta Clark, Soc. Com., Xi Alpha X737
Jackson, Mississippi

BRANDIED BANANAS

6 lg. bananas
3/4 c. (packed) brown sugar
Butter
Brandy
1 pt. vanilla ice cream
1/2 c. chopped walnuts

Peel bananas; halve lengthwise. Place halves, cut sides down, in greased shallow baking dish. Sprinkle generously with brown sugar; dot with butter. Pour in enough brandy to nearly cover. Bake at 325 degrees for 25 to 30 minutes. Remove to serving dish with broad spatula; top with scoops of ice cream. Ladle sauce from baking dish over top. Sprinkle with walnuts. Serve warm. Yield: 6 servings.

Hon. Elizabeth C. Wood
International Honorary Member, BSP
Ganges, British Columbia, Canada

SURPRISE FRUIT PUDDING

2 c. flour
1 1/2 c. sugar
1 tsp. soda
1 tsp. allspice
1 tsp. nutmeg
1 tsp. cinnamon
1 tsp. ground cloves
1 tsp. salt
1 1/2 c. grated carrots
1 c. raisins
1/2 c. candied pineapple
1/2 c. candied cherries
1 c. whole pecans
1 1/2 c. ground kidney suet
2 c. milk

Sift flour, sugar, soda, spices, and salt together; stir in carrots, raisins, candied fruit, and pecans. Add suet and milk; mix well. Spoon into mold. Steam for 4 hours.

Vanilla Sauce

1 c. sugar
1/4 tsp. nutmeg
1 tsp. vanilla
2 tbsp. cornstarch
2 tbsp. butter

Combine all ingredients in saucepan; add 3 cups cold water. Boil, stirring, until smooth and thickened. Serve sauce over pudding.

Mrs. Laurena Senter
International Honorary Member, BSP
Denver, Colorado

RHUBARB CRISP

4 c. diced red rhubarb
3/4 c. sugar
1/4 c. butter
3/4 c. (packed) brown sugar
1/4 c. flour
1/2 c. fine rolled oats
1/4 tsp. salt

Place diced rhubarb in greased baking dish; sprinkle with sugar. Cream butter with brown sugar; blend in flour, oats, and salt. Sprinkle brown sugar mixture over rhubarb mixture. Bake at 375 degrees for about 40 minutes or until rhubarb is soft and topping is golden brown.

Evelyn R. Wright, Soc. Spon.
Theta Xi Gamma No. 3819
Fredericton, New Brunswick, Canada

LIME FLUFF PIE

3 tbsp. melted butter
3/4 c. chocolate wafer crumbs
Whole chocolate wafers
1 env. unflavored gelatin
1/4 c. cold water
2 eggs, separated
1 c. sugar
1/2 tsp. salt
1/2 c. lime juice
1 c. whipping cream, whipped
6 drops of green food coloring
1/3 c. chopped toasted almonds
2 tsp. grated lime peel
Sweetened whipped cream

Line 8-inch round cake pan with narrow double-folded 15-inch strips of waxed paper in lattice fashion; place foil-covered cardboard circle in bottom of pan over strips. Stir butter into crumbs in small bowl; press to cover bottom of cake pan. Line whole wafers around side, overlapping slightly and pressing into crumb base. Sprinkle gelatin over water to soften. Beat egg yolks in saucepan; add 1/2 cup sugar and salt. Add lime juice gradually; cook over medium heat, stirring constantly, until thickened. Add gelatin; stir until gelatin is dissolved. Cool. Beat egg whites until soft peaks form; beat in remaining sugar gradually until stiff peaks form. Fold into lime mixture; fold in whipped cream and food coloring. Reserve 1 tablespoon almonds and 1 teaspoon lime peel; fold remaining almonds and peel into lime mixture. Turn into crust; sprinkle with reserved almonds and peel. Chill until set. Lift pie from pan holding opposite ends of waxed paper strips; place on chilled serving plate. Remove paper strips; serve with sweetened whipped cream. Yield: 8-10 servings.

Photograph for this recipe on page 123.

LEMON MERINGUE PIE

1/2 c. cake flour
1 1/4 c. sugar
Dash of salt
1 1/2 c. water
3 egg yolks, slightly beaten
1/2 c. lemon juice
1 tbsp. grated lemon rind
1 baked 9-in. pie shell

Combine flour, sugar, and salt in top of double boiler. Add water and egg yolks; mix thoroughly. Place over hot water; cook for 10 minutes, stirring constantly. Remove from water. Add lemon juice and grated rind; cool. Pour into pie shell.

Meringue

3 egg whites
3 tbsp. sugar

Beat egg whites until foamy. Add sugar, 1 tablespoon at a time, beating after each addition until sugar is blended. Beat until stiff peaks form. Pile lightly on filling; seal to edge. Bake in 350-degree oven for 15 minutes.

Mrs. W. F. Fredeman
International Honorary Member, BSP
Port Arthur, Texas

STRAWBERRY MOCHA CREAM TARTLETS

4 c. sifted all-purpose flour
2 tsp. salt
1 1/2 c. vegetable shortening
2 pt. fresh strawberries
Light corn syrup
1/2 c. strong coffee
1/2 c. sugar
6 egg yolks
1 tbsp. instant coffee powder
2 tbsp. cocoa
1 c. softened butter

Combine flour and salt in bowl; cut in shortening until consistency of coarse meal. Sprinkle with 1/2 cup cold water; toss with fork until mixed. Press into ball. Roll out 1/2 of the dough at a time on lightly floured surface to 1/8-inch thickness; cut into 3-inch circles. Fit inside 2 1/4-inch tart pans; prick with fork. Place on baking sheet. Bake in 425-degree oven for 10 minutes or until lightly browned. Cool; remove from tart pans. Brush strawberries with corn syrup; dry on racks. Combine coffee and sugar; cook to soft-ball stage or until candy thermometer registers 234 degrees. Beat egg yolks with instant coffee powder and cocoa until fluffy and thick. Add hot syrup gradually, pouring in thin, steady stream and beating constantly until light in color and cold. Beat in butter. Chill slightly, if necessary. Pipe ring of butter mixture around inside edge of each tartlet shell. Place a strawberry in each shell; chill until served. Yield: 50 servings.

Photograph for this recipe on page 3.

FRENCH APPLE PIE

Pastry for 1-crust pie
6 c. sliced tart apples
2/3 c. sugar
1 tsp. cinnamon
1 1/8 c. flour
1/2 c. butter or margarine
1/2 c. (packed) brown sugar

Line pie pan with pastry; flute edge. Mix apples, sugar, cinnamon, and 2 tablespoons flour together; turn into pastry. Cream butter and brown sugar together; blend in remaining flour to make a crumb mixture. Sprinkle over apples. Bake at 450 degrees for 10 minutes; reduce oven temperature to 350 degrees. Bake for 30 minutes longer or until brown.

Photograph for this recipe on page 88.

PASTEL CANDIED FRUIT PEEL

3 lg. grapefruit or 6 lg. oranges
1 6-oz. package fruit-flavored gelatin
2 c. sugar
1 stick cinnamon
1/2 tsp. whole cloves

Cut grapefruit in halves. Squeeze out juice; strain and use as desired. Cover grapefruit halves with water in a saucepan. Bring to a boil; boil for 15 minutes. Drain. Remove pulp from peel, then with bowl of spoon remove moist white membrane carefully. Cut peel with scissors into thin strips, about 1/4 inch wide. Return peels to saucepan; cover with water. Boil for 15 minutes or until easily pierced with fork. Drain. Mix gelatin with 2 cups water and 1 cup sugar in a heavy skillet. Add fruit peel and spices. Bring to a boil; reduce heat to medium. Cook, stirring occasionally, for about 50 minutes, until peel is translucent and syrup is almost all absorbed. Remove from heat. Lift peel, several at a time, from skillet with a fork. Toss in remaining sugar. Arrange pieces in single layer on waxed paper-lined trays; let dry for about 12 hours or overnight. Store in a tightly covered container. Parboiled peels may be cut in fancy shapes using hors d'oeuvre cutters or a pointed sharp knife for attractive food decorations, if desired. Yield: About 1 pound.

Photograph for this recipe on cover.

GRANDMOTHER'S LOVE

6 tbsp. (heaping) flour, sifted
1 1/8 c. sugar
1/4 tsp. salt
5 tbsp. (heaping) cocoa
3 egg yolks
3/4 c. evaporated milk
1/3 c. water
1/4 c. margarine
1 tsp. vanilla
1 baked pie shell
1 recipe meringue

Mix flour, sugar, salt, and cocoa in top of double boiler. Mix egg yolks, milk, and water; stir into flour mixture. Place over boiling water; cook over medium heat, stirring, until thick. Place top of double boiler in cold water to cool quickly. Add margarine and vanilla; beat with mixer until blended and smooth. Place in pie shell; top with meringue, sealing to pie shell. Bake at 400 degrees until meringue is brown.

Mrs. David N. Tischler, Alpha Pi No. 8106
Corpus Christi, Texas

ORANGE SHERBET DESSERT

2 3-oz. packages orange gelatin
2 tbsp. lemon juice
1 tbsp. grated orange peel
1 pt. orange sherbet
2 11-oz. cans mandarin oranges, drained

Dissolve gelatin in 2 cups boiling water; add lemon juice and orange peel. Cool. Soften sherbet; fold into gelatin mixture. Add orange slices; pour into mold. Chill until firm. Top with whipped cream for dessert.

Evelyn Martin, Pres., Xi Beta Epsilon X803
Freedom, California

INDEX

PHOTOGRAPHY CREDITS: General Foods Kitchens; International Tuna Fish Association; California Strawberry Advisory Board; Standard Brands Products: Bluebonnet Margarine, Fleischmann's Yeast, Fleischmann's Margarine; National Fisheries Institute; American Dairy Association; U. S. Department of Commerce: National Marine Fisheries Service; South African Rock Lobster Service Corporation; United Fresh Fruit and Vegetable Association; McIlhenny Company; Sterno Canned Heat; National Broiler Council; Best Foods, a Division of CPC International Inc.; American Lamb Council; Pie Filling Institute; Quaker Oats Company; Artichoke Advisory Board; National Macaroni Institute; Spanish Green Olive Commission; Peter Pan Peanut Butter; Brussels Sprouts Marketing Program; Filbert/Hazelnut Institute; National Kraut Packers Association; Louisiana Yam Commission; Western Growers Association; Apple Pantry: Washington State Apple Commission; Cling Peach Advisory Board; Pineapple Growers Association; California Raisin Advisory Board; Evaporated Milk Association; Canned Salmon Institute; Idaho Bean Commission; National Dairy Council; Rice Council; The American Spice Trade Association; National Pecan Shellers and Processors Association; Campbell Soup Company.

Printed in the United States of America.

Complete your Cookbook Library or Give These Perfect Gifts!

Fondue and Buffet

Holiday

Meats

Desserts

Casseroles

Salads

A complete cookbook library is available in **THE BETA SIGMA PHI INTERNATIONAL COOKBOOK** series! You must have all editions: the all-new **Fondue and Buffet** as well as the **Holiday, Meats, Desserts, Casseroles,** and **Salads** editions. Each recipe in each edition was contributed by a Beta Sigma Phi member. Each was also fully kitchen-tested in the homemaker's own kitchen. You can rest assured that each dish you prepare will turn out perfectly with these wonderful recipes. Be sure to order your complete cookbook library today!

And, remember — cookbooks make perfect gifts for all occasions. Consider your own gift-giving needs: birthdays, weddings, showers, anniversaries, Valentine's Day presents, Mother's Day gifts, and other special occasions when you need to give a gift. Be sure to give cookbooks this year. They are a much-appreciated and useful gift that will be treasured this year and for many years to come!

The Beta Sigma Phi International Cookbook

Use these handy order forms to order cookbooks for yourself and for gifts!

PERSONAL ORDER FORM
74102

Please send me the following cookbooks @ $3.95 each. My check or money order for the full amount is enclosed.

_____Fondue and Buffet (1-21-011)   _____Desserts (1-21-002)
_____Holiday (1-21-010)   _____Casseroles (1-21-006)
_____Meats (1-21-001)   _____Salads (1-21)

Name_____

Address_____

City_____State_____Zip_____

The Beta Sigma Phi International Cookbook, P. O. Box 3396, Montgomery, Alabama 36109

PERSONAL ORDER FORM
74102

Please send me the following cookbooks @ $3.95 each. My check or money order for the full amount is enclosed.

_____Fondue and Buffet (1-21-011)   _____Desserts (1-21-002)
_____Holiday (1-21-010)   _____Casseroles (1-21-006)
_____Meats (1-21-001)   _____Salads (1-21)

Name_____

Address_____

City_____State_____Zip_____

The Beta Sigma Phi International Cookbook, P. O. Box 3396, Montgomery, Alabama 36109

PERSONAL ORDER FORM
74102

Please send me the following cookbooks @ $3.95 each. My check or money order for the full amount is enclosed.

_____Fondue and Buffet (1-21-011)   _____Desserts (1-21-002)
_____Holiday (1-21-010)   _____Casseroles (1-21-006)
_____Meats (1-21-001)   _____Salads (1-21)

Name_____

Address_____

City_____State_____Zip_____

The Beta Sigma Phi International Cookbook, P. O. Box 3396, Montgomery, Alabama 36109